# Toward Filipino Self-Determination

SUNY series in Global Modernity

Arif Dirlik, editor

# Toward Filipino Self-Determination

## Beyond Transnational Globalization

E. San Juan Jr.

Cover images courtesy of Dreamstime.com. Photo of protesters © photographer: Antonio Oquias/Dreamstime.com and photo of fist in the air © photographer: Mladen Mitrinovic/Dreamstime.com

Published by State University of New York Press, Albany

© 2009 State University of New York

For information, contact State University of New York Press, Albany, NY
www.sunypress.edu

Production by Diane Ganeles
Marketing by Anne M. Valentine

**Library of Congress Cataloging-in-Publication Data**

San Juan, E. (Epifanio), 1938–
    Toward Filipino self-determination : beyond transnational
globalization / E. San Juan Jr.
        p. cm. — (SUNY series in global modernity)
    Includes bibliographical references and index.
    ISBN 978-1-4384-2723-2 (hardcover : alk. paper)
    ISBN 978-1-4384-2724-9 (pbk. : alk. paper)
    1. Filipino-Americans—History.   2. Filipino-Americans—Social conditions.
3. United States—Relations—Philippines.   4. Philippines—Relations—
Unied States.   I. Title.
    E184.F4S28 2009
    305.899'921073—dc22
                                                                2008047581

10 9 8 7 6 5 4 3 2 1

*For Maricris Sioson, Cecilia Gelio-Agan,*
*Flor Contemplacion, Delia Maga, Jocelyn Guanezo,*
*Sarah Balabagan, and millions of*
*Overseas Filipino Workers—victims of*
*transnationalism, cosmopolitanism, and*
*imperialist globalization.*

# Contents

# Acknowledgments

In undertaking this project, I owe immeasurable debt to my friend and colleague Delia D. Aguilar, whose criticism and knowledge have given edge and substance to my inquiries. I also want to thank the following colleagues and mentors for their generous help in the research and writing of this book: Arif Dirlik, Peter McLaren, Michael Martin, David Palumbo-Liu, Sam Noumoff, Kenneth Bauzon, Paul Wong, Doug Allen, James Bennett, Lester Ruiz, Alan Wald, Bruce Franklin, Bill Fletcher, and Paul Buhle. Since, as John Berger writes, "only worldwide solidarity can transcend modern homelessness" (1984, 67), I take pleasure in acknowledging my gratitude to my friends in Europe, Asia, and Latin America: Yoshiko Nagano, Lee Yu-cheng, Liao Ping-hui, Pin-chia Feng, Wolfgang Fritz Haug, Rainer Werning, Michael Lowy, Domenico Losurdo, William Boelhower, Wen-ching Ho, Pierre Lantz, Giovanna Covi, and Pauline Eadie.

I would also like to thank my compatriots and comrades in the Philippines, Europe, and in North America for their unstinting support: Lulu Torres, Tomas Talledo, Alex Remollino, Sarah Raymundo, Bobby Tuazon, Mike Viola, Jeff Cabusao, Anne Lacsamana, Freedom Siyam, Julia Camagong, Robert Roy, Jorshinelle Sonza, Joseph Lim, John Iremil Teodoro, Roland Tolentino, Bienvenido Lumbera, Clodualdo del Mundo Jr., Denis Guevarra, Leonor Aguilar, Francisco Nemenzo, Preachy Legasto, Elmer Ordonez, Roger Mangahas, Louie Jalandoni, Rio Mondelo, Fe Mangahas, Princess Nemenzo, Mila D. Aguilar, Ave Perez Jacob, Judy Taguiwalo, Carol Araullo, Rosario Bella Guzman, Elmer Aguilar, Esther Pacheco, Malou Jacob, and Karina Bolasco.

Last but not least, Eric A. San Juan and Karin Aguilar-San Juan provided both intellectual stimulation and spiritual encouragement, light at the shores from where, in the distant plain, one can apprehend the sound and shadow of armies fighting in the night.

# Introduction

The year 2006 marked the centennial of the arrival of Filipinos in Hawaii—workers recruited under contract for the Hawaiian Sugar Planters' Association—from the colonial territory of the Philippines. With the defeat of Spain in the Spanish-American War of 1898, the United States expanded its imperial might to overseas territories—Cuba, Puerto Rico, Guam, and the Philippines. Unlike Cuba and Puerto Rico, however, the natives of the Philippine Islands had already overthrown Spanish rule and established the first Philippine Republic in 1898 (Constantino 1975). But the United States could not be deterred: its ruling business elite was in search of a gateway to the China market, for one, and an assertion of its newly discovered global "Manifest Destiny" (Nearing and Freeman 1966; Williams 1962). This Republic and millions of its defenders were destroyed by thousands of U.S. military troops as the Filipinos resisted, first in pitched battles and then in guerilla warfare from 1899 up to 1913.

From 1898 to 1946, the Philippines was a colonial possession, a captured territory of the United States. The conquest of the Philippines after the Filipino-American War of 1899–1913 is now celebrated by the neoconservative prophets of the "American Century" as the inaugural humanitarian accomplishment of imperial power (Kaplan 2004; Katz 2004). On October 18, 2003, while visiting Manila, Philippines, President George W. Bush declared that war of violent occupation as a model for Iraq. He claimed that American soldiers "liberated the Philippines" for democracy—by killing 1.4 million Filipinos.

U.S. occupation of the Philippines, by force and cooptation of the native oligarchy, converted the Philippines into a classic colony, a supplier of cheap raw materials and human labor, as well as a regulated market for surplus goods. It also provided strategic military bases for U.S. intervention in China, Korea, Vietnam, Indonesia, and the Middle East before World War II and during the Cold War up to 1992. Despite nominal independence in 1946, the war-devastated Philippines failed to industrialize due to the onerous terms imposed by the United States and later by the World Bank and the International Monetary Fund. The United States wholly supported the native landlords and compradors trained as subaltern surrogates to govern a sharply divided class society. The current GDP per person is $5,100, with over 30 percent of the population living in poverty. According to the United Nations Development Program, the Philippines ranked number 98 in the 1994 Human Development Index (Instituto del Tercer Mundo 1999, 71). Its economy lags way behind other "postcolonial" formations such as Singapore, South Korea, Malaysia, and Thailand in Southeast Asia. Its underdevelopment, maintained by structural inequalities in the control of productive property and distribution of resources, explains why, today, the Philippines is forced to export "warm bodies"—one million Filipinos are forced to leave every year in search of employment around the world, remitting billions of dollars enough to pay the country's foreign debt and sustain the privileges of the few oligarchical families who benefit from the exploitation and oppression of the majority of its citizens. This condition persists, confronted with the insurgency of millions of peasants and workers, as well as the armed insurrection of over eight million Moros (Muslims) trying to recover and protect their ancestral habitat.

The Filipino diaspora, then, is not a symptom of "discrepant cosmopolitanism" (Clifford 2006) or of postcolonial hybridity and neoliberal globalization. It is an effect of U.S. imperial coercion and transnational corporate violence. While the concept of diaspora problematizes the idea of national identity, the idea of the nation as an "imagined" or realized community, the Filipino version seeks to reconstitute the nation as a late-modern invention, a product of revolutionary social transformation. It may be that the almost universal sense of banishment and loss afflicts the plight of Filipinos lacking any strong attachment to a nation, affiliated only to a region, hometown, or birthplace; that nation was being born in the womb of the revolution against Spain and the United States at the turn of the last century. In any case, as I argue throughout this book, Filipino migration and expatriation coincide with a worldwide process of metamorphosis occurring among marginalized, subjugated peoples. This process is bound to disrupt the ideology of modernity founded on Eurocentric instrumentalism and the sacred unity of the "rational" consumer. It is possible, to adapt John Berger's speculation, that this scattering of a people with a long, durable tradition of revolutionary patience and creativeness will substitute for the shelter of a national homeland "not just our personal names, but our collective conscious presence in history, and we will live again at the heart of the real" (1984, 67). I articulate the problematic of this desire, hope, and promise in the closing paragraphs to this preface.

Meanwhile, a brief overview may be useful here. Filipinos in the United States today number more than three million, arguably the largest of the Asian American ethnic category. Six percent of the $12 billion remitted last year by Overseas Filipino Workers (OFW) came from North America, the United States, and Canada (Yap 2006). Although this emerging Filipino diaspora of ten million souls/bodies around the world does not yet match the Chinese worldwide dispersal of 35 million followed by the Indian diaspora of 22 million, it is more consequential because it constitutes about 10 percent of eighty-nine million citizens and decisively affects the balance-of-payments problem (IBON 2006;. OFW Philippines Online 2002; Wikipedia 2006). They are even considered the Philippines' "lost middle class," investors needed to feed the consumer-driven, acquisitive polity, the "coping mechanism of an economy in crisis" (Hernandez 2004). First institutionalized by then President Ferdinand Marcos in the early years of his dictatorship (1972–1986) to relieve social unrest due to unemployment, corruption, and neocolonial exploitation, the OFWs were extolled by his successor, Corazon Aquino, as "modern heroes" (*bagong bayani*). Since then, the export of Filipino workers—chiefly domestic help and semiskilled labor for Hong Kong, Taiwan, Singapore, the Middle East, Europe, and elsewhere—has become an almost integral component of the economy and culture of the country (Montinola 2006; Paddock 2006). Sailors or seamen constitute 28.5 percent (about 217,000) of the total OFWs (Luci 2004). They are found in 126 countries, with the concentration in Saudi Arabia, Japan, Hong Kong, the United Arab Emirates, and Taiwan.

And so it is not because a handful of Filipinos, fugitives from the Spanish galleon trade in the eighteenth century, somehow got lost in the marshes of Louisiana that the centennial of Filipino arrival in the United States is being commemorated. We cannot preempt the Mayflower settlement by this dubious primordialism. From the hindsight of this epoch of globalization and global war on terrorism, the presence of Filipinos in Hawaii may be taken as the beginning of a historic Filipino diaspora in the making. What is the nature of this peculiar dispersal of a whole community in late modernity? How is it connected to the political and economic situation of contemporary Philippines? What are its immediate and long-term consequences? Breakdown of families; crudely avaricious materialism; rape, imprisonment, and murder of so many women; the arrival of three to five corpses of OFWs at the Manila International Airport every day; and so on. So what else is new?

In terms of the alleged "clash of civilizations" and disintegration of nation-states, we pose the philosophical question: What are the implications of this nascent diaspora for the dialectic of identity and difference that underlies the "ethnographic operation" that defines the determinants of nationality, ethnic belonging, and civilizational profiles (Surin 1999)? If the old world system of center-periphery, core and margin, is breaking down, as Stuart Hall (2005) contends, how will a diasporic Filipino community register this momentous change when a Filipino nation-state, or an emergent nationality, will no longer be viable and substantially authenticate Filipino belonging, a singular Filipino identity?

Initiated as a series of essays written after the crisis of 9/11, this book may be considered a sequel to my previous works dealing with U.S.–Philippine relations from an interdisciplinary, cultural-studies approach (see, in particular, *The Philippine Temptation* [1996]; *From Exile to Diaspora* [1998b]; and *After Postcolonialism* [2000]). It endeavors to explore answers to those key questions, surveying the present situation (chapter 1) and tracing the genealogy of this collective uprooting in the U.S. colonization of the Philippines and the situation of early Filipino migrant workers, with a focus on the exemplary life of Philip Vera Cruz (chapter 2). In chapters 2 and 3, I address the lived predicament of Filipinos in the context of the general ethico-political questioning of identity, national belonging, citizenship, cultural affiliation, and so on. In chapters 4 and 5, I engage in a more personal and philosophical meditation on the plight of Filipino intellectuals expatriated or exiled by force of historical circumstances. Here the writer-activist Carlos Bulosan serves as a pedagogical locus for exploring the limits and possibilities of individual and collective emancipation. In chapters 6 and 7, I examine the problem of Filipino dislocation as a dialectical predicament of objective historical situation and sedimented, dis-integrated, subjugated consciousness in the context of untamed globalization. In the process, I inquire into the oppositional project of inventing a singular national-popular will/subject-position as a response to the loss of national sovereignty, commodity-centered alienation, and the general crisis of Enlightenment-oriented modernity.

In May 2004, a talented Filipina student, Patricia Evangelista, won a prize in the International Public Speaking competition sponsored by the English Speaking Union in London, by pontificating on the rewards of the Filipino diaspora. She tried to compensate for her country's underdevelopment by the Filipinos' unsolicited offer of help and resources to the developed, rich societies. She sought to deconstruct the irony by positing a hypothesis: "A borderless world presents a bigger opportunity, yet one that is not so much abandonment but an extension of identity. Even as we take, we give back. . . . A borderless world doesn't preclude the idea of a home. I'm a Filipino, and I'll always be one. It isn't about geography; it isn't about boundaries. It's about giving back to the country that shaped me" (2005). But who is the person speaking? Do we recognize her? And to whom is she addressing her words? What is the context of this utterance? I engage these questions in the last chapter by situating the emergent Filipino diaspora against the background of diverse forces converging in the vortex of an irresistible globalization process, at present epitomized in the "global war on terrorism," that seems to distill the sharp contradictions of race, class, gender, and ethnicity that make up the singular crisis of our late modern transitional epoch. Can the Filipino as a singular speaking subject survive this cathartic process, this suicidal war of barbaric capitalism against humanity?

Finally, at the risk of being repetitious, it seems appropriate to conclude with the following observations requested from me recently by the organizers of the Migrant Heritage Commission in Washington, DC, to commemorate the centennial of Filipino migration to the United States (specifically, to Hawaii) on the eve of June 12, 2006, Philippine Independence Day. This date was chosen in honor of the day when the first Republic of the Philippines was proclaimed in 1898 in Malolos, Bulacan, by President Emilio Aguinaldo and the revolutionary Congress. I reproduce this souvenir message as a distillation of my brief for the potential for an evolving praxis of Filipino self-determination.

> While there are now close to three million Filipinos in the United States, either as citizens or permanent residents, the majority by habit or conscious decision still consider the Philippines their real and only homeland. Even if they modify their ethnic identity as "Filipino American," they are still perceived as "Filipino." Their country of origin, their nationality, is reproduced by the ironic paradigm of a homogenizing pluralism that underlies U.S. immigration policy and its logic of naturalization. Until the nature of the U.S. racial polity (Mills 1999) is changed, the "Filipino" will survive despite assimilation or self-denial. And despite globalization, the system of nation-states and the hierarchy of international power politics will persist until genuine equality among nations and peoples becomes a reality.

Despite the unrecognized majority status of Filipinos in the Asian American segment of the U.S. polity, Filipinos remain marginalized and racialized due to physical markers, accent, association by name, and other reasons. One key reason is historical: the first Philippine Republic, victorious over Spanish rule, was destroyed by invading U.S. forces in the Filipino-American War of 1899-1902 (the "official" end of the war). More than one million Filipinos died fighting for national self-determination. We became colonial subjects, confiscated or captured properties of the U.S. empire. Throughout the twentieth century, Filipinos revolted and fought for justice and independence. We Filipinos are proud to have a long and durable revolutionary tradition that identifies our collective belonging. The first Filipinos recruited by the Hawaiian plantations—and, later on, by the Alaskan canneries and California agribusiness—distinguished themselves not only by diligent work but by militant resistance to exploitation. We use this occasion to pay homage to Pablo Manlapit, Pedro Calosa, Chris Mensalvas, Ernesto Mangaong, Carlos Bulosan, Philip Vera Cruz, Silme Domingo,

Gene Viernes, and nameless others (in the International Longshoreman's and Warehouseman's Union; United Farm Workers; and other cooperative, self-managed agencies) who sacrificed their lives to uphold Filipino dignity and autonomy, as well as the principles of a participatory, egalitarian democracy. They not only fought for principles of class, gender, and racial equality, but also for respect for their nationality and their ethnic integrity.

Since the end of the Marcos dictatorship in 1986, more than ten million Filipinos, now known as "Overseas Filipino Workers," have been scattered around the planet. Because the homeland remains a neocolonized dependency, economic backwardness and unrestrained oligarchic greed accounts for severe unemployment. Hence Filipinos have to "sell" themselves in the predatory globalized market. It is timely to celebrate the centennial by noting that Filipinos in the United States form a decisive contingent of this evolving diaspora because of its location in the metropole of the global hegemon. The pathos of the OFW's predicament is captured powerfully by Angelo de la Cruz's response after his release by his kidnappers in Iraq in July 2004: "They kept saying I was a hero, . . . a symbol of the Philippines. To this day I keep wondering what it is I have become." So what have we become as displaced and diasporized Filipinos outside our homeland, the imagined but realizable and knowable community of our fears, loves, and longings? "By the waters of Babylon, there we sat down, yea."

We are not transmigrants or transnationals, to be sure, despite the theories of academic pundits and exoticizing media. We are Filipinos uprooted and dispersed from hearth and communal habitat. We will find our true home if there is a radical systemic change in the metropole and, more crucially, a popular-democratic transformation in the Philippines. Only a free, prosperous, genuinely sovereign Philippines can give Filipinos here and Pinays/Pinays everywhere their authentic identity and empower them as creative, resourceful humans in a world of free, equal associated producers, thus invoking the "Eden lost" of the revolutionary hero Jose Rizal: "Farewell, my adored Land, region of the sun caressed,/Pearl of the Orient Sea, our Eden lost."

# 1

# Imperial Terror in the Homeland

We did what we ourselves [Filipino working people] had decided upon—
as free people, and power resides in the people. What we did was our
heritage . . . We decided to rebel, to rise up and strike down the sources of
power. I said "We are Sakdals! We want immediate, complete, and absolute
independence." No uprising fails. Each one is a step in the right direction.

—Salud Algabre, in an interview with David Sturtevant

In spite of the universal horror at the perverse torture of prisoners at Abu
Ghraib and the ruthless devastation of Iraq and Afghanistan by U.S. occupation forces, the U.S. ruling class seems undeterred in pursuing its relentless
quest of world domination by military means. Opportunistically seizing the
catastrophe of September 11, 2001, the U.S. power elite is desperately trying
to resolve the crisis of finance capital by unilateral state terrorism. Whether
Democratic or Republican, U.S. politicians all justify the invasion of Iraq and
Afghanistan. Selected American intellectuals have been mobilized to legitimate this version of "just war" by theorizing the "clash of civilizations" and
the defense of neoliberal democracy by fascist violence. While empire has
been disavowed as part of American "exceptionalism," apologias for "humanitarian" imperialism are now fashionable. Professor Amy Kaplan, former
president of the American Studies Association, strongly denounced the USA
PATRIOT Act and the idea of homeland security as "violent" acts of secrecy
and deception (2004, 3). One example of this attempt to vindicate a long history of violent interventions—preemptive wars for regime change—is the
rewriting of the brutal war of the United States to suppress the Filipino independence struggle a century ago. The repressed returns—in the guise of triumphalist celebrations of imperialist barbarism and genocide (Shalom 2004).

When U.S. occupation troops in Iraq continued to suffer casualties
every day after the war officially ended, academics and journalists began

1

in haste to supply capsule histories comparing their situation with those of troops in the Philippines during the Filipino-American War (1899–1902). A *New York Times* article summed up the lesson in its title, "In 1901 Philippines, Peace Cost More Lives Than Were Lost in War" (July 2, 2003, B1), while an article in the *Los Angeles Times* contrasted the simplicity of McKinley's "easy" goal of annexation (though at the cost of 1.4 million Filipinos killed, 4,234 U.S. soldiers slain, and 3,000 wounded) with George W. Bush's ambition to "create a new working democracy as soon as possible" (July 20, 2003, M2). *Wall Street Journal* writer Max Boot extolled the counterrevolutionary victory of the U.S. armed forces in destroying the revolutionary Philippine Republic (2002).

To learn critically from the lessons of the past, we need to place historical conjunctures in the context of present circumstances in the Philippines and of the international crisis of globalized capital. What is the real connection between the Philippines and the current U.S. war against terrorism?

## Missionary Retribution

With the death of Martin Burnham, the hostage held by Muslim kidnappers (who called themselves "Abu Sayyaf") in Mindanao, the southernmost island of the Philippines, one would expect that the more than twelve hundred American troops (including FBI and CIA) training Filipinos for that rescue mission would have headed home in late 2002. Instead of being recalled, reinforcements were brought in and more joint military exercises were announced for the future. Since September 11, 2001, U.S. mass media and Filipino government propagandists have dilated on the Abu Sayyaf's tenuous links with Osama bin Laden. A criminal gang that uses Islamic slogans to hide its kidnapping-for-ransom activities, the Abu Sayyaf is a splinter group born out of the U.S. war against the Soviet Union in Afghanistan and used by the government to sow discord among the insurgent partisans of the Moro Islamic Liberation Front and others fighting for genuine substantive autonomy. Protected by local politicians and military officials, the Abu Sayyaf's persistence betokens the complicated history of the centuries-long struggle of about ten million Muslims in the Philippines for dignity, justice, and self-determination (Bauzon 1991; Stauffer 1981).

What is the background to the return of the former colonizer to what was once called its "insular territory" administered at the start by the infamous Bureau of Indian Affairs? With Secretary Colin Powell's decision to stigmatize as "terrorist" the major insurgent group that has been fighting for forty years for popular democracy and independence—the Communist Party of the Philippines (CPP) and its armed wing the New People's Army (NPA), both members of the National Democratic Front, the introduction of thousands of U.S. troops, weapons, logistics, and supporting personnel has been given an imprimatur of legitimacy. More is involved than simply converting the archipelago to instant military facilities for the U.S. military—a bargain exchange for the strategic outposts Clark Air Base and Subic Naval Base formerly "owned" by the United States and scrapped by a resurgent Filipino nationalism a decade ago. With key military officials practically managing the executive branch of government, the Philippine nation-state will once again prove to be more an appendage of the Pentagon than a humdrum neocolony administered by oligarchic compradors, a dependent formation since nominal independence in 1946. On the whole, Powell's stigmatizing act is part of the New American Century Project to reinstall a new pax Americana after the Cold War.

Immediately after the proclaimed defeat of the Taliban and Al-Qaeda forces in Afghanistan, the Philippines became the second battlefront in the U.S. war to impose its "pax Americana in a grossly unequal world" (Foner 2004). Raymond Bonner, author of *Waltzing with Dictators* (1987), queries the obvious rationale: "the desire for a quick victory over terrorism, . . . the wish to reassert American power in Southeast Asia. . . . If Washington's objective is to wipe out the international terrorist organizations that pose a threat to world stability, the Islamic terrorist groups operating in Pakistan-controlled Kashmir would seem to be a higher priority than Abu Sayyaf" (*New York Times*, June 10, 2002), or those in Indonesia, a far richer and promising region in terms of oil and other abundant natural resources. As in the past, during the Huk rebellion in the Philippines in the Cold War years, the United States acted as "the world's policeman," aiding the local military in "civic action" projects to win "hearts and minds," a rehearsal for Vietnam. Given this time-tested modus operandi, Washington used the Abu Sayyaf as a cover for establishing a forward logistics and operation base in Southeast Asia to be able to conduct swift preemptive strikes against its perceived enemies in Indonesia, Malaysia, Vietnam, China, and elsewhere.

Overall, however, the intervention of U.S. Special Forces in solving a local problem inflamed Filipino sensibilities, its collective memory still recovering from the nightmare of the brutal Marcos dictatorship. What disturbed everyone was the Cold-War practice of "Joint Combined Exchange Training" exercises. In South America, Africa, and Indonesia, such U.S. foreign policy initiatives merged with counterinsurgency operations that channeled military logistics and personnel to favored regimes notorious for flagrant human rights violations (Ray and Schaap 2003). In El Salvador, Colombia, Guatemala, and other parts of the hemisphere, the U.S. role in organizing death squads began with Special Operations Forces advisers who set up "intelligence networks" ostensibly against the narcotics trade but actually targeting leftist insurgents and nationalists. The well-known CIA operative Colonel Edward Lansdale, who later masterminded the Phoenix atrocities in Vietnam, rehearsed similar counterinsurgency techniques during the Huk insurrection in the fifties (Schirmer and Shalom 1987).

Today, U.S. soldiers deployed with the local military (a blatant violation of the Philippine Constitution) are pursuing those "terrorists" defined by the U.S. State Department—guerillas of the New People's Army, Moro resistance fighters, and other progressive organizations. Scarcely has the first decade of the new millennium ended, predatory American troops are again haunting the boondocks (from *bundok*, in Tagalog, means "mountain" refuge for guerillas) in search of prey.

# Crusade of "Manifest Destiny"

A moment of reflection returns us to what historian Bernard Fall called "the first Vietnam," the Filipino-American War, in which 1.4 million Filipinos died. The campaign to conquer the Philippines was designed in accordance with President William McKinley's policy of "Benevolent Assimilation" of those they treated as unchristian natives, a "civilizing mission" that Mark Twain considered worthy of the Puritan settlers in the proverbial "virgin land." In Twain's classic prose: "Thirty thousand killed a million. It seems a pity that the historian let that get out; it is really a most embarrassing circumstance" (1992).

In *"Benevolent Assimilation": The American Conquest of the Philippines, 1899-1903* (1982), Stuart Creighton Miller recounts the U.S. military's "scorched earth" tactics in recalcitrant Filipino guerilla strongholds, atrocities from "search and destroy" missions reminiscent of Song My and My Lai in Vietnam. This episode in the glorious history of the U.S. empire is usually accorded a marginal footnote, or a token paragraph in school textbooks. Miller only mentions in passing the U.S. attempt to domesticate the unhispanized Moros, the Muslim Filipinos in Mindanao and Sulu islands. On March 9, 1906, four years after President Theodore Roosevelt declared the war over, Major General Leonard Wood, commanding 540 soldiers, killed a beleaguered group of 600 Muslim men, women, and children in the battle of Mount Dajo. A less publicized but horrific battle occurred on June 13, 1913, when the Muslim sultanate of Sulu mobilized about five thousand followers (men, women, and children) against the American troops led by Captain John Pershing. The battle of Mount Bagsak, twenty-five kilometers east of Jolo City, ended with the death of 340 Americans and of 2,000 (some say 3000) Moro defenders. Pershing was true to form—earlier he had left a path of destruction in Lanao, Samal Island, and other towns where local residents fought his incursions. Anyone who resisted U.S. aggression was either a "brigand" or seditious bandit; the "anti-brigandage" campaigns of the first three decades suppressed numerous peasant revolts and workers' strikes—a carnage of genocidal proportion. Eventually the islands became a model of a pacified neocolony (Pomeroy 1992)

Except for Miller's book and assorted studies, nothing of consequence about the effects of that process of barbaric subjugation has disturbed American Studies scholarship despite the recent "transnationalization" of cultural studies in general. This is usually explained by the theory that the United States did not follow the old path of European colonialism, and its war against Spain (now compared to the war against Iraqi and Afghani insurgents) was pursued to liberate the natives from Spanish tyranny. If so, that war now rescued from the dustbin of history signaled the advent of a globalizing U.S. interventionism whose latest manifestation, in a different historical register, is Bush's "National Security Strategy" of "exercising self-defense [of the Homeland] by acting preemptively," assuming that might is right, imposing "regime change" for the sake of corporate profit-making—this latter is always glamorized in the slogan of America delivering "freedom and democracy" to the ravaged lands of Iraq and Afghanistan.

# Comprador and Tributary Barbarism

Since nominal independence in 1946, especially during the U.S.–Marcos dictatorship (1972–1986), neocolonial state terrorism first in the name of anticommunism, and then later of "law and order," has inflicted havoc on the lives of millions of Filipinos. Despite the appeals of human rights organizations, religious groups, and international opinion, nothing seems to have stopped the Arroyo military in its campaign of deliberate slaughter. If the security and health of millions of workers, peasants, and indigenous peoples in Mindoro, Mindanao, and other embattled regions cannot be protected by the neocolonial state that commands the legal monopoly of violence and other coercive means, then that government has lost legitimacy. In fact, it is open to being convicted for state terrorism in the court of world opinion (San Juan 2007b). Since the Philippine polity is defined as a constitutional republic, citizens from whom all power emanates have the right to alter the social contract if the government has failed to answer their needs. All signs indicate that the social contract has been broken, violated, damaged many times over since the country became a mock-sovereign nation in 1946.

It is precisely on this ground—the massive state terrorism of the military bureaucracy, police and paramilitary forces of the neocolonial state—that Luis Jalandoni (2002), the chairperson of the National Democratic

Front spearheading the revolution, responded to the Colin Powell–Arroyo doctrine of summary condemnation of the Communist Party of the Philippines and the New People's Army as "terrorist" organizations. Jalandoni called on the present regime to renounce state terrorism and indemnify its numerous victims: thousands of prisoners and activists killed in assassinations, extrajudicial executions, and indiscriminate massacre by the military. It would indeed be traumatic to recount the litany of human rights violations that burden our history since the Marcos dictatorship, nay, since the Filipino-American War, with millions of Filipinos and Moros killed by the "civilizing" missionaries of U.S. "Manifest Destiny."

## Serfs of the Global Bourgeoisie

For the moment, before addressing the struggle for decolonization, I want to shift your attention first to this unprecedented phenomenon in Philippine history, a qualitative change in our geopolitical status in the present world-system linkage of industrialized centers and peripheral or dependent social formations. This is the diaspora of close to ten million Filipino OFWs, 10 percent of the population of ninety million, around the world—about four million in North America and roughly six million more in the Middle East, Europe, Africa, Asia, and elsewhere.

During the U.S. colonial period, thousands of Filipinos migrated to the metropole, first as recruited workers for the sugar plantations in Hawaii, and then as seamen, U.S. Navy personnel, nurses and doctors, and so on (San Juan 1999). Since the Marcos martial-law regime, the "warm body export" (including mail-order brides, children, and modern "slaves" in the global sex traffic) accelerated tremendously. This is explained by the worsening crisis of a neocolonial society—chronic unemployment, rampant poverty, corruption, criminality, military atrocities—that coincides with what Stefan Engel, in his powerful book *Twilight of the Gods—Gotterdammerung over the New World Order*, indicts as "the policy of neoliberalism with its propaganda of unrestricted flow of capital, privatization, deregulation," and so on (2003, 368).

Every day three thousand Filipinos leave for abroad as the servants/maids of the globalized world order. In Hong Kong alone, over 150,000 Filipina domestics service the middle strata and elite. Moreover, 25 percent of the world's seafarers, and cruise waiters, are Filipinos. With 10 percent of the population scattered around the three continents as cheap or affordable labor, mainly domestics and semiskilled workers, the Philippines has become the world's leading supplier of what is euphemistically called "human capital"—in actuality, hands to do work for minimal pay, tied to jobs often humiliating and sometimes unpaid, producing enormous surplus value (profits) for transnational corporations as well as for affluent sectors in Europe, North America, the Middle East, and Asia.

Everyone knows that these Filipino workers' remittance of billions of dollars—$10 to $12 billion annually—(aside from exorbitant government fees and taxes) is the major earner of dollars needed to pay the onerous foreign debt and keep the system afloat. It guarantees the privileges of the comprador and landlord oligarchy. It preserves and aggravates the impoverishment of over half of the working population. Despite the unrelenting cases of inhumane treatment, rape, all kinds of conceivable deprivation, and murder—about three to four coffins of OFWs arrive daily at the Manila International Airport, reminiscent of Flor Contemplacion and others—the humorless Labor Secretary Patricia Santo Tomas was quoted as saying: "It's not politically correct to say you're exporting people, but it's part of globalization, and I like to think that countries like ours, rich in human resources, have that to contribute to the rest of the world" (Diamond 1999). It seems that more than four hundred years of colonization are not sufficient for Filipinos to sacrifice themselves to the white-supremacist bourgeoisie at the altar of consumerism and commodity-fetishism.

Generations of Filipinos have contributed prodigiously to the accumulation of surplus-value and total wealth of the planet—except to our own country, the very soil and land of which have been depleted, polluted, plundered, its people exploited and oppressed in diverse ways. One commentator advises Filipinos to be versatile, in keeping with "flexible" capitalism: "Look Asian, think Spanish, act American. . . ." Is this a joke? I doubt the appropriateness of this maxim, something that not a few traditional social scientists delight in when they proclaim that Filipino culture is one proud of its diversity, hybridity, cosmopolitanism, and other disingenuous rubrics to compensate for the horrific reality. Some usually resort to an apologetic reprise about how the "third world" poor excel in spiritual beauty. But inner wealth, like inner beauty, is precisely the symptom of the profound alienation and disenchantment afflicting the benighted recipients of Western modernity—multitudes of colonial subalterns blessed by commodity-exchange (their bodies, among others), by the freewheeling market and the relentless commodification of everything under the aegis of sacred private property.

Now we know that all things develop via contradictions and the dialectical process of their unending resolution. The diaspora of ten million Filipinos is bound to generate forces of critique and transformation with their own self-generated leadership. They will surely emancipate themselves, for nobody else can do it for them. Already OFWs in Hong Kong, Canada, and elsewhere have organized as far as the laws will allow; our compatriots in Europe, in countries where they are subjected to vicious racist treatment, have also become more politically aware and have mobilized to raise consciousness and protest their inhumane conditions. If and when they return, we hope that they will not be cadavers but vibrant bodies ready for militant engagements in the political arena, not just with the panicked pursuit of the creature comforts of a frayed if not mystifying bourgeois public sphere, the pleasures of a "cannibalistic" (if this term has not been demystified by the black market selling of body parts such as kidneys, hearts, eyes, and so on) predatory civil society.

## Festivals of the Oppressed

The revolutionary upsurge in the Philippines against the Marcos dictatorship (1972–1986) stirred up dogmatic cold war complacency. With the inauguration of a postmodernist stage in cultural and humanistic studies in the post–cold war era, the historical reality of U.S. imperialism (inaugurated by the genocide of Native Americans and confirmed by the subjugation of the indigenes of the Philippines, Puerto Rico, Cuba, and Hawaii) is finally being excavated and reappraised. But this is, of course, a new development brought about by the confluence of multifarious events, among them: the demise of the Soviet Union as a challenger to U.S. hegemony; the sublation of the sixties in both Fukuyama's "end of history" and the interminable "culture wars," the Palestininan intifadas; the Zapatista revolt against the North American Free Trade Agreement; the vicissitudes of the ongoing U.S. anti-Islamic fundamentalist holocaust in Afghanistan and Iraq; and the fabled "clash of civilizations." Despite these changes, the old frames of intelligibility have not been modified or reconfigured to understand how nationalist revolutions in the dominated territories cannot be confused with the chauvinist patriotism of the hegemonic metropole, or to grasp fully how the mode of U.S. imperial rule after World War II differs in form and content from those of the British or French in the nineteenth century. The received consensus of a developmental, modernizing impact on the colonized by the capitalist taskmasters remains deeply entrenched. Even deconstructionist thinkers commit the mistake of censuring the liberatory projects of the subalternized peoples because these projects (in the condescending gaze of these scholastics) have been damaged by emancipatory passion and soon to become perverted into despotic postcolonial regimes, such as those in Ghana, Algeria, the Philippines, and elsewhere. The only alternative, it seems, is to give assent to the process of globalization under the aegis of the World Bank/International Monetary Fund/World Trade Organization, and hope for a kind of "enlightened" patronage in the style of Bush's "compassionate" conservatism.

What remains to be carefully evaluated, above all, is the historical specificity or singularity of each of these projects of decolonization and national liberation, their class composition, historical roots, programs, ideological tendencies, and political agendas within the context of "humanitarian" imperial supremacy (for a background on the capitalist crisis, see Dickhut 1986; Fitt, Faire, and Vigier 1980). It is imprudent if not fatuous to pronounce summary judgments on the character and fate of nationalist movements in the peripheral formations without focusing on the complex manifold relations between colonizer and colonized, the dialectical interaction between their forces as well as others caught in the conflict (Weightman 1970). Otherwise, the result would be a mendacious ethical utopianism such as that found in U.S. "postnationalist" discourse that, in the final analysis, functions as an apology for the machinations of the transnational corporate powers ensconced in the nation-states of the North, in particular for the hegemonic rule of the only remaining superpower claiming to act in the name of everyone's freedom and salvation.

The project of national liberation acquires substance in the Filipino critique of imperialist ideology and its vision of a truly sovereign, just, egalitarian society. Among Filipino progressive intellectuals, Renato Constantino (1978) is distinguished for his acute grasp of how the profound Americanization of the Filipino psyche, mediated through the instrumentalities of education, mass media, elections, and so forth, prevented the majority from seeing through the myths of American democracy, free trade, altruism, and so on. Constantino exposed the Filipino elite, the "new *ilustrados*," as effective conduits for neocolonial control, a fact witnessed by the sycophancy to the United States of succeeding administrations since the country's nominal independence in 1946. The criminal regime of Ferdinand Marcos at the height of the cold war epitomized the demagoguery, corruption, and brutality of the neocolonial state manipulated by U.S. overseers (Sison and de Lima 1998). Not to be outdone, the treacherous policies of President Gloria Macapagal-Arroyo have not only abetted the barbaric U.S. aggression in Afghanistan and Iraq but also surrendered the country's sovereignty to the Pentagon as well as to the onerous diktat of the managers of globalization: the World Bank and the International Monetary Fund and the World Trade Organization (Tuazon et al. 2002).

From the Marcos dictatorship to the politically bankrupt regimes of Corazon Aquino, Fidel Ramos, Joseph Estrada, and up to Macapagal-Arroyo, the Filipino people suffered intolerable hardships and unconscionable deprivations. Countless atrocities and human rights violations (extrajudicial political killings, forced "disappearances," torture, and so on committed with unconscionable impunity) perpetrated by the neocolonial state since the Marcos era are still unpunished up to this day. Severe unemployment caused by the International Monetary Fund-World Bank "structural conditionalities," and government policies of privatization and deregulation, have driven millions of Filipinos to seek work abroad (Gonzalez 1999). With a corrupt oligarchy that supervises not only the state apparatus but also the institutions of civil society, the U.S. strategy of "low intensity democracy," which accompanies "low intensity" counterrevolutionary measures, continues to wreak havoc on the daily lives of workers, peasants, women, urban poor, and middle strata (white-collar workers and petite-bourgeois professionals). Taking account of the U.S. military presence in the Philippines for almost a century, and the U.S. stranglehold over its economy, culture and politics, Filipino jurist Romeo Capulong recently handed out this judgment based on a substantial inventory of evidence: "I find the U.S. government accountable for war crimes and crimes against humanity it committed and continues to commit against the Filipino people and peoples of other countries in over more than a century of colonial and neocolonial rule in the Philippines" (2004). The verdict still awaits execution by the masses of victims.

## Scholastic Complicity

We may ask at this point to what extent the discipline of cultural studies (of which I am a practitioner), for all its claims to offer oppositional critiques of establishment orthodoxies, has engaged the crisis of transnational globalization, in particular U.S. terrorism against the peoples of the world. The answer is: Precious little, from the perspective of the OFWs and the victims of ruthless U.S. bombing in Iraq and Afghanistan. In my books *Racism and Cultural Studies* (2002) and *Working through the Contradictions* (2004), I called attention to recent developments in cultural studies in North America and Europe that have subverted the early promise of the field as a radical transformative force. In every attempt to inquire into ideological practices and discourses, one is always carrying out a political and ethical agenda, whether one is conscious of it or not. There are many reasons for this, the chief one being the inescapable political-economic constitution of any discursive field of inquiry, as historical-materialist critiques have convincingly demonstrated. And even without invoking that famous theoretical couplet that Foucault and Bourdieu have popularized, knowledge/power, the production of knowledge is always already implicated in the ongoing struggles across class, nation, gender, locality, ethnicity, and so on, which envelop the total sensibility of the would-be knower, learner, investigator, scholar, and so forth.

This is the moment when I would like to open the topic of why problems of culture and knowledge-production are of decisive political importance. Although we always conceive of ourselves as citizen-subjects with inalienable rights, it is also the case that we are all caught up in a network of obligations whose entirety is not within our conscious grasp. What is our relation to Others—the excluded, marginalized, and prostituted Others who affirm our existence and identity—in our society? In a sense we, all Filipinos, are responsible for the plight of the Moros—yes, including the existence of the Abu Sayyaf—insofar as we claim to live in a community of responsible if not rational persons who alternatively occupy the positions of speakers and listeners, I's and you's, and who have obligations to one another, and reciprocal accountabilities.

Here I am following an argument elaborated by the late Canadian scholar Bill Readings in his provocative book *The University in Ruins* (1996). Speculating on the impossibility of subjective self-identity, of being free from obligation to others, Readings comments on an attitude of cynical self-congratulation prevalent in the United States. I am referring to a widely shared stance or posture that became more articulate when, after September 11, 2001, most Americans, newly self-anointed as victims, refused to see any responsibility for what happened to them and disclaimed any share in causing such horrendous disaster, what is indeed a terrible tragedy because it is uncomprehended and disconnected from the flaws of the "egotistical sublime," hence the hunger for revenge. No doubt Readings includes his fellow Canadians in the following remark whose pedagogical lesson we can immediately apply to our own relations with members of ostracized communities, marginalized minorities, or invidiously categorized neighbors whom we encounter every day and who share our common habitat:

> It is the desire for subjective autonomy that has led North Americans, for example, to want to forget their obligations to the acts of genocide on which their society is founded, to ignore debts to Native American and other peoples that contemporary individuals did not personally contract, but for which I would nonetheless argue they are *responsible* (and not only insofar as they benefit indirectly from the historical legacy of those acts). In short, the social bond is not the property of an autonomous subject, since it exceeds subjective consciousness and even individual histories of action. The nature of my obligations to the history of the place in which I live, and my exact positioning in relation to that history, are not things I can decide upon or things that can be calculated exhaustively. No tax of "x percent" on the incomes of white Americans could ever, for example, make full reparation for the history of racism in the United States (how much is a lynching "worth"?). Nor would it put an end to the guilt of racism by acknowledging it, or even solve the question of what exactly constitutes "whiteness." (1996, 186)

Underpinned by an ideology of white supremacy, the racialized U.S. nation-state controlled by finance capital mystifies its violent strategy of maintaining post–cold war global hegemony by claiming that it is giving freedom and democracy to the people of Iraq, Afghanistan, the Philippines, Colombia, Haiti, and others, whatever the cost in terms of suffering, injustice, deaths, and other "collateral damage" in its endless genocidal war of reprisal, occupation, and remorseless self-aggrandizement (Mann 2002; Meszaros 2001).

## In the Belly of the Beast

What about the beleaguered situation of Filipinos in the fabled "land of promise," the quasi-utopian "new world" wrested from the American Indians? In the United States, the Filipino Americans have suffered, as everyone knows, from the latest act of vengeance against what it designates as Islamic extremism or terrorism: the USA PATRIOT Act. We are struggling against what may be the initial stage of authoritarian rule, "friendly fascism," in the new guise of Homeland Security. We have to fight a version of pragmatic patriotism more arrogant than anticommunism, a self-righteous Manichean worldview intent on preemptive strikes and other unilateral interventions against "Jihad International," against all those resisting the hegemony of the "only remaining superpower." Civil liberties and constitutional rights have been annulled if not eviscerated. What Susan Sontag (2002) calls the "dangerous lobotomizing notion of endless war," the pseudowar of the civilized versus barbarians, has already encouraged all sorts of repressive excesses— racial profiling, incarceration of suspects, killing of innocents who look like Arabs or "terrorists," contingent on the demonology of the day. If "measure and proportionality require the language of law and justice" (Asad 2002, 38), then the mad rush to war against Iraq after the merciless devastation of Afghanistan has broken all records. A climate of fear and suspicion reigns hidden by the fog of mindless consumerism and patriotic hysteria.

Noam Chomsky, as well as other public intellectuals, have called the United States "a leading terrorist state" (2001, 16). Just to give an example of how this has registered in the lives of Filipinos in the United States: In June, sixty-two Filipinos (among them, doctors and engineers) were apprehended by the U.S. Immigration and Naturalization Services for overstaying their visa or for lack of appropriate documentation. They were arrested as "absconders," handcuffed and manacled in chains while aboard a plane on the way to the former Clark Air Base in Pampanga, Philippines. Roughly three hundred thousand Filipinos were scheduled for deportation, some were treated as hardened criminals; several planeloads had already been dispatched before their relatives in the Philippines could be notified. Over three thousand persons, most of them people of color, have been detained as suspects, already being punished as "war combatants," without benefit of any public trial or legal assistance (Mahajan 2002). I am not referring to the prisoners captured in Afghanistan and confined to quarantine cells in Guantanamo, Cuba; I am referring to U.S. citizens who have been jailed on suspicion that they have links with Osama bin Laden or other terrorist groups listed by the U.S. State Department, groups that now include the CPP/NPA. One may ask: How many more Filipinos, and for that matter U.S. citizens with an immigrant background, will suffer arbitrary state terrorism led by the U.S. ruling elite, a fate that may befall any one of us who as citizens (here or in the Philippines) may be branded as unpatriotic or traitors because we dare to criticize, dare to think and resist with our uncompromising conscience?

As a background/prologue to the Filipino collective project of actualizing self-determination, I would like to delineate briefly the historical trajectory of the ongoing people's war in the Philippines. The case of the national-democratic struggle in the Philippines may be taken as an example of one historic singularity in this new millennium. Because of the historical specificity of the Philippines' emergence as a dependent nation-state controlled by the United States in the twentieth century, national democracy as a mass movement has always been defined by events of anti-imperialist rebellion. U.S. conquest entailed a violent racist, genocidal suppression of the Filipino revolutionary forces for decades. The foundational inspiring "event" by public consensus is the 1896–1898 revolution against Spain and its sequel, the Filipino-American War, together with the Moro resistance up to 1914 against U.S. colonization. Another political sequence of events was the Sakdal uprising in the thirties followed by the Huk uprising in the forties and fifties—a sequence that was renewed in the First Quarter Storm of 1970 against the neocolonial state. While the local feudal, comprador, and bureaucratic power-elite under U.S. patronage utilized elements of the nationalist tradition formed in 1896–1898 as their ideological weapon for establishing moral-intellectual leadership, their attempts have never been successful. Propped by the Pentagon-supported military, the Arroyo administration today, for example, uses the U.S. slogan of democracy versus Moro (or Muslim) terrorism, supplemented by the fantasies of the neoliberal free market, to legitimize its continued exploitation of workers, peasants, women, and ethnic minorities. Following a long and tested tradition of grassroots mobilization, Filipino nationalism has always remained centered on the peasantry's demand for land closely tied to the popular-democratic demand for equality and genuine sovereignty spearheaded by the progressive elements of the organized working class and radical democratic intelligentsia. Its proletarian orientation continues to draw nourishment from the vital and sustainable living tradition of Marxist-Leninist anti-imperialism.

For over a century now, U.S.-backed developmentalism and modernization have utterly failed in the Philippines. The ongoing resistance against global capital and its neoliberal extortions is constituted and defined by a national-democratic mass movement of which the National Democratic Front remains the most viable socialist vanguard. We have a durable proletarian-led insurgency that seeks to articulate the "unfinished revolution" of 1896 in its demand for genuine national independence and social justice for the majority of citizens, including ethnic minorities and indigenous peoples. Meanwhile, the Muslim community in the Philippines initiated its armed struggle for self-determination during the Marcos dictatorship and continues today as a broadly based movement for autonomy, despite the religious orientation of its teacher-militants. Recalling the genocidal U.S. campaigns against the Muslims cited earlier, BangsaMoro nationalism cannot forget its Muslim singularity, which is universalized in the principles of equality, justice, and the right to self-determination.

In the wake of past defeats of numerous peasant revolts, the Filipino culture of popular-democratic nationalism rooted in proletarian militancy constantly renews its anti-imperialist vocation by mobilizing new forces (women, youth, and church people in the sixties and the indigenous or ethnic minorities in the seventies and eighties). It is organically embedded in emancipatory social and political movements whose origin evokes in part the Enlightenment narrative of sovereignty and secular humanism. And though mediated by third world nationalist movements (Fanon, Ho Chi Minh, Mao), its sites of actualization may be witnessed in the local events of mass insurgency against continued U.S. hegemony (San Juan 1998a, 2000). The Philippines cannot thus be reduced merely to an "imagined" community in an idealist construal. It is embodied and enacted in actually experienced practices of communities, collective bodies of workers and peasants, dynamic social blocs in motion, whose habitat remains in the process of being constructed primarily through modes of political and social resistance against finance-capitalist transnationalism (or globalization, in the trendy parlance) and its technologically mediated ideologies. Sustained and enriched by the conscious, organized participation of the working masses, the current national-democratic revolution in the Philippines and in the Filipino diaspora is fashioning thereby the appropriate concrete forms of dissent, resistance, and subversion worthy of its history of uninterrupted revolts and its internationalist socialist vision.

# 2

# In the Belly of the Beast

On the Asiatic coast, washed by the waves of the ocean, lie the smiling Philippines. . . . There, American rifles mowed down human lives in heaps.

—Rosa Luxemburg, "Martinique"

They are even afraid of our songs of love, my brother.

—Carlos Bulosan, "Poem for Chris Mensalvas"

It was as if many of us Filipinos were living behind hidden identities for fear of associating with the realities of our lives, our real names, and therefore, our real identities. . . . My life here was always an emergency.

—Philip Vera Cruz, *Autobiography*

Thirty thousand Filipinos work in Lebanon today and about the same number in Israel, with thousands more in war-ravaged Iraq and Palestine, several millions in the entire Middle East. Since the bombardment of Beirut and other regions of Lebanon, several hundred Filipinos have been repatriated, thanks to the International Office of Migration. Despite billions of pesos in taxes and fees collected from these workers by their own government, the Arroyo administration has again proved completely helpless, unable to do anything to save or protect its citizens, officially designated as OFWs. As everyone knows, their burgeoning remittances have continually saved the government from endemic bankruptcy and earned them the celebrity status of "modern heroes," phenomenal investors to the country's and the world's development. Recent interviews of OFWs in Lebanon have confirmed again the bitter truth of their collective plight: many prefer to stay in their place of work at the mercy of bombs and missiles rather than return to the Philippines and die of starvation. The choice for OFWs, in almost all cases, was instant death or slow extinction. How did we reach this point of awful, unashamed desperation?

15

An estimated three thousand Filipinos leave the country every day, roughly a million every year. In 2004, 8.08 million Filipinos, out of 80 million, left the country. In 2008, with a population totaling 89.5 million, that would run to about 9–10 million, with about 3–4 million in North America, and the rest scattered around the world. About three to five cadavers of overseas Filipinos (now an entry in *Wikipedia*), or OFWs, land at the Manila International Airport—not as famous as Flor Contemplacion or Maricris Sioson, but scandalous enough to merit attention. According to Connie Bragas-Regalado (2006), chair of Migrante International, at least fifteen "mysterious deaths" of these government "milking cows" (her term for Filipino remittance senders) remain unsolved since 2002, with more brutalization to come in the wake of the U.S.-led war of "shock-and-awe" against anyone challenging its global superiority. Alternatively, Filipinas/Filipinos may be classified as "collateral damage," in the lexicon of neoliberal, capitalist globalization.

Balikbayan cadavers? This may prove that despite the borderless world of predatory global capitalism today, as the English-speaking Pinay celebrity Patricia Evangelista once orated, Filipinos always return to their home—or "the idea of a home," after thousands of Filipino nurses have served the United Kingdom's National Health Service, or a quarter of a million Filipino seafarers have sweated it out on foreign commercial ships. Not to worry; many come home alive, if bruised or brutalized; never mind, the dollars (amounting last year to $10.7 billion) of these new investors, or "bagong bayani"—as Tita Cory (2007) acclaimed them—have saved Gloria Macapagal-Arroyo's skin, sustained the meretricious lives of a few oligarchic families, and glorified the Philippines as a proud supplier of skilled human power for the world's affluent citizens in the North (Europe, North America, and Japan), and in the developing nations (the Middle East, Africa, and the Asian "Tigers").

So we are indeed extremely generous. We are investing more in the overdevelopment of Europe and petrodollar-rich Arab kingdoms than in our country where we are witnessing, in slow motion, the irreversible collapse of the health care system. Who cares, anyway? Not the hustlers in Malacanang or the Batasan. With drastic cutbacks in funding for education and other social services, with more than one billion pesos siphoned off to fund a counterinsurgency "total war" to kill dissenting Filipinos, some in the New People's Army, the rest as ordinary journalists, lawyers, public servants, Bayan Muna activists, and so on. Meanwhile, the notorious Armed Forces of the Philippines continues its rampage of massacring Muslims, Igorots, Lumads, left and right, aside from more than a thousand activists killed and forcibly made to disappear. We are faced with the impending total breakdown of Arroyo's kingdom, confronted by disgruntled businessmen, Catholic bishops, and millions of workers and peasants amassing in various metropolitan centers to mount rallies before the guns of ruthless police and soldiers and hired thugs.

Keep the dollars flowing in to pay the debt, oligarchs pray, or the World Bank and financial despots will come in and pronounce doom. Can a remittance society survive in the long run? The uninterrupted flow of remittance is contingent on an inherently unstable precarious labor market, a market completely unpredictable, mortgaged to the essentially precarious, crisis-ridden globalized capitalist economy. The "war on global terrorism" threatens the smooth flow of remittance every day, the value of currency, computer servers, and so on. The first and second Iraq wars led to the dislocation of thousands of contract workers. War measures against Iran, North Korea, and other U.S.-declared "axes of evil" are bound to choke off, if not totally cut off, this flow of dollars to keep afloat Arroyo, her bureaucratic clique, and the comprador elite—the privileged minority who, for a century, have colluded with the United States and other foreign corporate interests in keeping the country an underdeveloped, dependent, subordinate appendage of the empire. With the environment ruined, the infrastructure wasted, and most educated Filipinos abroad schlepping along with their "damaged culture," as one American journalist put it, there might be no viable "home" to which Patricia Evangelista's compatriots can return and spend their golden years.

Meanwhile, the fabled ascendancy of this overseas "middle" class—a freakish diaspora of sorts mimicking the Indian and Chinese migration in modern times—has led to stagnation and near collapse. As Richard Paddock noted in a *Los Angeles Times* report (April 20, 2006) on this phenomenon, the much touted "booming economy" of Arroyo and her generals "can't create even the 1.5 million jobs a year needed to keep up with population growth." No wonder the Philippine health care system is in ruins, the public schools are a wreck, families are disintegrating, and the system is corrupted thoroughly by the profits gained by bureaucrats, politicians, recruiting agencies, and so on, from the misery of millions of OFWs. Who cares, anyway?

Let us turn to the erstwhile land of promise, the "land of the free and home of the brave." While there are now close to three million Filipinos in the United States (not counting the "TNT"s, those trickster "aliens" dodging and hiding from the "migras"), who are either citizens or permanent residents, the majority by habit or prudent decision still consider the Philippines their real and only homeland. This unless they have opted to become Anglos by sheer self-denial, shame, or suicide by self-delusion. Even if they modify their ethnic identity as "Filipino American," they are perceived as "Filipino" by the majoritarian optic in this racial polity governed by the ethos of white supremacy. Their country of origin, their nationality, is reproduced by the logic of cultural pluralism that underlies

U.S. immigration and naturalization ideology and policy. This logic is demonstrated every day in the immigration debate, by the proponents of a liberal "guest worker" program or by the neoconservative scheme of a heavily militarized border. To be sure, the immigration problem masks the fundamental reality of fierce class war waged every day by the corporate elite, hitherto led by Bush and his neoconservative clique, against the majority of citizens, in particular against people of color. Did Patricia Evangelista proclaim a "borderless" world where love for one's neighbor is dutifully observed?

But Filipinos will continue to leave, according to the cliché, "come hell or high water." Or the daily bombing in Lebanon, Iraq, and elsewhere. Recall how many Filipinos reacted when the government prohibited travel to Iraq on account of Angelo de la Cruz's kidnapping, that they would rather go to Iraq to work and be killed instantly rather than die a slow death in their "beloved Philippines." Lives of quiet desperation? Survival of the fittest by adaptation to a fixed environment, or to the pressure of changing historical circumstances? Thoreau! Darwin! Hegel! The wisdom of the sages is needed; but, alas, the Hobbesian Leo Strauss and Rortyan pragmatism seem to trump everything in our born-again computerized Disneyland.

History, however unpredictable, can be ultimately understood through our acts of intervention. Until the nature of the U.S. racial polity (founded on white supremacy/*Herrenvolk* Exceptionalism) is changed, the "Filipino" will survive despite assimilation or self-denial. What this "Filipino" might be remains to be seen. And despite globalization, the system of nation-states and the hierarchy of international power politics will persist until genuine equality among nations and peoples becomes, via a revolutionary transformation, a reality.

Despite the unrecognized majority status of Filipinos within the Asian American category, Filipinos remain marginalized and racialized due to physical markers, accent, association by name, and other knowable reasons. One key reason is historical: the first Philippine Republic, victorious over Spanish rule, was destroyed by invading U.S. forces in the Filipino-American War of 1899 up to 1913. Over one million Filipinos died fighting for national self-determination. We became colonial subjects, subalterns of the U.S. empire. Throughout the twentieth century, Filipinos rebelled—via strikes, seditious theater, peasant insurrections, clandestine newspapers, and so forth—and fought for justice and independence. We wanted boundaries to mark and delineate the territory of the Filipino nation as well as the sovereignty of the nation-state called the Philippines.

What follows are propositions that can be examined and debated, depending on one's perspective. Some may appear as tired banalities, some may offer catalyzing provocations. In any case, here they are for discussion.

# In Quest of Singularity

We Filipinos are proud to have a long and durable revolutionary tradition that identifies our collective belonging. The first Filipinos recruited by the Hawaiian plantations—and later on by the Alaskan canneries and California agribusiness—distinguished themselves not only by diligent work but by militant resistance to exploitation. We use this occasion to pay homage to Pablo Manlapit, Pedro Calosa, Chris Mensalvas, Ernesto Mangaong, Carlos Bulosan, Philip Vera Cruz, and many others (in the International Longshoremen's and Warehousemen's Union, United Farm Workers, and so on) who sacrificed their lives to uphold Filipino self-respect and autonomy. At the least, they fought for human dignity. They not only fought for principles of class, gender, and racial equality, but also for respect for their nationality and ethnic integrity. Personal honor, class identity, and nationality constituted one dialectical constellation of values and norms.

Reality is always contradictory, and changes are never uniform and reducible to easy generalizations. Since the end of the Marcos dictatorship in 1986, more than nine million Filipinos, now known as Overseas Filipino Workers have been scattered around the planet. Because the homeland remains a neocolonized dependency, economic backwardness accounts for severe unemployment. In the fifties, Magsaysay promised and delivered some token homesteads to Huk surrenderees, at the expense of the Moros. But that propaganda frontier, that illusory "safety valve," is gone. After all, it was simply a cold war "promise" designed to defeat the impatient Huk Politburo.

Today, the Philippines has been integrated into the neoliberal global market, thanks to Aquino, Ramos, Estrada, and Arroyo. This is Patricia Evangelista's borderless dreamworld of buy and sell, of the certain freedom of starving if no one buys your labor-power. Filipinos have to "sell" themselves in the predatory globalized market. Can we envision Filipinos as part of a world proletariat arming themselves for a general mass strike, as Rosa Luxemburg prophesied for twentieth-century Europe? Will Filipinos participate in storming the barricades of Wall Street and other centers of corporate power? One recalls the mass demonstrations organized by MIGRANTE and other groups in Hong Kong, North America, Italy, and other countries, against Arroyo's Proclamation 1017 and the continuing brutalization of opponents by torture, extrajudicial killings, "disappearances," and so on.

Once upon a time, according to a self-serving family album entitled *Filipinos: Forgotten Asian Americans*, Filipinos died for "Americanism." We are told that Filipinos wanted to be 200 percent Americans as they fought side by side with their colonizers in Bataan and Corregidor. Recently, Itty Abraham (2006) of the East-West Center in Hawaii, noted how "the imperial wheel had turned full circle" when, in 1945, Filipino veterans were finally awarded full U.S. citizenship for their military service to the country. Unfortunately, in 1946 the U.S. Congress rescinded the rights of these same veterans. Of the original 141,000, only 29,000 survive; 8,000 reside in the United States, the rest in the Philippines. Even if the Filipino Veterans Bill is approved, benefits will not be extended to those veterans living in the Philippines. "Americanism," anyone?

Meanwhile, immediately after 9/11, over 465 Filipinos, some already U.S. citizens, were deported as criminals, manacled during the twenty-two-hour chartered flight to the homeland. Under the white-supremacist USA PATRIOT Act, according to the organization FOCUS, the entire Filipino community—not just individuals like the Cuevas family of Fremont, California—is under attack (Mendoza 2003). An estimated three hundred thousand Filipino immigrants will be deported from the United States, according to a Department of Foreign Affairs official in the Philippines. Whither Americanism a century hence?

What signifies this centennial? Could it be the rebirth of the Filipino as multicultural citizen of a borderless world, as zealous hawkers of the nomadic, multivocal, heterogeneous Pinoy contend? Certainly it is not the resurrection of the "Flip" or the "little brown brother" as a refurbished Stephen Fetchit in a nonstop minstrelsy "Pilipino Cultural Night" of *tinikling*, *kiyeme*, and *Maganda dogeaters*. In any case, it is instructive to celebrate the centennial by noting that Filipinos in the United States form a decisive contingent of this evolving diaspora because of its location, not yet because of their collective praxis, in the metropole of the global hegemon. The ideology of "Americanism" retooled to fit the neoconservative "civilizing mission" of the "New American Century" still prevails, despite the Foucauldian negotiations of assimilated "model minority" cheerleaders of the community.

Of course, location is not enough; but being dis-located is a strategic disadvantage since you need orientation to find your direction and accomplish collective goals. Otherwise, you are at the mercy of sharks, sirens, and destructive currents. The pathos of the OFW's predicament is captured powerfully by Angelo de la Cruz's response after his release by his kidnappers in Iraq in July 2004: "They kept saying I was a hero, . . . a symbol of the Philippines. To this day I keep wondering what it is I have become." What have I become? So what have we become as displaced and transported Filipinos outside our homeland, the imagined but realizable and knowable community of our fears, loves, and longings? "By the waters of Babylon, there we sat down, yea . . ." yearning for our lost Eden, singing forbidden songs under constant surveillance by the FBI, the CIA, border patrols, Minutemen, and so on.

We are not transmigrants or transnationals, to be sure, despite the lucubrations of academic pundits and the exoticizing mantra of the patronizing media. To speak plainly, we are Filipinos uprooted and dispersed from hearth and communal habitat. We will find our true home if there is a radical systemic change in the metropole and, more crucially, a popular-democratic transformation in the Philippines. Short of a world without classes and nation-states, without the bourgeoisie "screwing" (to quote the idiom of some famous rappers) the masses, in the meantime, we need to "cultivate our garden," as a French *philosophe* once said. What else bears repeating? Only a free, prosperous, genuinely sovereign Philippines can give Filipinos here and Pinays/Pinoys everywhere their authentic identity and empower them as creative, resourceful humans in a world of free, equal associated producers. Confronting this arena of struggle in Lebanon, the sweatshops of Los Angeles, or the domestic work sites in Hong Kong, Italy, Saudi Arabia, and other countries, let us join together and celebrate our fate as OFWs: *Mabuhay ang sambayanang Pilipino*!

# Rediscovering the "New World"?

What, then, could be the significance of celebrating the one-hundred-year anniversary of the advent of Filipino contract labor in Hawaii? Are Filipinos (or Filipino Americans) the new compradors of the militarist U.S. empire? Or are they harbingers of a new generation of combatants from the oppressed communities, from the internal colonies of the metropoles? At the turn of the last century, the revolutionary leader Rosa Luxemburg elegized the plight of the subjugated natives in "*las islas Filipinas*." Today, U.S. Special Forces are back to reconquer the neocolony, with the natives no longer smiling, now up in arms, united with people of color in Mexico, Venezuela, Palestine, Lebanon, Hawaii, Nepal, and other battlefronts of our beleaguered planet. Whither the emerging Filipino diaspora? Before we can answer this question, let us review briefly the history of Filipino transplantation into this North American continent, a history shrouded with conundrums and plagued with misconstruals.

Claims that "Luzon Indios" from the Spanish possessions of Las Islas Filipinas first landed in Morro Bay, California, in the sixteenth century and "Manillamen" settled near what is now New Orleans, Louisiana, in the eighteenth century are made to preempt or mimic the Puritan settlement of the United States. But they cannot overshadow the historical fact that Filipinos, unevenly hispanized Malays with dark brown skin, first entered the American consciousness with their colonial subjugation as a result of the Spanish-American War at the turn of the century.

After the defeat of the first Philippine Republic in the Filipino-American War, this Southeast Asian archipelago became a source of raw materials and a reservoir of human capital. Peasants were recruited by the Hawaiian Sugar

Planters Association as cheap contract labor when the Gentlemen's Agreement of 1908 cut off the Japanese supply. Feudal oppression and colonial brutality drove rural Filipinos from their homes while the lure of adventure and easy wealth blurred the hardships formerly endured by Mexican farmhands now restricted by the Immigration Act of 1924.

About four hundred students (called *pensionados*) on U.S. government scholarship are often cited as the first "wave" of immigrants (1903–1924). In reality, the new rulers invested in their education so that they could return to serve as the middle stratum of loyal natives who, subordinated to landlords and compradors, would legitimize U.S. domination. From this segment would come the bureaucrat-capitalists of the Commonwealth and the postwar Republic. An ironic sequel to this initial moment of the Filipino diaspora is the influx of "brain-drain" professionals (doctors, nurses, and technicians) in the sixties and seventies who now function as part of the "buffer race" displacing tensions between whites and blacks. Meanwhile, the political exiles and economic refugees during the Marcos dictatorship (1972–1968), like president Corazon Aquino, returned home to further reinforce Filipino subalternity and promote the massive export of Filipino "overseas contract workers."

Over one hundred thousand "Pinoys/Pinays" and "Manongs" (affectionate terms of address) helped build the infrastructure of U.S. industrial capitalism as the major labor force in agribusiness in Hawaii and on the West Coast. From 1907 to 1933, Filipino "nationals," neither citizens nor aliens, numbered 118,436—7 out of 10 percent of Hawaii plantation workers. Severely exploited and confined to squalid barracks, Filipinos joined with Japanese, Chinese, Korean, and other nationalities in a series of militant strikes in 1920 and 1924. One of these agitators, Pedro Calosa, was forced to return to the islands where he figured prominently in the Sakdal insurrection in 1935 against feudal exploitation and U.S. imperial rule.

As late as 1949, six hundred workers from the independent Republic of the Philippines were imported by the sugar planters to break up strikes led by the International Longshoremen's and Warehousemen's Union. The 1990 census indicates that 168,682 Filipinos resided in Hawaii, most of them employed in the service industries (restaurants, hotels, tourist agencies, entertainment) as low-paid semiskilled labor. The election of Benjamin Cayetano as governor of Hawaii offers a signal lesson: his success depends more on Japanese and white support than on the political mobilization of his own fractious ethnic constituency.

The theory of "migration waves" breaks down when sizable numbers of Filipinos moved from Hawaii to California, Oregon, and Washington according to the business cycle and local contingencies. Predominantly male (only one out of fourteen Filipinos were women), a majority of thirty thousand Filipinos in bachelor communities circulated from farm to farm in seasonal rhythm. Others worked in the Alaskan canneries, as Pullman porters in Chicago, volunteers in the U.S. Navy, and more frequently as domestics: janitors, kitchen helpers, cooks, house cleaners, and hospital attendants. Stoop labor generally received $2.50 a day for six days, half of what factory workers got in the late twenties. Without benevolent associations or credit cooperatives like other Asians, Filipinos participated with other groups in union organizing and other progressive, multicultural initiatives in the thirties and forties.

The Depression aggravated the racism toward Filipinos, already victimized by previous anti-"Oriental" legislation. Up to 1942, longtime residents were denied the right to own land, marry whites, or apply for welfare. Citizenship was still reserved for "white persons," as stipulated by a 1934 court ruling that upheld the 1790 naturalization law. Racist violence culminated in the 1930 riots at Exeter, Watsonville, and Stockton, California. These attacks were motivated by the belief that Filipinos lowered the standard of living while also enjoying "the society of white girls." Carlos Bulosan, the radical writer-activist, captured the saga of Filipino resistance from the thirties to the outbreak of World War II in his testimony, *America Is in the Heart* (1973). Displacing the fixation on taxi-dance hall, bar, poolroom, and Manilatown, union organizer Philip Vera Cruz memorialized the evolution of the indeterminate sojourner to the pioneer militant of the United Farm Workers of America in the sixties.

Immigration was virtually halted by the Philippine Independence Act of 1934. Enormous Filipino sacrifices in Bataan and Corregidor fighting with their American comrades had a positive effect on public opinion. In 1942, Filipinos became eligible for naturalization. Thousands volunteered for military service. Due to unequal power relations between the two countries, however, about seventy thousand veterans of World War II are still awaiting full benefits. The liberation of the Philippines from Japanese Occupation (1942–1945) restored the unjust social structure on top of the incalculable physical and spiritual damage wrought by the war. Neocolonial "Americanization" plus a continuation of "free trade" and privileges for a minority elite intensified the impoverishment of the peasantry, women, petite-bourgeois entrepreneurs, government employees, and urban workers, hence the push to search for jobs in the United States and elsewhere.

From 1946 to 1965, 35,700 Filipinos entered as immigrants. Most of these families, residing in the big cities of Hawaii, California, Washington, New York, and Chicago, earned their livelihood from industrial occupations and blue collar work. The post–1965 contingent of Filipinos decisively altered the character of the Filipino community: 85 percent were high school graduates, most were professionals and highly skilled personnel who fitted the demands of the U.S. economy. But because of race-biased licensing and hiring practices, they found themselves underemployed or marginalized. Family reunification fostered by new legislation contributed to the leap from a total of 343,000 in 1970 to more than one million in the early nineties. In 2000, Filipinos number nearly three million, with over seventy thousand coming every year—the largest of the Asian Pacific Islander category.

The Filipino American community at present occupies a peculiar position in the socioeconomic landscape. Although highly educated, with professional, military, or technical backgrounds, fluent in English and nestled in large relatively stable families (average households include 5.4 persons of which 2 at least are employed), Filipinos in general earn less than whites and all other Asian groups, except the Vietnamese. With women workers in the majority, Filipinos are invisible or absent in the prestigious managerial positions. Erroneously considered part of the mythical "model minority," they are denied benefits under Affirmative Action and "equal opportunity" state laws. Labor market segmentation, cultural assimilation under U.S. neocolonial hegemony, and persistent institutional racism explain the inferior status of Filipinos.

Owing to the rise of anti-imperialist mass movements in the Philippines since the sixties and the recent outburst of nationalist insurgency, the Filipino community has undergone profound changes. While the "politics of identity" born in the civil rights struggles finds resonance among the informed middle sector, Filipino Americans as a whole tend to identify with mainstream society. Despite antagonisms arising from linguistic and regional diversity, Filipino youth are wrestling with the limitations of patriarchal authority, family togetherness, kinship, and filial piety. They are beginning to problematize and explore their commonality with other racialized communities (African Americans, Latinos, American Indians, Arab Americans, and others).

A reciprocal interaction between ethnic consciousness and historical determination characterizes the subjectivity or social behavior of Filipino Americans. Generalizations can only be haphazardly ventured here. While intermarriage continues, particularly worsened by the "mail-order bride" business, and while ethnic enclaves are being eroded amid residential segregation, Filipinos—both U.S. born and "foreign born"—are acquiring a more sophisticated sense of themselves as a historically specific nationality. In the last two decades, Filipino American intellectuals have begun to articulate a unique dissident sensibility based not on nostalgia, nativism, or ethnocentrism but on the long durable revolutionary tradition of the Filipino masses and the emancipatory projects of grassroots movements in the Philippines where their parents and relatives came from.

Claims that Filipino uniqueness springs from a cooperative family structure and egalitarian gender relation need to be questioned on the face of internal class conflicts, sexism, individualist competition, and color prej-

udice. It is impossible to divorce Filipinos from the problems of the larger
class-divided society and from the effects of the global power conflicts configuring United States–Philippine relations. What needs more critical inquiry is not the supposed easy adaptation or integration of Filipinos in U.S.
society, but the received consensus that Filipinos remain unassimilable if
not recalcitrant elements. That is, they are not quite "oriental" or hispanic,
at best they appear as hybrid diasporic subjects (more than nine million of
ninety million Filipinos are now scattered around the planet) with suspect
loyalties. Filipinos, however, cannot be called the fashionable "transnationals" because of racialized, ascribed markers (physical appearance, accent, peculiar nonwhite folkways) that are needed to sustain and reproduce
Eurocentric white supremacy. Ultimately, Filipino agency in the era of
global capitalism depends not only on the vicissitudes of social transformation in the United States but, more crucially, on the fate of the struggle
for autonomy and popular-democratic sovereignty in the homeland.

It might be instructive to demonstrate the veracity of this thesis with
the exemplary life of Filipino labor union organizer Philip Vera Cruz, one
of the founders of the United Farmworkers of America. His life may be
read as a testimony of national self-determination in the making.

## Proletarian Intervention

On July 21, 1994, the Honorable Lucille Roybal-Allard of the U.S. House
of Representatives delivered a brief homage to Philip Vera Cruz (1904–
1994), who died on June 10 at the age of ninety. Vera Cruz left a "legacy
of commitment and dedication to social justice," Representative Roybal-
Allard stated, which survives "in the work of grassroots organizers"
everywhere. This legacy is now inscribed in his memoir (2000), coau-
thored by Lilia Villanueva and Craig Scharlin. From his arrival in this
country in 1926 as a "colonial ward," neither alien nor citizen, from beleaguered Asian territory annexed by the United States after the Spanish-American War (1898) and the Filipino-American War, to his leadership
(together with Larry Itliong) of the historic 1965 Delano Grape Strike,
the course of Vera Cruz's life followed a typical pattern—youthful initiation, crisis (*peripeteia*), discovery—memorably delineated in his contemporary Carlos Bulosan's writings, in particular the classic ethnohistory of
the Filipino migrant worker, *America Is in the Heart* (1973).

In contrast to the international stature of Bulosan, now part of the
ethnic canon in Asian American Studies, Philip is almost unknown despite his being vice president of the United Farm Workers from its founding up to 1977. His memoir (first published in 1992 by the Labor Center
and the Asian American Studies Center of the University of California,

Los Angeles) has not really circulated as widely, despite or maybe because of its candid yet tempered criticism regarding the leadership style of Cesar Chavez. Chavez's place in the pantheon of heroic Americans, like that of Martin Luther King, appears secure. But Philip's name, for various reasons, has remained in limbo. Except for a handful of Filipino academics, most Filipino Americans (close to three million, the largest Asian American contingent [Paddock 2006; Takaki 1989, 432; Wikipedia 2006]), nor the Latinos whom he championed, I am sure, have never heard of Philip Vera Cruz. Nor will his compatriots, chiefly preoccupied with the "American Dream of Success," spend time and energy to find out about Philip's life and his significant contribution to the popular-democratic struggles of the working people in this country and around the world.

Before attempting an explanation why, I want to pose the general problem of how to make sense of the life of any individual, how to understand its distinctive physiognomy and meaning. Are all human lives alike? Yes and no. We all belong to the natural species of Homo sapiens/*faber*, sharing common needs and aspirations. Praxis, our interaction with nature to produce and reproduce our social existence, unites all humans. However, we are all different because our lives are shaped by multiple contexts in history, contexts that are often variable and unpredictably changing, so that one needs the coordinates of the body, psyche, and society to map the trajectory of any single individual's life history. Writing on Luther and Gandhi, Erik Erikson focused on the identity crisis of individuals in the life cycle framed by the structure of ideological world images. He noted in particular the centrality of identity problems as omnipresent in the "mental baggage of generations of new Americans, who left their motherlands and fatherlands behind to merge their ancestral identities in the common one of self-made men. . . . Migration means cruel survival in identity terms, too, for the very cataclysms in which millions perish open up new forms of identity to the survivors" (1975, 43). Philip was a survivor, indeed, but was he a self-made man in the stereotypical cast of the Horatio Alger models?

Instead of following a psychohistorical approach, I want to engage the challenge of Philip's *testimonio* as more than a personal confession. We can read his biography as a reconfiguration of personal experiences, a constellation of events that can be read as an allegory of the Filipino community's unspoken project of fashioning subjects capable of fidelity to promises and commitments, and thus invested with self-respect and self-esteem. Winning reciprocity and recognition, Philip held himself accountable to his family, ethnic compatriots, and coworkers in terms of universal maxims and norms that suggest a collective project for the "good life" envisaged within and through the contingencies and risks of late capitalist society. Narrating one's life translates into telling the story of the life of the group to which one belongs or seeks to belong, a matter of filiation and affiliation, what Edward Said discerned as "contrapuntal ensembles" (1993, 52).

# Configuring the Self and Its Situations

Today, given the debate on multiculturalism, the nature of identity is almost equivalent to cultural belonging, to genealogy and affiliation. In the culture wars in which everyone is engaged, whether one likes it or not, the politics of identity seems to have repudiated any universal standard or "metanarrative," so that one's life can only be situated within the frame of limited localities, specific zones of contact, particularities of time and place. Relativism and nominalism dictate the parameters of intelligibility. I do not subscribe to the postmodernist doctrine of nominalist relativism—that only atomistic sense-data, not general concepts, can provide experimental knowledge (for a critique of nominalism, see Rochberg-Halton 1986). As Charles Sanders Peirce argued, consensual belief can be fixated at the end of any inquiry provided we agree that the reasons for any belief are fallible and open to modification (on Peirce's "fallibilism," see Brent 1998, 17–18). Whatever the position one takes in the dialectic of global and local, the singular and the universal, it is difficult to avoid the question of how to adjudicate the relative power of social/cultural and individual/psychic factors in the shaping of subaltern lives. Nietzsche and Derrida cannot so easily reject the Enlightenment legacy of doubt and critique without pulling the rug from under their feet; such a legacy, on the other hand, has been put on trial by its victims—by feminists and by thinkers such as Frantz Fanon, Aime Cesaire, Jose Carlos Mariategui, C. L. R. James, and others.

One can hazard a hypothesis for exploration. I submit that the life pattern of an individual such as Philip Vera Cruz is unique and at the same time typical for a colonized subaltern in the U.S. empire. But it is not idiosyncratic since he, like thousands of his compatriots from the Philippines (or other subjugated territories such as Puerto Rico, Cuba, Micronesia, and so on), was exposed to the same political, economic, and ideological forces that shaped the lives of the majority of migrant workers in the United States in the last century. This occurred in varying degrees, with nuanced complexities, depending on their ethnic/racial, gender, class, and national positions at particular historical conjunctures. In the case of the Filipino subject—the "nationals" in the first three decades of the last century—the crucial context for understanding the ethos or subject-position of this group is none other than the violent suppression of the revolutionary struggle of Filipinos against colonial domination, first by Spain and then by the United States. This coincided then with the beginning of segregation enforced by lynching mobs, the confinement of Native Americans to reservations, and mass war hysteria against the "Black Legend" (*leyenda Negra*; see Retamar 1989) during the Spanish-American War. In this charged climate, nationality, racialized physiognomy, and social class marked all Filipinos, and continues to mark them, as stigmata difficult even for assimilationists to erase.

Despite the defeat of the anti-imperialist insurgency, Filipinos who grew up in the first three decades of the last century absorbed the ideals and passion for independence that saturated the milieu and resonated up to the outbreak of World War II. Philip's will to autonomy is displayed in his realistic attitude to religion—for him, "churches are only as good as what they do, not what they say" (2000, 80)—a practicable stance easily harmonized with his emphasis on what he calls traditional values of helpfulness, understanding, and loyalty. Both the resonance of a persistent communal tradition and the impact of the revolutionary resistance to U.S. colonialism are registered in Philip's contextualization of his life in Philippine history.

The racialized subjugation of the natives, the arguably genocidal extermination of more than one million Filipinos resisting U.S. aggression, continued through a dual policy of coercion and "Benevolent Assimilation." Eventually the United States co-opted the elite and used the patron-client system to pacify the seditious peasantry. The Americanization of the Filipino through selective education and the liberal *habitus* of a "free-market" order, side by side with feudal or tributary institutions, produced the subaltern mentality that one will find in most Filipinos then (and up to now, in the professional stratum and the petite bourgeoisie in general), particularly those recruited for work in the Hawaiian plantations, the student *pensionados* sent by the colonial government, or those who, like Philip and Bulosan, chose on their own to pursue the adventure of making their fortune in the United States in the years of the Great Depression (see Constantino 1978; San Juan 1996a).

Unlike in Iraq and Afghanistan today, the U.S. colonizing strategy in the early twentieth century drew from the experience of the brutal taming of the American Indians and the juridical/ideological policing of blacks, Tejanos, Chinese, and so on. This underlies the emergence of the United States as a racial polity (Janiewski 1995; Mills 1999). Class and ethnic stratification via mass public education regulated the rigor of industrialization while the few exceptional cases of successful careers gave an illusion of mobility and possibilities of change. The gradual but inexorable movement from the impoverished rural village to the modern city and then to the North American continent replaced the lure of revolutionary ideals. The impact of the defeat of the armed nationalist movement registered in different ways for every Filipino migrant—one needs to qualify here that Filipinos were not technically immigrants until the establishment of the Philippine Commonwealth in 1935 when entry of Filipinos was limited to fifty every year (McWilliams 1997). One can say that the primal scenario of defeat bred suspicion, not trust; however, every Filipino of peasant or working-class origin had to settle account with that "curse" by sly, cunning accommodation or by hidden forms of civil disobedience if she or he wanted to show fidelity to the promise of being responsible to family and community.

For Bulosan, the personal experience of peasant revolts brutally put down by the United States in the twenties allowed him to see in collective suffering a promise and hope of liberation. He interpreted every episode in his life as part of this narrative of transformation. Thus, early union organizing by the Congress of Industrial Organizations on the West Coast and the popular front of intellectuals—especially the international front against fascism in Spain and Europe—made it possible for him to withstand the cruelties of the McCarthy repression in the fifties and the equally brutal suppression of the Communist-led peasant uprising in the Philippines in the late forties and fifties. The symbolic action of the native's laughter at his fate produced a catharsis that helped him recover from disillusionment. Hence the pattern of life for the Bulosan protagonist in his fiction is that of the young peasant who gets his education from community/worker struggles, pan-ethnic solidarity with all the oppressed (including women), and from his conviction that underneath the ruin of his dreams, the temporary deprivations and exclusions, survives the image of "America" as the embodiment of equality, dignity, and material prosperity for all, a condition that will be brought about by mass struggles and personal sacrifices. It was a narrative of maturation, learning from collective experience, and a celebration of universal togetherness, a belonging to a redemptive fraternity (Bulosan 1995b). Bulosan arrived in Seattle in the thirties without any possessions and died in Seattle in the fifties penniless, but he was supported and acclaimed by a large vibrant community of workers and colleagues of various ethnic and racial backgrounds throughout the country.

With Philip Vera Cruz, this prototypical narrative of a Filipino "national" acquired some telling, if commonplace, deviations. It was a narrative of emancipation, no doubt, but it was also a story of disenchantment and a caustic tale of reserved affirmation of the human comedy. In broad outline, Philip's life conforms to Bulosan's in that both were colonized subjects from the Philippines, and both participated in the anticapitalist reform-minded struggle of multiethnic farmworkers. But they were also two unique individuals. As Jean-Paul Sartre (1974) once said in wrestling with the problem of how one can define the individuality of members of the same group: "Valery is a [petite] bourgeois intellectual, no doubt about that. But not every [petite] bourgeois intellectual is Valery." Philip shared the same subject-position as millions of his countrymen: "Because of our colonial education we looked up to anything American as good" (2000, 11); but he diverged in overturning the dominant hierarchy of values, valorizing integrity and faithfulness to one's words, solidarity, as the universal measure. That is, he tried to decolonize his mind and body.

Key to the difference lies in Philip's more independent temperament that was manifest early; for example, he defied his parents in going to school despite their refusal or indifference. Philip was able to pay for his passage from the sale of the last piece of family property. Moreover, his family did not go through the more arduous ordeals of Bulosan's clan in strife-torn Pangasinan province. Philip accepted the beneficent claims of U.S. education, not questioning its ideological function; so he finished high school in Washington in between hoeing beets in North Dakota, earning income as a busboy in a country club in Spokane, Washington, and doing various chores in Chicago. In Chicago, however, Philip engaged in intellectual pursuits. He was active in various community organizations where professionals participated; he also studied for a while at Gonzaga University in Spokane before being drafted into the army in 1942. What is unusual is that even though Philip learned the art of survival in the cities where Filipinos were discriminated against and ostracized, he did not experience the violent racist attacks that Bulosan and other Filipinos suffered in California and Washington in the thirties and forties. Philip quietly accepted subaltern status as long as he could send money to his family back home.

It was not until Philip settled in Delano, California, in 1943 and began working in the grape vineyards that he would be exposed to the overt racial segregation, hostility, and institutional harassment that Filipinos experienced every day. I think it was Philip's knowledge of diverse settings, modalities of survival and adjustment, as well as his uninterrupted devotion to supporting his brother and sister by regular remittances, that enabled him to maintain some distance from the plight of the Filipino community even while being categorized as belonging to that politically and economically subordinated group. His civic consciousness was dormant, his capabilities as a citizen untapped by any mediating political or social institution that could turn them into actual powers. In short, the subaltern had no choice of either speaking or refusing to speak.

Another disparity may be noted. It is revealing that Philip did not display the more reflexive astuteness that Bulosan showed in his dealings with compatriots, perhaps due to the latter's health problems and physical inability to really earn a living. Philip was able to manage and still save money to send home to his mother, a fulfillment of his vow to his father. Despite accommodation to city life, Philip expressed an appreciation not for the pastoral innocence of the countryside but for the independence of the farmer cultivating productive land, for the self-disciplined industriousness of "simple folk," which contrasted sharply with the deceit and betrayal rampant in urban life. After leaving his birthplace, Saoang, Ilocos Sur, and "crossing the Pacific in search of a better life, wandering around the United States for many years," Philip finally returned to a rural place resembling his natal village, though he also was painfully cognizant of the disparity: "Saoang was green, lush, tropical . . . and there was always the sight of the blue ocean that contrasted so beautifully with the rolling green foothills that came down almost to the water, whereas Delano is flat, hot but dry, with almost no green vegetation except what's planted on the farms, and no bodies of water" (2000, 7). In contrast, as in stories such as "As Long As the Grass Shall Grow," Bulosan displayed a tendency to romanticize the "virginal" land where migrant workers were abused and exploited (see San Juan 1998b).

Philip celebrated the "Saong tradition of migrant work" in the forties when the New Deal was being tested in factories and fields. Despite his direct acquaintance with racism, Philip never showed any tendency to chauvinist exclusivism; he acknowledged the influence of his Anglo friend Bill Berg from New York—Philip would talk to Filipinos about how "white people had also fought for freedom and are also revolutionaries, that the minority in this country cannot fully succeed without the help of all freedom fighters, whatever the color of their skin" (2000, 23). After the victory over fascist Germany and militarist Japan, the United States entered the era of the Cold War. Times changed and labor-capital antagonisms, muted by white supremacy and Western chauvinism, simmered under the surface (for a good historical background of the farmworker's movement, see Kushner 1975).

## Crucible of Circumstance

One of the major events that produced a decisive swerve in Philip's life, even if not consciously recognized in words, took place in his witnessing the 1948 Stockton strike led by the veteran labor organizers Chris Mensalvas and Ernesto Mangaong, close friends of Carlos Bulosan. Both organizers were officers of the Cannery Workers Union, International Longshoremen's and Warehousemen's Union Local 37, in Seattle where Filipinos predominated. (Bulosan edited the 1952 yearbook of this militant Union Local 37.) Of great significance to Philip was Mensalvas and Mangaong's successful effort to thwart the government's attempt to deport them under the anticommunist McCarran Act. Earlier in his life, as field help or restaurant worker, Philip never experienced any sustained involvement in strikes or worker protests.

What is problematic, and at the same time revealing, is Philip's silence about his views regarding the witch hunt of progressive activists who were suspected as communists or "fellow-travelers." Nor does he make any mention of the Huk uprising in the Philippines, nor Mao's triumph in liberating China, nor of the Korean War. Instead he comments on why Filipinos who entered the United States before 1936 (like himself) could not be deported because they were nationals, not aliens. In any case, he emphasizes the importance of the Stockton strike as "the first major agricultural workers strike" before the 1965 Delano strike. The process of his self-education seems to have reached the stage of narrating its genealogy and future direction.

Philip's education materialized in the school of arduous labor in households, restaurants, factories, and fields, and in his solidarity meditations. Personal witnessing of farmworker organizing, as well as the testimony of actual participants in the struggle for humane treatment, helped shape Philip's trust in the competence and sustainable strength of the organized masses to influence the course of their lives, even to the point of converting their passive resignation into active self-determination. Before touching on Philip's decision to resign from the United Farm Workers (UFW) as a critique of Chavez's top-down style, I want to introduce the two aspects of identity, the idem and ipse identity, theorized by the philosopher Paul Ricoeur, as pivotal elements in the construction of an ethnic autobiography.

So far, what I have reviewed are the events of Philip's development as reflexive protagonist of his adventure in the United States. This is a narrative of the development of character, what Ricoeur calls the "self" (idem/sameness) as a permanent structure of qualities or dispositions by which a person is recognized. This structure consists not just of acquired habits but also learned identification with values, norms, ideals, models, and heroes, in which the person or the community recognizes itself. This continuity of character should be distinguished from the self as ipse (selfhood) embodied in the phenomenon of promise, "that of keeping one's word in faithfulness to the word that has been given. Keeping one's word expresses a self-constancy that, far from implying temporal changelessness, meets the challenge of variation in beliefs and feelings. . . . The continuity of character is one thing, the constancy of friendship quite another" (1983, 106). The question "What am I?" differs from "Who am I?" in this manner: the former is sameness without selfhood and the latter selfhood without sameness. It subtends Philip's narrative of articulating a Filipino identity with a difference.

The practice of belonging implies accountability. We have seen Philip prove his faithfulness to his father and to his family by sharing his hard-won wages, denying himself the opportunity for an education or even for a relatively comfortable life. He has in effect been fulfilling an unspoken promise to maintain his organic linkage with the community. This is itself a mark of character as well as a sign of selfhood, although the practice of helping the family back home is shared by the majority of Filipino workers in one degree or another. This truth is confirmed today in the huge remittance of ten million Filipino migrant workers around the world, a return of wages enough to bail out a shipwrecked economic and political nation-state (Montinola 2006). Another subcultural characteristic of Philip's generation is what he calls pride, the refusal or failure to convey the forbidding reality of their lives to their parents and relatives back home. In other words, lying turns out to be necessary to safeguard or salvage the truth. Everyone in the colony believed in America as the "land of promise," a place where hard work would reward you with success, status in terms of money and material possessions. Conditioned by this ideological expectation, Philip and the "Manongs" lived a life of suspended utopian longing, if not stubborn self-deception. Philip did not want to disappoint his brother so he persuaded him not to follow and join him: "I was trying to be truthful but at the same time I didn't want to tell him the details of how hard life was here." Philip confessed the nature of the collective predicament:

> I couldn't tell them some of the truths about my life here because I wanted to make them believe that America was good as I believed before I left. I had to struggle to make it good, at least for myself. Most of my Filipino compatriots felt this way too, and that's why very few of us wrote truthfully about our lives here to our families back home. Many of us were guilty of fooling our families in the Philippines into believing we were something here that we really were not. (2000, 29)

## What Is to Be Done?

For the most part, Philip never dwelt at length or in-depth on the illusions most colonials cherished about the United States. To be sure, the schooling and ideological apparatuses of the state conditioned every native to believe in the equivalence of prosperity and everyday life in the metropolis. So efficient was this mass indoctrination that it had to take the daily ordeals of survival for these young Filipinos to get rid of years of what Filipino historian Renato Constantino (1966) calls "mis-education." An emblematic symptom of this may be found in Philip's discovery of his ignorance when he disembarked from the ship that took him to Vancouver, Washington: he saw that the wealthy class enjoyed themselves above the deck while hundreds of his companions suffered in the steerage. This "shock of recognition" precipitated a turn or reversal that reinforced the latent streak of independence already manifested in his childhood.

We can speculate then that Philip's narrative of his life is an attempt to explain his character, the *habitus* (to use Pierre Bourdieu's term [1992]) of the self shared with his ethnic group. But what distinguishes Philip from the others, and in what way is this selfhood (ipse) a departure from the typical paradigm of the immigrant fable of success in America? What kind of moral or ethical subject is exemplified in Philip's decision to reveal his judgment of Chavez as a consequence of his being faithful to the demand of the larger Filipino community that was prior to his obligation to the bureaucratic constraints or rules of being an official of the union?

Philip's critique of Chavez's authoritarian style is nothing new, as Frank Bardache (1993), Rodolfo Acuna (1988), and others have elaborated on. Qualified by profuse praise of Chavez's charismatic stature and his self-sacrificing devotion to the welfare of the farmworkers, Philip's objection to Chavez's top-down management was long suppressed for the sake of the public image of UFW unity. However, the struggle for popular democracy in the Philippines and in the United States preempted Philip's devotion to UFW bureaucracy. It was only when Chavez embraced the brutal Marcos dictatorship in the Philippines, and invited the fascist labor minister Blas Ople to speak to the UFW rank and file at the August 1977 convention, while muzzling his own vice president Philip, that Philip could no longer restrain himself.

This crisis is significant for configuring Philip's narrative because it ushered the rupture, the ethical choice, that defined his character from idem-sameness to ipse-selfhood: his opposition to the authoritarian rule of Ferdinand Marcos in the Philippines coincided with a national upsurge of radicalism among Filipino Americans, in particular the second- or third-generation youth, who were mobilized in the late sixties and seventies by the civil rights and antiwar campaigns. This is the youth that he appeals to at the end, his audience, his hope for a new future. No such turning point can be found in the early stages of Philip's life that equals this episode in intensity and resonance. Patient and forgiving, self-effacing to the point of seeming to be fatalistic or indifferent, Philip finally disrupted postcolonial inertia and connected his present with other moments in his life when he rebelled, contradicted abusive authority, and tried to help sustain a community of honest, dignified, morally capable citizens of equal status. At last the postcolonial subaltern dared to speak.

In the section of his autobiography entitled "The Movement Must Go Beyond Its Leaders," Philip opposed the irrational cult of a leader and the suppression of criticism that deprived union members of "their right to reason for themselves." Capability for moral choice needs to be actualized by democratic public institutions such as unions and the like. Notwithstanding the praise of Chavez by Peter Mathiessen (1969) and the biographers Richard Griswold del Castillo and Richard A. Garcia (1995), Jacques

Levy (1975), Joan London and Henry Anderson (1970), John Gregory Dunne (1971), and others, Philip's reservation may be explained by his identification with the plight of his compatriot Larry Itliong who initiated the Delano grape strike and had never really been credited for his part in this historic event. Philip regretted not having been closer to Larry whose self-contradictions, tied to the apathy and suspicion of his ethnic group, limited his efficacy. Responding to those who wanted to preserve the mythical aura of Chavez and the movement, Philip writes: "For me, we need the truth more than we need heroes" (2000, 91). He has broken from the circumscribed locus of family and ethnic kinship; defamiliarized, he joins a larger family of citizens united by the solidarity of civic cooperation and the humanizing telos of transformative political praxis.

Truth, in Philip's eyes, concerned principles, not personalities. Although he resigned from the union after he publicly distanced himself from Chavez's support of the Marcos dictatorship, Philip remained supportive of the UFW and the entire unionizing movement. Although he bewailed the fact that he sacrificed too much in his struggle to survive (a duty to support his family in the Philippines) and maintain his dignity as a Filipino assisting his community and fighting for workers' rights, Philip was never bitter or cynical. He affirmed an internationalism that transcended the narrow parochial claims of ethnicity, racial affiliation, and nationality: "I respect the differences between people through their cultures, and I think all efforts, energies, and money should be concentrated to serving the people instead of making profits for a select group or country here and there" (2000).

The narrative climaxes with an invocation to his successors, the youthful workers whose representatives here may be his editors Scharlin and Villanueva. Philip's message to the young generation in whom rests the future of any country clearly serves as the leitmotif of his chronicle: "The success of any positive changes in this country depends on the strength of the workers and the organizations that hold the workers together are the unions. . . . Nothing will really change in this country without the total support of the working class" (2000, 154). He was seventy-three when he chose the popular, democratic resistance against the right-wing Marcos dictatorship over Chavez's open support for it, a stand that also confirmed his internationalist, progressive spirit of opposing capitalism as a system whose destructive exploitative logic was the lesson and truth that Philip wanted to impart by recording his life.

In retrospect, Philip's life is in search of a narrative scheme that would contradict if not interrupt the commodified story of immigrant success, a narrative that would capture what Sartre calls (with reference to Kierkegaard) "the singular universal" (1974, 141). It would be a narrative that would assume the world-historical objectivity of human character but also recognize the active subject who fills the "holes of history" and opens up the space for global transformation. Such is the lesson we can infer from studying the autobiography of Philip Vera Cruz, a revolutionary Filipino worker, who replied to the perennial question we often hear addressed to us, ourselves as others: Why don't you go back where you came from? He couldn't—until he could account for why he stayed and fought. While narrating the life of a Filipino in the process of self-transformation, he also had to narrate an epoch in the history of the United States that witnessed significant sociopolitical changes, the civil rights struggles of the sixties and seventies, which gave birth to a multiculturalist if not an egalitarian, social-justice–minded consciousness still active despite the terror of racial profiling in a "National Security" homeland.

# 3

# Subaltern Silence: Vernacular Speech Acts

From the time Filipinos arrived in the United States as "colonial wards," or subaltern subjects, in the first decade of the twentieth century, the practice of speaking their vernacular tongues (whether Ilokano, Cebuano, Tagalog, or any of the other dozen regional languages) has been haunted by an interdiction. This accompanied the defeat of the revolutionary government of the first Philippine Republic at the end of the Filipino-American War (1902) and the institutionalization of English as the official medium of communication in government, business, education, and so on. American English became an instrument of political and ideological domination throughout colonial rule (1898–1946) and neocolonial hegemony (1946–present). With competence in English as the legal and ideological passport for entry of Filipinos into the continental United States as *pensionados* and contract laborers, the native vernaculars suffered virtual extinction in the public sphere. In exchange, the Philippines acquired the distinction of belonging to the empire of English-speaking peoples, texting messages intelligible at least to the merchants of global capitalism if not to George W. Bush and the Homeland surveillance agents at the airport. That is also the reason why Filipina domestic workers are highly valued in Hong Kong, Taiwan, Singapore, and countries in Europe and the Middle East for their ability to speak English, which fits their employers' needs.

U.S. linguistic terrorism has continued via subtle co-optation and juridical fiat. Up to the last quarter of the twentieth century, the custom of speaking the vernacular in the workplace was discouraged if not prohibited. Filipino nurses and government employees talking in Filipino/Pilipino were penalized, triggering legal suits by the aggrieved immigrants or naturalized citizens. "English only" needs to be vindicated. Filipinos need not be heard or listened to as long as they perform according to expectations.

37

Why learn or study the Filipino vernaculars when "they" can speak and understand English? With the sudden increase of Filipino migrants after 1965 and the growth of the multicultural ethos of the eighties and nineties, Filipinos discovered anew that they had always been speaking their native languages even while they ventriloquized in English. Filipino (the pre-1987 designation was "Pilipino") has indeed become a lingua franca for recent immigrants in the "land of the free," making it possible for the newly arrived from the "boondocks" to read U.S. Postal Service guidelines and tax regulations in Filipino.

However, Filipino is still an exotic language, despite its vulgarization and accessibility via the Internet and satellite media. While today courses in Arabic have become necessary aids for preparing all students for global citizenship, a college course in Filipino is a rarity. In the fifties and sixties, when the Huk insurgency disturbed the peace of the Cold War Establishment, courses in Tagalog were introduced in the universities as part of Area Studies; experts were trained at least to read captured documents from the underground, if not to assist in the propaganda and psywar effort of the local military (San Juan 2000). In the seventies, politicized Filipino Americans successfully initiated projects to teach Tagalog inside and outside the academy. With the displacement of the Philippines as a contested zone in Southeast Asia (despite the Abu Sayyaf and the Moro Islamic Liberation Front), administrators have shifted resources to the study of Indonesian, Thai, and Vietnamese cultures. After all, isn't the Philippines now a suburb of California? And hasn't the current Arroyo administration reversed the trend of Filipinization by promulgating English as truly the privileged language for individual success, prestige, and acceptance?

Historical necessity has once more intervened in the "belly of the beast." Filipinos have become the largest group in the Asian American ethnic category and are slowly beginning to realize the political impact of this demographic trend. With the upsurge of Filipino Americans entering college and moving on to graduate schools, and given the heightened racial and ethnic antagonisms in this period of the borderless war against terrorism (recall, after September 11, 2001, the hundreds of Filipinos summarily deported in handcuffs and chains), a new "politics of identity" seems to be emerging, this time manifesting itself in a demand for the offering of credited courses in Filipino as part of the multiculturalist program (San Juan 2002). In 2002 I was requested by the community of Filipino and Filipino American students at the University of California–Irvine, to share my ideas about the "language question." The following provisional theses attempt to address this question in the context of the struggle of the Filipino nationality in the United States for democratic rights and the Filipino people in the Philippines and in the diaspora for national self-determination. It goes without saying that there are other still undiscerned factors overdetermining this complex conjuncture, particularly in this stage of the advanced corporatization of the U.S. university in late modernity; the following observations are meant to induce an exploration of the totality of social relations subtending this issue.

# I

In dealing with the issue of linguistic freedom and bondage, I begin with the thesis that language cannot be separated from material-social activity, from human interaction. Marx and Engels (1978) write in *The German Ideology*: "Language, like consciousness, only arises from the need, the necessity, of intercourse with other humans." Language is essentially a social phenomenon, embedded in collective human activity. Consciousness and language cannot be divorced; both are social products; they originate from work, from the labor process, whose historical changes determine the function of language as a means of communication and, as an integral component of everyday social practice, a signifier of national or ethnic identity.

Work or social labor, then, explains the structural properties of language. This does not mean, however, that given the unity of thought and language, linguistic structures imply different ways of thinking, world outlooks, and others. Race, culture, and language are not equivalent, as proclaimed in Hitler's idealizing slogan: "Ein Volk, Ein Reich, Ein Sprache" (One People, One Empire, One Language). We do not live in isolated language compartments with singular "takes" on reality. Forms of thought manifest a certain universality that is not affected by linguistic differences, even though speech acts derive their full import from the historical contexts and specific conditions of their performance. "Ideas do not exist separately from language" (Marx 1993, 163). And since the ideas of the ruling class prevail in every epoch as the ruling ideas, the uses of a particular language often reveal the imprint of this ruling class. Various classes may use the same language or operate in the same linguistic field, hence this domain of sign usage becomes, to quote Bakhtin and Voloshinov (1986, 23), "an arena of class struggle." For example, Jose Rizal (1912) used Spanish to counter the corrupt abuses of the friars and reach his Spanish-speaking compatriots as well as reform-minded Spanish liberals in Spain. Likewise, Tagalog and other vernaculars were used by the Filipino elite in persuading peasants and workers to conform to American policies and ideas.

In sum, language as a practice of signification is not only reflective but also productive and reproductive of antagonistic social relations and political forces. It is a vehicle and an embodiment of power. It is both a means of expressive self-identification and an instrument for cognitive communication (Ives 2006). Language usage manifests the pressure of contradictory class relations and concrete ideological structures that are registered on the level of special subcodes and idiolects. Idiolect in general refers to those aspects of an individual's speech pattern that deviate from group norms; the idiolect of, say, a Christian or Islamic fundamentalist believer represents a code of free variants mimicking certain sociocultural patterns of thought (Ducrot and Todorov 1979, 57). An idiolect, then, becomes intelligible as a departure from the normal usage of words (Rifatere 1983) and resembles what Mikhail Bakhtin (1981) calls "ideologeme," or "utterance," amenable to rational semantic analysis. In sum, then, language is a socioideological phenomenon whose empirical manifestation can be investigated with scientific rigor. Using this frame of inquiry, let us examine the status of Filipino/Pilipino vis-à-vis English within the Filipino community (totaling nearly three million) in the United States. A historical background is imperative in assessing the worth of languages relative to each other, specifically in the context of the fraught relations between the Philippines as a former colony, now a neocolony, of the United States, and the hegemonic nation-state, now the "only remaining superpower" in this period of "endless war" against terrorist multitudes.

With the violent conquest of the Philippines after the Filipino-American War of 1899–1914 (I include the wars that tried to pacify the Moros) that cost 1.4 million Filipino lives, the United States imposed colonial institutions on the subjugated natives. The process of what Renato Constantino (1966) famously called "the mis-education of Filipinos" began with the imposition of English as the chief medium of instruction. This was not because the teacher-volunteers in the St. Thomas knew no Spanish, as one historian puts it (Arcilla 1971), but because this was the language of the U.S. ruling class, the vehicle in which to inculcate the American "way of life," its institutions and normative practices, in their colonial subjects. Contrary to the supposed intention of democratizing society, the use of English "perpetuated the existence of the *ilustrados*—American *ilustrados*" loyal to the United States, analogous to the Spanish-speaking Filipino elite who sought reforms within Spanish hegemony. Constantino cites Simoun's denunciation of the latter in Rizal's novel *El Filibusterismo*:

> You ask for equal rights, the Hispanization of your customs, and you don't see that what you are begging for is suicide, the destruction of your nationality, the annihilation of your fatherland, the consecration of tyranny! What will you be in the future? A people without character, a nation without liberty—everything you have will be borrowed, even your very defects! . . . What are you going to do with Castilian, the few of you who will speak it? Kill off your own originality, subordinate your thoughts to other

brains, and instead of freeing yourselves, make yourselves slaves indeed! Nine-tenths of those of you who pretend to be enlightened are renegades to your country! He among you who talks that language neglects his own in such a way that he neither writes it nor understands it, and how many have I not seen who pretended not to know a single word of it! (1966, 55)

In 1913, the American scholar Najeeb Saleeby deplored the imposition of English as the means of trying to accomplish what Alexander the Great and Napoleon failed to accomplish, that is, impose the conqueror's language on the multitudinous groups speaking different tongues. It had been a failure twenty-five years since the United States established schools in the pacified regions. In preserving imperial hegemony, however, the policy was not a failure at all. It has proved extremely effective: English as linguistic capital has functioned to sustain the iniquitous class hierarchy and maintain the subordination of the nation-state to the power that monopolizes such capital in the form of control over the mass media, information, and other symbolic instruments and resources in a globalized economy. I think the purpose was not to make every Filipino a speaker of English, just those classes—the elite and intelligentsia—that have proved crucial in reinforcing and reproducing consent to U.S. imperial rule.

The historical record is summed up by Constantino: "Spanish colonialism Westernized the Filipino principally through religion. American colonialism superimposed its own brand of Westernization initially through the imposition of English and the American school system which opened the way for other Westernizing agencies" (1978, 218). Superior economic and technological power certainly enabled the American colonizers to proceed without serious resistance. Inscribed within the state educational apparatus, American English as a pedagogical, disciplinary instrument contributed significantly to the political, economic, and cultural domination of the Filipino people. American English performed its function in enforcing, maintaining, and reproducing the values and interests of the imperial power and the dominant native class. Its usage was not neutral or merely pragmatic; it was a deliberately chosen ideological weapon in subjugating whole populations (including the Muslims and indigenous communities), in producing and reproducing the colonial relations of production, and later of neocolonial relations.

Again, as I said in the beginning, no language (like English) as a system of signs is by itself exploitative or oppressive. It is the political usages and their historical effects that need evaluation. Consequently, the use of the colonizer's language cannot be separated from its control of the educational system, the panoply of commercial relations and bureaucratic machinery that instilled consumerist values, White supremacy, and acquisitive individualism within the procedural modus operandi of a so-called free enterprise system. More than a half century of tutelage de-Filipinized youth and "taught them to regard American culture as superior to any other, and American society as the model par excellence for Philippine society" (Constantino 1974, 39). Individual and public consciousness had been so Americanized that a Filipino national identity was aborted, suppressed, unable to emerge fully except in outbursts of revolt and insurrection—a durable tradition of revolutionary resistance that we should be proud of.

What of Filipino and the other vernaculars? When the Philippines was granted commonwealth status in 1935, an attempt was made to develop a national language based on Tagalog. Pilipino evolved, despite the objections of other regional groups, so deep was the legacy of the "divide-and-rule" strategy that undermined the weak Filipino elite. Note that, of course, the ruling bloc of local landlords, compradors, and bureaucrats was completely subservient to the United States diktat even up to and beyond formal independence in 1946. Up to now, it is no secret that the Philippine military is completely dependent on U.S. largesse for its weaponry and logistics, including the training of its officers in counterinsurgency warfare (as witness the prolongation and systematization of joint training exercises against the Abu Sayyaf and other insurgents in violation of the constitution). More than 80 percent of Filipinos can speak or understand Filipino in everyday transactions throughout the islands. While some progress has been made today in institutionalizing the use of Filipino as an intellectual medium in university courses, English remains the preferred language of business and government, the language of prestige and aspiration. Decolonization of the Filipino mind has not been completed; hence Filipino remains subordinate, marginalized, or erased as a language of power and self-affirmation of the people's sovereign identity. Just as in other colonized parts of the world, the Philippines was a multilingual society during the heyday of Spanish imperialism. While formal colonialism no longer obtains, a linguistic imperialism continues, with English employed as the international language of science, technology, business and finance, world communications, and international academic studies—despite some nativization of American English in the Philippines. This will continue unless the political economy and power relations in the whole society are changed.

## II

The rise of the U.S. empire in Asia beginning with the defeat of Spanish power translated into a reassertion of Anglo-Saxon "manifest destiny." This is a continuation of a long saga of territorial expansion from the eastern seaboard of the continent. When the Filipino entered U.S. metropolitan territory, first in Hawaii as recruited plantation workers in the first three decades of the last century, the United States was already a racial polity founded on the genocidal confinement of the indigenous Indians, the slavery and segregation of blacks, the conquest of Spanish-speaking natives, and the proscription of Asian labor. The United States was and is a multilingual polity, with English as the hegemonic language.

A language community is not by itself sufficient to produce an ethnic or national identity. English cannot by itself define the American national identity as such, even though it is within this linguistic community that individuals are interpellated as subjects, subjects as bearers of discourse—persons defined as subject-positions sutured within discourses of law, genealogy, history, political choices, professional qualifications, psychology, and so on. This construction of identity by language is open to incalculable contingencies; what makes it able to demarcate the frontiers of a particular people is a principle of closure or exclusion. And this fictive ethnicity is accomplished in the historical constitution of the U.S. nation-state based on the discourses of the free market and white supremacy.

Etienne Balibar has shown how the French nation initially gave privileged place to language or linguistic uniformity as coincident with political unity; the French state democratized its citizens by coercively suppressing cultural particularisms, the local patois. "For its part," Balibar observes, "the American 'revolutionary nation' built its original ideals on a double repression: that of the extermination of the Amerindian 'natives' and that of the difference between free 'white' men and 'black' slaves. The linguistic community inherited from the Anglo-Saxon 'country' did not pose a problem—at least apparently—until Hispanic immigration conferred upon it the significance of class symbol and racial feature" (Balibar and Wallerstein 1991, 104). In other words, the phantasm of the American race defined as English speakers materialized when the Spanish-speaking indigenes of the Southwest were defeated in the war of 1848. Thus, the national ideology of the "melting pot" of a new race emerged "as a hierarchical combination of the different ethnic contributions," based on the inferiority of Asian labor immigrants and "the social inequalities inherited from slavery and reinforced by the economic exploitation of the blacks" (ibid.). It is within this historical process of ethnicization of the American identity on an assimilative or pluralist ideology that we can then locate the supremacy of American English over the other languages of various ethnic groups within the polity. It is also in this historical context of the formation of the American multicultural pluralist imaginary that problems of citizenship—equality of rights, multilingualism, neocolonialism, nationalism, or internationalism—should be placed and analyzed.

In the United States today, we have various languages spoken and practiced everywhere—Spanish being the most widespread; Black English vernacular (BEV); Creole in Louisiana and New York City; Russian in Brooklyn; and so on—testifying to a multilingual society. Yet as studies have demonstrated, the failure of the school authorities in the United States to recognize BEV as a separate language has continuously retarded the educational progress of black children (Spears 1999). BEV, as well as the other varieties of Spanish, functions as symbolic markers signifying membership in a particular ethnic group.

Why is one's use of a particular language important? Language usage or behavior is closely connected with the individual's perception of herself and her own identity. The British sociolinguist Robert Le Page has proposed a theory of language use in terms of acts of identity. According to Le Page, "the individual creates his or her own language behavior so that it resembles that of the group or groups with which he wishes to be identified, to the extent that: he can identify the groups; observe and analyze such groups; is motivated to adapt his behavior; and is still able to adapt his behavior. By so doing the individual is thus able to locate himself in the 'multidimensional' space defined by such groups in terms of factors such as sex, age, social class, occupation and other parameters for social group membership, including ethnicity" (quoted in Cashmore 1984, 173). In Britain, the use of a modified Jamaican Creole by second-generation Britishers of Caribbean descent is an example of acts of identity-formation, an assertion of an ethnic identity associated with such cultural interests as Rastafarianism, reggae, and so on. By consciously adopting this Creole or patois, the youth are expressing their solidarity, ethnic pride, and symbolic resistance to what they perceive as a repressive and racist society.

One may ask: Has the Filipino community in the United States considered language as one of the most important social practices through which they come to experience themselves as subjects with some critical agency, that is, not merely as objects trained to consume and be consumed? Have Filipino scholars examined language as a site for cultural and ideological struggle, a mechanism that produces and reproduces antagonistic relations between themselves and the dominant society? In my forty years here, except for a few academics influenced by the late Virgilio Enriquez, I have not encountered among our ranks any special awareness of the importance of Filipino and the other vernaculars.

In the dismal archive of ethnic studies of Filipino Americans, we encounter a species of identity politics that is unable to escape the hegemonic strategies of containment and sublimation. Ironically, this politics is really designed for encouraging painless assimilation. For example, Antonio Pido's *The Pilipino in America* (1986) is a repository of scholastic clichés and a rehash of received opinions, at best an eclectic survey that tries to coalesce the contradictory tendencies in the research field as well as those in the community during the Marcos dictatorship. Recently, the collection

*Filipino Americans: Transformation and Identity* (1997), edited by Maria
P. P. Root, tried to advance beyond the Establishment banalities, but to no
avail, although gays and lesbians have succeeded in occupying their niches
amid the cries for "healing the cultural amnesia and sense of shame." I
have no problem celebrating Filipino firsts, but I think historical memory
of this ingratiating kind cannot decolonize our psyches since we use such
memory to compete with other people of color in grabbing a piece of the
American pie. Pido's contribution to this anthology compounded the mud-
dle in its reflection of a neoconservative climate of the nineties with the
multiculturalist belief that Filipinos have transcended their ethnicity in assuming some kind of mutant or freakish existence: "Such solidarity did
not happen to the Pilipino Americans because they are Pilipinos who are
in America, as their parents and grandparents were, but rather because
they are Americans who are Pilipinos" (1997, 37). An ambivalent oppor-
tunist indeed if not an enigmatic trickster figure. None of the essays, if I recall, deal with the discrimination of Filipinos on account of their speaking
Pilipino/Filipino at the workplace, or elsewhere.

In a study on Filipino Americans, Pauline Agbayani-Siewert and Linda
Revilla comment on the Filipino group's lack of a "strong ethnic identity."
They give a lot of space to the issue of whether Filipino should be spelled
with an "F" or "P." In spite of disagreements among post-1965 and
pre-1965 immigrants, they note that Filipinos are distinguished by their ad-
herence to "traditional Filipino values" relating to family togetherness and
respect for elders. So what else is new? What is interesting about their survey is that they touch on the issue of language, remarking that "language
is a questionable indicator of Filipino immigrants' acculturation," without
adding that, of course, their country of origin has been thoroughly Americanized in language, if not in customs and habits. They cite a study that in-
dicated that 71 percent of Filipinos speak a language other than English at
home, although 91 percent of them claimed being able to speak English
well or very well. Their conclusion: "This suggests that most Filipinos who
have been naturalized citizens [Filipinos have a 45 percent naturalization
rate, the highest among Asian groups] and who can speak English well still
prefer to speak their native language at home" (1995, 152). What does this
signify? In general, third-generation children no longer speak the languages
of their grandparents.

One interpretation is that of Yen Le Espiritu, author of the ethnographic collection, *Filipino American Lives* (1995). Despite some mobility
and cultural adaptation, Filipino settlers in the United States are still not
fully accepted as "Americans." This is not bad because Espiritu claims that
Filipinos are really "transmigrants," that is, they resist racial categorization
and at the same time sustain "multistranded relations between the Philippines and the United States" (27). This hypothesis is flawed. Espiritu wants

Filipinos to have their cake and eat it too. While some may succeed in manipulating their identities so that they both accommodate and resist their subordination within the global capitalist system—a tightrope performance not really warranted by the biographies she presents—they do not constitute the stereotype. Especially in the case of those who came in the last two decades, Filipinos have not really become full-blown hybrids conjured by postmodernists-postcolonial academics. The majority of the testimonies gathered by Espiritu provide incontrovertible proof that despite sly forms of resistance, institutional racism has continued to inflict damage on the lives and collective psyche of the Filipino community, whether some of them are perceived as transmigrants or not.

In fact, the transmigrant paradigm cannot explain adequately the linguistic behavior of Filipinos. Siewert and Revilla (1995) report that Filipinos have begun to challenge the "English-only" policies at the workplace. They cite one case in the Harborview Medical Center in Seattle, Washington, where seven Filipino workers filed a grievance for having been penalized for being told to use English-only for business purposes. The policy was eventually rescinded, but we are not informed what the views of the experts are. Since they are obsessed with acculturation or cultural assimilation, they probably feel that the case was not really significant since Filipinos are bilingual anyway, and they can be flexible or versatile in adapting to the exigencies of their minority situation. Never mind that they have to suppress their need to speak in Filipino.

To recapitulate: The development of U.S. capitalism concomitant with the growth and consolidation of American English proceeded up to 1898, with the onset of imperial expansion. The civil rights movement succeeded (through the Civil Rights Act of 1964 and later the Bilingual Education Act of 1968) to mandate the use of non-English voting ballots and the funding of bilingual education programs serving primarily Hispanics to expedite their transition to competent English users. Due to various revisions, bilingual education programs (which started in 1963 in Miami, Florida, to help the children of Cuban exiles) only serve a small proportion of the total population. And yet some were alarmed by the increase of Hispanics in many states. One of them, Senator S. I. Hayakawa, a naturalized Canadian immigrant of Japanese descent, founded the U.S. English in 1983 after sponsoring a bill in 1981 to make English the official language of the United States (Fischer et al. 1997).

In actuality, what has been happening in the last decades involves an implicit "reorganization of cultural hegemony" by the ruling elite faced with a sharpening political, social, and economic crisis of the system since the end of the Vietnam War. We may interpret this English-only movement as an index to the resurgent nativist hostility to the recent influx of immigrants from Latin America and Asia—aliens who supposedly disunite America and threaten the supremacy of the "American Way of Life" (Nunberg 2000). The English First anti-immigrant phenomenon can easily be demystified and translated as the symptom of a moral panic, a fanatical zeal to preserve the status quo, "a fear of cultural change and a deep-seated worry that European Americans will be displaced from their dominant position in American life" (Douglas Massey, quoted in Zelinsky 2001, 192). This symptomatic reading finds its rationale in Antonio Gramsci's insight:

> Each time that in one way or another, the question of language comes to the fore, that signifies that a series of other problems is about to emerge, the formation and enlarging of the ruling class, the necessity to establish more intimate and sure relations between the ruling groups and the popular masses, that is, the reorganization of cultural hegemony. (1971, 16)

## III

In 1985 then Education Secretary William Bennett judged bilingual education a failure because it only promoted ethnic pride despite the fact that programs such as the Transitional Bilingual Education program and the Family English literacy programs no longer seek to fund classes conducted in the original ethnic languages. Four million language-minority students are now herded to monolingual "immersion" English classrooms that, according to one expert, often fail to teach anything but English. And this is supposed to explain why they don't have equal educational opportunities and become complete failures.

One opponent of the bills to make English the official language, Representative Stephen Solarz, expressed a sentiment shared by many liberals who endorse pluralism or multiculturalism under the shibboleth of a common civic culture. Language is a matter of indifference as long as the cement of the civic culture holds the market system, individual rights, and private property together. Solarz argued that the proposals "represent a concession to nativist instincts and are incompatible with the cultural diversity and ethnic pluralism that constitute fundamental strengths of our nation. . . . We are . . . a tapestry of many races, creeds, religions, and ethnic backgrounds—each independent, but all interwoven with one another. . . . The glue that bonds these diverse communities together is not commonality of language, but a commitment to the democratic ideals on which our country was founded" (1997, 251). Aside from these banalities, Solarz also opined that those proposals could pose significant threats to the civil and constitutional rights of citizens with little or no English proficiency.

In this he was right because English triumphalism signifies a mode of racialization: the institutional subordination of other communities and other languages to white supremacy and its cultural hegemony. This was in part the thrust of the challenge made in the class-action suit of 1970, *Lau v. Nichols*, in which 1,790 Chinese children enrolled in the public schools in San Francisco, California, argued against the San Francisco Unified School District that they were not being provided with an equal education because all instruction and materials were in English, which the children did not understand. Furthermore, the plaintiffs contended that English-only education for non–English-speaking children was unconstitutional because it violated the Fourteenth Amendment, which guarantees to all citizens the equal protection of the laws. Moreover, such education was illegal under Title VI of the Civil Rights Act, which rules that "no person in the United States shall be . . . subjected to discrimination under any program receiving Federal financial assistance" (the district was receiving funds from the federal government). The Supreme Court ruled unanimously in favor of the Chinese students, but only on the basis of the Civil Rights Act; the constitutional issue was avoided and the Court left the remedy to local school boards (Fischer et al. 1997, 242–45).

It is this 1974 *Lau* decision that can serve as the basis for litigation against public educational institutions that refuse to provide language services to students of limited English-speaking ability. It is a legal precedent on which institutions receiving federal money can be held accountable. It is not one, however, that engages the question of injustice, discrimination, and inequality in a racial polity such as the United States. It is not one that addresses, more specifically, the subordination of nationalities (such as Filipinos) and their diverse languages as a consequence of the past colonial subjugation and present neocolonial status of the Philippines, their "national origin." This is not a matter of personal opinion, feeling, or subjective speculation, but a matter for historical inquiry and empirical verification.

Following the mandate of federal laws, Tagalog, or Filipino, is now being used in census forms, ballots, postal notices, and even in public announcements of flights to the Philippines in some airports. Is this a sign that the racial polity has changed and abolished institutional impediments to the recognition of the identity and dignity of the Filipino as a cultural-political subject? Are we now living in a classless and race-blind society? Scarcely. Such events as Filipino History Month or Independence parades confirm the hierarchical placing of the various ethnic communities within the pluralist schema that reproduces monolingualism and Anglocentrism in everyday life. Even the concession to fund classes in Filipino, or, to cite a recent trend, Arabic—suddenly classes in Arabic multiplied after 9/11—may be a deceptive means of convincing a few that linguistic, racial, and sex discrimination are amenable to such piecemeal reforms.

Apart from the neoconservative backlash of the eighties and nineties, the advent of post–9/11 hegemony of the "only remaining superpower" entrenched in a National Security State, the imperiled "Homeland," almost guarantees a regime of unmitigated surveillance and policing of public spaces where ethnic differences are sometimes displayed. Calling attention to their "peculiar" speech/communication network, Filipinos speaking Tagalog make themselves vulnerable to arrest—recall the case of sixty-two overstaying Filipinos deported last June, handcuffed and manacled like ordinary criminals throughout the long flight back to Clark Air Base, Philippines; and recently, the case of eight Filipino airport mechanics in Texas, victims of racial profiling and suspected of having links with Arab terrorists.

Filipino sounds completely unlike Arabic or Russian. What has made Filipino, or Tagalog, visible in our multicultural landscape is, of course, the huge flow of recent immigrants who are not as proficient in English as the earlier "waves" after 1965. Movies, music, and other mass-media cultural products using Filipino are more widely disseminated today than before. In addition, the resurgent nationalist movement in the Philippines, despite the lingering horrors of the Marcos dictatorship from 1972 to 1986, has brought to center stage the nightly televised images of rallies where the messages of protest and rebellion against U.S. imperialism are often conveyed in Filipino. The nationalist resurgence in the Philippines, as well as in the diaspora of seven to nine million Filipinos around the world, has rebounded miraculously from the sixties and has continued to revitalize Filipino as the language of critical protest and nationalist self-determination. I don't have to mention the anxiety and tensions provoked when children cannot understand their parents who, as Siewert and Revilla indicate (1995), prefer to use Filipino or other vernaculars at home.

# IV

We are surrounded now by a preponderance of newly arrived Filipinos who use Filipino to make sense of their new experiences, a necessary stage in their arduous life here, before they are able to gain mastery of standard English and feel more capable of directing their lives. Learning English language skills alone, however, does not automatically translate to access to limited opportunities, not to mention genuine empowerment, as witness the plight of black Americans, or the sixty million functionally illiterate citizens in this affluent, technically superior society. Meanwhile, these Filipinos feel dispossessed and marginalized, completely alienated, either resentful or more servile, depending on the complex circumstances of daily life. If and when they enter school (formal or informal), their language experience (in Filipino or other indigenous languages) is delegitimized by a pedagogical system that operates on the assumption that knowledge acquisition is a matter of learning the standard English, thus abstracting English from its ideological charge and socioeconomic implications. Correct me if I am wrong, but I don't recall any time when Filipinos have demanded access to bilingual education in the same way that Latinos and Chinese Americans have, as noted earlier. And I know that Filipino American students' request for classes in Filipino/Tagalog is nothing compared to the substantial programs in bilingual education among Hispanics. Still, it might be useful to quote the educational scholar Donaldo Macedo's comments on the current philosophy:

> The view that teaching English constitutes education sustains a notion of ideology that systematically negates rather than makes meaningful the cultural experiences of the subordinate linguistic groups who are, by and large, the objects of its policies. For the education of linguistic minority students to become meaningful it has to be situated within a theory of cultural production and viewed as an integral part of the way in which people produce, transform and reproduce meaning. Bilingual education, in this sense, must be seen as a medium that constitutes and affirms the historical and existential moments of lived culture. . . . [S]tudents learn to read faster and with better comprehension when taught in their native tongue. The immediate recognition of familiar words and experiences enhances the development of a positive self-concept in children who are somewhat insecure about the status of their language and culture. For this reason, and to be consistent with the plan to construct a democratic society free from vestiges of oppression, a minority literacy program must be rooted in the cultural capital of subordinate groups and have as its point of departure their own language. (2000, 309)

Macedo rightly emphasizes the daily lived experiences of linguistic minorities rooted in collective and individual self-determination. He considers their language as "a major force in the construction of human subjectivities," since language "may either confirm or deny the life histories and experiences of the people who use it." Again, I refer to my earlier premise that it is language use that is decisive and consequential. We need to underscore the role of language as cultural or symbolic capital, a theme that Pierre Bourdieu (1991; 2000) has elaborated on.

Literacy must be based on the reality of subaltern life if it is to be effective in any strategy of real empowerment, in the decolonization of schooling for a start. Only by taking into account the language of everyday lived experience, and connecting this with the community's struggles to survive and maintain its integrity and autonomy, can we fully grasp what role the use of Filipino plays in the nationality's pursuit of a truly dignified and creative life as full-fledged citizens. This is, to my mind, a pursuit that cannot be achieved except as part of the collective democratic struggles of other people of color and the vast majority of working citizens oppressed by a class-divided, racialized, and gendered order.

And this system—globalized or neoimperialist capitalism—is the same one suppressing the possibilities for equality, justice, and autonomy in the Philippines. There is as yet no truly sovereign Filipino nation. I believe it is still in the process of slow, painful becoming. If so, how do we size up or assay persons who claim to be Filipinos, or whose geopolitical identities are somehow linked to the nation-state called the Philippines? Benedict Anderson theorized that modern nations are "imagined communities" made possible by print-capitalism and the "fatal diversity of human language" (1994, 95). If that is true, then the Philippines was imagined through American English mediated in schools, mass media, sports, and other cultural practices. Both the institutions of print capitalism and the schools were controlled and administered by the United States for half a century; long after formal independence, most of us continue to dream and fantasize in English mixed with Tagalog (Taglish), or one of the vernaculars.

We see then that language and the process of thinking form a dialectical unity. While Filipino has become the effective lingua franca, the community in the Philippines is still imagined in a babel of languages, with Cebuanos, for example, refusing to recite the Pledge of Allegiance unless it is in Cebuano. Less a political gesture than a symptom, this situation reflects the inchoate or abortive project of constructing a Filipino national identity, the clearest proof of which is the failure to develop one language through which the intellectual, political, and economic development of the masses can be articulated.

We have no alternative. We need to continue the task of reshaping our cultural identity as Filipinos whether here or in the Philippines, in this perilous age of antiterrorism. I want to quote Paulo Freire, the great Brazilian educator, whose work *Pedagogy of the Oppressed* has been a profound influence everywhere. Freire reminds us:

> At a particular moment in the struggle for self-affirmation, when subordinated to and exploited by the ruling class, no social group or class or even an entire nation or people can undertake the struggle for liberation without the use of a language. At no time can there be a struggle for liberation and self-affirmation without the formation of an identity, and identity of the individual, the group, the social class, or whatever. . . . Without a sense of identity, there can be no real struggle. I will only fight you if I am very

sure of myself. . . . This is why colonized peoples need to preserve their native language. . . . They help defend one's sense of identity and they are absolutely necessary in the process of struggling for liberation. (1985, 186)

Whether here in the United States or in the Philippines, we are, whether we like it or not, still entangled, caught, implicated in this ongoing process of struggling for liberation. A liberatory and radical approach to language as part of cultural production and pedagogical praxis is in order. How can we tell our stories in our own words? How do we retrieve the lost voices of our people, valorize their lived experiences, and in the process transform the way Filipinos as a group is treated in the metropolis?

To reappropriate the submerged or erased revolutionary legacy of our people, we need a language that is an integral and authentic part of that culture—a language that is not just "an instrument of communication, but also a structure of thinking for the national being" (Freire 1985, 184), that is, a tool for self-reflection and critical analysis, a creative and transforming agent committed to solidarity, social responsibility, and justice for the masses. That language needed to reconstruct our history and reappropriate our culture cannot be English but an evolving Filipino, which draws its resources from all the other vernaculars. If we allow English to continue in the Philippines as a hegemonic cultural force, this will simply perpetuate the colonial legacy of class-racialized inequalities—need I remind you that we are still a genuine neocolony—and allow imperial ideology to determine the parameters of our historical and scientific development, the future not only of the Philippines but also the future of those who choose to leave and settle in other lands that, however, remain, alas, still part of an inescapable globalized market system. This is the task challenging us today and for as long as we speak English to request or demand the authorities that the teaching and learning of Filipino be given some space in the university.

The paramount importance of a communal language or speech in the forging of a democratic and truly egalitarian society, let alone an emancipated socialist order, cannot be overemphasized. This is what the national liberation struggle in the Philippines is engaged with, first and foremost, rather than simply the fashionable copying of a market-centered multiculturalist polity. In struggling for a truly independent Filipino nation equal in standing with other nation-states, on the face of the flattening and leveling thrust of capitalist globalization, it is instructive to recall what Lenin taught on the question of the equality of languages: "Whoever does not recognize and champion the equality of nations and languages, and does not fight against all national oppression or inequality, is not a Marxist; he is not even a democrat. . . . For different nations to live together in peace and freedom or to separate and form different states (if that is more convenient for them),

a full democracy, upheld by the working class, is essential. No privileges
for any nation or any one language! . . . such are the principles of working-class democracy" (1983, 100, 116).

# V

In the current situation of portentous upheaval in the Philippines, any discussion of the "language question," like the "woman question," is bound
to be incendiary and contentious. The issue of language is always explo-
sive, a crux of symptoms afflicting the body politic. It is like a fuse or trig-
ger that ignites a whole bundle of inflammable issues, scandalously
questioning the existence of God in front of an audience of believers. Or
the immortality of souls among the faithful. Perhaps my saying outright
that I am a partisan for a national language, Filipino, may outrage the
postmodernists and cosmopolites among you—how can you say such a
thing when you are speaking in English? Or, as Senator Diokno once said,
"English of a sort." How dare I infuriate the loyal speakers of Cebuano,
Ilocano, Pampagueno, Ilonggo, Taglish, Filipino English, and a hundred
or more languages used in these seven hundred islands. One gives up: it
can't be helped. Or we can help lift the ideological smog and draw the
lines of demarcation in the battleground more lucidly.
    One suspects that this is almost unavoidable, in a society where to raise
the need for one national language, say "Filipino" (as mandated by the
Constitution) is bound to arouse immediate opposition. Or, if not immediately, it is deferred and sublimated into other pretexts for debate and argu-
mentation. Fortunately, we have not reached the point of armed skirmishes
and violent confrontations for the sake of our mother-father tongue, as in
India and other countries. My partisanship for Filipino (not Tagalog) is
bound to inflame Cebuanos, Bicolanos, Ilocanos, and so on, including Filipino speakers-writers of English, or Filipino English. We probably try to defuse any brewing conflict quickly by using the colonizer's tongue, or
compromise Babelwise. My view is that only a continuing historical analysis can help explain the present contradictory conjuncture, and disclose the
options it offers us. Only engagement in the current political struggles can
resolve the linguistic aporia/antinomy and clarify the import and consequence of the controversy over the national language, over the fate of Filipino and English in our society.
    One would expect that this issue had been resolved a long time ago.
But, given the dire condition of the Philippine political economy in this
epoch of globalized terrorism of the U.S. hegemon, a plight that is the
product of more than a century of colonial/neocolonial domination, all
the controversies surrounding this proposal of a national language since

the time of the Philippine Commonwealth when Quezon convened the Institute of National Language under Jaime de Veyra, have risen again like ravenous ghouls. I believe this specter can never be properly laid to rest until we have acquired genuine sovereignty, until national self-determination has been fully exercised, and the Filipino people—three thousand every day, more than one million every year—will no longer be leaving in droves as overseas contract workers, the whole nation becoming a global subaltern to the transnational corporations, to the World Bank-World Trade Organization, the International Monetary Fund, and the predatory finance capital of the global North. If we cannot help but be interpellated by the sirens of the global market and transformed into exchangeable warm bodies, we can at least interrogate the conditions of our subordination—if only as a gesture of resistance by a nascent, irrepressible agency.

In the hope of avoiding such a situation, which is almost ineluctable, I would like to offer the following seven theses that may initiate a new approach to the question, if not offer heuristic points of departure for reflection. In contrast to the dominant neoliberal idealist-culturalist, metaphysical approach, I apply a historical materialist one whose method is not only historicizing and dialectical—not merely deploying the "Aufhebung" of Hegel within an eclectic, neoWeberian framework (as Fernando Zialcita does in his provocative book *Authentic Though Not Exotic: Essays on Filipino Identity* (2005)—but also, as Marx said, standing it on its head in the complex and changing social relations of production within concrete historical settings. The materialist dialectic offers a method of analysis and elucidation of the context in which questions about a national language can be clarified and the nuances of its practical implications elaborated.

In addition, I would like to stress the key distinction that needs to be made, following Gramsci's teaching on hegemony and the national-popular strategy discussed earlier, when we apply a historical-materialist optic on this terrain. First, as Peter Ives (2006) reminds us, we need to establish a dialectical connection between the communicative or pragmatic aspect of language with its expressive dimension, its role in identity and cultural formation integrally tied to the development of the nation-state. Those two aspects are engaged in the complex protracted process of the ongoing national-democratic revolution. In contrast to the liberal/neoliberal emphasis on the utilitarian/communicative function of language, a historical-materialist mode of critical analysis would concern itself with how language use interacts with the concepts and empirical actualization of "passive revolution," "subalternity," and "common sense," in particular, with the formation of a national-popular collective needed for the radical egalitarian transformation of the feudal/capitalist mode of production and social relations toward a democratic, socialist mode of production relations. Ultimately the policy debate on choosing a national language is a political question. Without investigating these linkages, any inquiry into the "national language" predicament would simply replicate the old exploitative order and reinforce imperialist hegemony based on "global English" and its various seductive alibis.

Thesis 1: Language is not an entity or phenomenon in itself but a component of the social forms of consciousness of any given social formation. As such, it can only be properly addressed within the historical specificity of a given mode of production and attendant social-political formation. It has no history of its own but is a constituent and constitutive of the ideological terrain on which the struggle of classes and historic blocs are fought, always in an uneven and combined mode of development. It forms part of the conflicted evolution of the integral state, as Gramsci conceived it as the combination of political society and civil society. The issue of language is located right at the heart of the construction of this integral state. Hence not only its synchronic but also diachronic dimensions should be dialectically comprehended in grasping its worth and contribution to the liberation and fulfillment of the human potential.

Thesis 2: The function and nature of language then cannot be adequately discussed in a neutral and positivistic-empiricist way, given its insertion into conflicted relations of production, at least since the emergence of class-divided societies in history. In the Philippines, the status and function of various languages—Spanish, English, and the numerous vernaculars or regional languages—cannot be assayed without inscribing them in the history of colonial and neocolonial domination of the peoples in these islands. In this regard, the terms "national-popular" and "nation-people"— as Gramsci employed them in a historical-materialist discourse—should be used in referring to Filipinos in the process of expressing themselves as diverse communities, interpellating other nationalities, and conducting dialogue with themselves and other conversers.

It is necessary to assert the fundamental premise of the "national-popular," the nation as constituted by the working masses (in our country, workers and peasants), not the patricians. Otherwise, the nation (in the archive of Western-oriented or Eurocentric history) is usually identified with the elite, the propertied classes, the national bourgeoisie, or the comprador bourgeoisie and its allies, the bureaucrats and feudal landlords and their retinue of gangsters, private armies, paramilitary thugs, and so forth. Actually, today, we inhabit a neocolony dominated by a comprador-bureaucratic bloc of the propertied classes allied with and supported in manifold ways by the U.S. hegemon and its regional accomplices.

Thesis 3: The Filipino nation is an unfinished and continuing project, an unfinished work, constantly being reinvented but not under conditions of its own making. Becoming Filipinos is a process of decolonization and radical democratization of the social formation, a sequence of collective choices. This is almost a cliché among the progressive forces with a nationalist orientation. It bears repeating that Filipino sovereignty is a dynamic totality whose premises are political independence and economy self-sufficiency. We have not yet achieved those premises.

Given the current alignment of nation-states in the world system under U.S. hegemony, whose hegemony is unstable, precarious, sustained by manifold antagonisms, and perpetually challenged by other regional blocs, becoming Filipino is an ever-renewing trajectory of creation and re-creation, a process overdetermined by legacies of the past and unpredictable incidences of the present and the future. Within this configuration, an evolving, emergent Filipino language may be conceived as both a medium and substantive element in fashioning this sequence of becoming-Filipino, a sequence grasped not as a cultural essence but a network of dynamic political affiliations and commitments. It is also an aesthetic modality of hegemonic expression.

Thesis 4: Only within the project of achieving genuine, substantive national independence and egalitarian democracy can we argue for the need for one national language as an effective means of unifying the masses of peasants, workers and middle strata and allowing them integral participation in a hegemonic process.

Note that this is not just a question of cultural identity. Without changing the unequal and unjust property/power relations, a distinctive Filipino culture incorporating all the diverse elements that have entered everyday lives of the masses cannot be defined and allowed to flourish. Without the prosperous development of the material resources and political instrumentalities, a Filipino cultural identity can only be an artificial, hybrid fabrication of the elite—an excrescence of global consumerism, a symptom of the power of transnationalized commodity-fetishism that, right now, dominates the popular consciousness via the mass media, in particular television, films, music, food and fashion styles, packaged lifestyles that permeate the everyday practices of ordinary Filipinos across class, ethnicities, age, and localities.

# VI

The consumerist *habitus* (to use Bourdieu's concept) acquired from decades of colonial education and indoctrination has almost entirely occupied the psyche of every Filipino, except for those consciously aware of it and collectively resisting it. With the rise of globalization, it has been a fashionable if tendentious practice among the floating litterateurs, mostly resident in colleges and universities, to advocate the maintenance of the status quo; that is, English as the prestigious language, Taglish as the media lingua franca, and Filipino and the other languages as utilitarian devices for specific tasks. But soon we find that this imitated pluralistic/multiculturalist stand only functions as the effective ploy of neoliberal finance capital. This seemingly pragmatist, accommodationist stance ultimately serves neocolonial goals: the Filipino as world-citizen as compensation for its lack of effective national sovereignty. Its obverse is regional/ethnic separatism. The culturalist or civilizationalist program, often linked to nongovernmental organizations and deceptive philanthropic schemes, skips the required dialectical mediation and posits an abstract universality, though disguised in a self-satisfied particularism now in vogue among postcolonial deconstructionists eulogizing the importance of place, locality, indigeneity, organic roots, and so on.

We discover in time that this trend serves as a useful adjunct for enhancing the festishistic magic, aura, and seductive lure of commodities—from brand-name luxury goods to the whole world of images, sounds, and multimedia confections manufactured by the transnational culture industry and marketed as symbolic capital for the petite bourgeoisie of the periphery and other subalternized sectors within the metropole.

Thesis 5: Spanish and English are global languages needed for communication and participation in world affairs. They are recognized as richly developed languages of aesthetic and intellectual power useful for certain purposes—English particularly in the scientific and technical fields. But they have a political history and resonance for "third world peoples" who have suffered from their uses. Its sedimented patterns of thought and action cannot so easily be ignored or elided. The discursive genres of law, business, and so forth in English and their institutionalized instrumentalities cannot be judged on their own terms without understanding the political role they played as effective instruments in the colonial domination of the various peoples in the Philippines and their total subordination to the political-cultural hegemony of the Spanish empire, and then of the American empire from 1899 to 1946, and of U.S. neocolonial control after formal independence in 1946.

Everyone knows that while Rizal used Spanish to reach an enlightened Spanish public and an *ilustrado*-influenced audience, the masses who participated in the Malolos Republic and the war against the Americans used Tagalog, and other vernaculars, in fighting for cultural autonomy and national independence. Historically the national and democratic project of the Philippine revolution—still unfinished and continuing—provides the only viable perspective within which we can explore the need for a national language as a means of uniting and mobilizing the people for this project.

Thesis 6: The use and promotion of a national language does not imply the neglect, elimination, or inferiorization of other regional languages spoken and used by diverse communities involved in the national-democratic struggle. In fact, it implies their preservation and cultivation. But that is contingent on the attainment of genuine national sovereignty and the emancipation of the masses, their integration into active participation in governance. Meanwhile, in the course of the national-liberation struggle, all languages should and are being used for mobilization, political education, and cultural self-affirmation. Simultaneously, the dissemination and development of one national language becomes a political and economic-cultural necessity for unifying the diverse communities under a common political program—which does not imply a monolithic ideological unity—in front of the monstrous power of finance-capital using English as an instrument of subordination and neocolonial aggression.

In this regard, I would argue that the unity and collective pride attendant on the use of one national language provides the groundwork and fundamental requisite for the promotion and development of other ethnic/regional languages within the national polity. This is a psychological-ideological imperative that cannot be deferred.

Thesis 7: Hegemony, the moral and intellectual leadership of the Filipino working masses, the scaffold within which an authentic Filipino identity can grow, assumes the rise of organic Filipino intellectuals who will use and develop Filipino as the evolving national language. Again, this does not mean suppressing other regional languages. Nor does it mean prohibiting the use and teaching of English or other international languages (Spanish, French, Chinese, etc.). It simply means the establishment of a required platform, basis, or foundation, without which the productive forces of the people within this particular geopolitical boundary can be harnessed, refined, and released in order to benefit the physical and spiritual health of Filipinos, repair and recover the damage inflicted by centuries of colonial oppression and exploitation, and thus be able to contribute to the cultural heritage of humankind.

Without national self-determination, there is no way Filipinos can contribute their distinctive share in global culture. In fact, it is impossible to be a global citizen unless you have fully grown and matured as an effective democratic participant in the making of a prosperous, egalitarian nation-people in a historically specific territory defined by a concretely differentiated sequence of events not replicated elsewhere.

Historical examples are often misleading, but sometimes elucidatory. It may be irrelevant and even Eurocentric to invoke the examples of Italy and Germany as nations that experienced unified mobilization through the affirmation of national-popular languages, Italy vis-à-vis the Papal ascendancy, and Germany vis-à-vis Latin/Roman Catholic hegemony. In any case, again, the social and historical function and character of language cannot be adequately grasped without situating them in the complex dynamics of the conflict of social classes in history since the break-up of the communal tribes in the hunting-gathering stage, since the rise of private property in the means of production, and the intricate dialectics of culture and collective psyche in the political economy of any social formation. In short, language is not just a permanently undecidable chain of signifiers, always deconstructing itself and falling into abysmal meaninglessness, but a social convention and a site of struggle, the signifier as "an arena of class struggle," to use Mikhail Bakhtin's phrase. I believe that only from this historical materialist perspective, and within the parameters of the political project of attaining genuine autonomy as a nation-people, can the discussion of a Filipino national language be intelligible and productive. But, again, such a discussion finds its value and validity as part of the total engagement of the people for justice, equality, and all-sided emancipation from the nightmares of the past and the terrorist fascism of the present.

# 4

# Revisiting Carlos Bulosan

"Go out into the world and live, Allos. I will never see you again. But remember the song of our birds in the morning, the hills of home, the sound of our language." What a beautiful thing to say to a young man going away! The sound of our language! It means my roots in this faraway soil; it means my only communication with the living and those who died without a gift of expression. My dear brother, I remember the song of the birds in the morning, the hills of home, the sound of the language.

—Carlos Bulosan, *The Sound of Falling Light*

When the Bush administration made the fateful decision in March 2003 to invade Iraq after its incursion into Afghanistan in the wake of September 11, 2001, the Philippines—its only colony in Asia for over a century—became the second battlefront in the global war against terrorism. U.S. "Special Troops" landed in the southern region of the country (Mindanao and Sulu) hunting for Al-Qaeda–linked Muslims called the Abu Sayyaf. Up to 2006, which officially marked the centennial anniversary of the arrival in U.S. territory of the first twenty-five natives from its new colonial possession, U.S. troops were still actively intervening in what was basically an internal civil war in a neocolonial theater of conflict (Aquino 2005; San Juan 2007b). The current crisis in the Philippines characterized by unprecedented extrajudicial political killings and forced "disappearances" carried out by state agents backed by Washington/Pentagon thus cannot be understood without keeping in mind the continuing involvement of the former colonial power in the affairs of ninety million Filipinos, three million of whom have settled in the United States as part of the ten million–strong Filipino diaspora around the world.

The Philippines, together with Puerto Rico and Cuba, was acquired as one of the spoils of the Spanish-American War at the turn of the twentieth century. One may speculate that the twenty-five dark-skinned "subalterns" (as trendy postcolonialists would now categorize them), first recruited by the Hawaiian Sugar Planters Association, may have been veterans of the Filipino-American War, America's "first Vietnam," in which more than four thousand American soldiers and 1.4 million Filipinos were killed (Schirmer and Shalom 1987, 19). Today, approximately three million Filipinos constitute the largest of the Asian American immigrant group originating from one nation-state, the Republic of the Philippines, which is also perhaps the biggest exporter of low-paid migrant contract workers (chiefly female domestics) to all the continents (Takaki 1989, 432; also see Beltran and Rodriguez 1996; San Juan 2007a).

Apart from the pioneering efforts of now forgotten chroniclers such as Carey McWilliams (1997) and Emory Bogardus (1976), only one Filipino among several thousand—Carlos Bulosan—succeeded in capturing in expressive form the ordeals and traumatic experiences of Filipino workers (called "Manongs" on the West Coast and in Hawaii) in the United States in the first half of the last century. This is itself a revealing symptom of the transition from classic colonial underdevelopment to neocolonial marginality. Although elevated to the status of a "politically correct" ethnic icon by the civil rights struggles of the sixties and seventies, Bulosan's position as an authoritative "spokesperson" of this expatriated, deracinated community—now mainly "middle-class" after the 1965 relaxation of immigration law—has always been precarious from the start, contingent on the vitality of the progressive social movements that inspired his own singular artistic development (San Juan 1995; Solberg 1991). Today, many doubt if Bulosan's "message" is still relevant or meaningful for thousands of Filipinos working in the Las Vegas casinos or in the caregiver industry of Florida, California, and other states. With the decline of labor insurgency during the Cold War and the predominance of the neoconservative ethos of the last decades, we can now begin to take a critical, skeptical look at the way the formation of the academically sanctioned "Bulosan" may have contributed to the demobilization, if not defusing, of the radically subversive energies immanent in the subterranean folds of the author's "unread" texts. Pluralist Eurocentric assimilationism begets its opposite: the quest for national localizing singularity as a stage in the process of regaining a destroyed historical specificity and universality (Lowy 1998). An attempt to internationalize—that is, resituate in the context of U.S.–Philippines' asymmetrical interstate dynamics—Bulosan's genealogy as a producer of historically determinate texts might help us understand the nature of scholastic canon-making in the putative U.S. multicultural archive and hopefully recover its original democratizing, emancipatory impulse. This is an integral part of the project of national liberation of the oppressed and exploited Filipino masses in this post–9/11 era of corporate-directed globalization.

On September 11, 2009, it will be fifty-three years since Carlos Bulosan
died in Seattle, Washington. This is based on a birth year of 1956; however, up to now the correct year of his birth has not been settled on, whether
1911, 1913, or 1914. Commentaries on his work abound, but a definitive
reliable biography is still wanting; Susan Evangelista's pioneering effort
(1985) in this regard is valuable for suggesting what more needs to be done:
a temporally differentiated remapping of Bulosan's intellectual itinerary or
genealogy. What is certain is that he has become canonized: his 1946 *testimonio* called *American Is in the Heart* (originally titled "In Search of America"; hereafter *AIH*) is celebrated as a classic ur-text of the Asian American,
more specifically, Filipino American experience. Because Bulosan is now required reading for thousands of college students and an icon for local folks,
he is in danger of becoming an allergy or aversion. Like Jose Rizal, the national hero, Bulosan is in danger of becoming inutile, taken for granted,
and museumified as a literary "high priest," or monumental *anito* (ances-
tor). Which triggers the cynical quip: so what else is new?

# I

First, a qualified mea culpa. In hindsight, I am perhaps chiefly to blame
for having started a trend when in 1972 the University of the Philippines
Press published my *Carlos Bulosan and the Imagination of the Class
Struggle*, the first book-length commentary on his major texts. Subsequently I edited the first anthology of his writings as a special issue of
*Amerasia Journal* (May 1979) and also Bulosan's only extant novel, *The
Power of the People* (1977; originally titled *The Cry and the Dedication*,
hereafter *The Cry*), which was issued by Tabloid Books in Ontario,
Canada, and subsequently by National Bookstore in 1986. This was followed by a volume of stories hitherto dormant in the archives of the University of Washington Library, *The Philippines Is in the Heart* (published
in 1978 in Quezon City, Philippines), most of which were excluded from
*The Laughter of My Father* (hereafter *The Laughter*). By the time the next
collection of his works—*On Becoming Filipino: Selected Writings of Carlos Bulosan* (Temple University Press) came out in 1995, Bulosan was already a canonical author, included in Paul Lauter's *Heath Anthology of
American Literature* and in assorted readers. This sums up my complicity with the canonizing orthodoxy.

Whatever the claims of other impresarios, the real "angel" of Bulosan's
works is the late Dolores Feria, a lifelong friend of Bulosan, to whom all
of us owe a great debt. Aside from several insightful commentaries on Bulosan, Feria edited the indispensable selection of Bulosan's letters, *Sound
of Falling Light* (1960); her effort to publicize his works and call attention

to the plight of Bulosan's compatriots remains unacknowledged and in fact unconscionably forgotten. I should like to rectify here this "sin" of omission. Meanwhile, when the Filipino youth movement burst into the scene inspired by the civil rights movement in the late sixties and ripened into the antimartial law movement from 1972 up to 1986, Bulosan's *AIH* (reprinted in 1973 by the University of Washington Press) was already being quoted in Filipino community newspapers, programs, forums, and ethnic festivals. I understand that *AIH* has gone through fifteen printings and is selling at least four thousand copies every year. And yet, especially in the last two decades, I have found many Filipinos and Filipino Americans who have never heard of Bulosan or read any of his now acclaimed works. It now seems a sign of idiosyncratic atavism or retrogression to be caught reading Bulosan in this "war-on-terrorism" epoch.

One truth cannot be doubted: the changes in the political and social milieu from the thirties to the fifties here and internationally, in particular the relations between the Philippines and the United States, will explain to a large extent the position, meaning, and significance of Bulosan's writings—why they were forgotten immediately after coming out, why they were rediscovered and acquired new significance, and why they have become institutionalized and rendered safe. This is the task of a historical-materialist hermeneutics and epistemology. Lest I be charged for being guilty, or at least complicit, for the direction history is taking with regard to the unpredictable reception of Bulosan's texts, and also in fear of repeating myself, I take this occasion to speculate on possible answers to these specific questions and by implication to the vicissitudes of the Filipino presence in the United States—only a part, of the ten million–strong Filipino diaspora around the planet. I undertake here a prolegomenon of transnational poetics between the hegemonic metropolis and the subalternized dependency.

I begin with actuality sutured to potentiality—to use Charles Sanders Peirce's terminology (see Merrell 1997). On the seventy-fifth anniversary of his arrival in Seattle on July 22, 1930, a news report in the *News Tribune* (Estrada 2005) juxtaposed two items that signify two themes often replicated in response to Bulosan's life and work. First, a quotation from a letter dated April 27, 1941: "Yes, I feel like a criminal running away from a crime I did not commit. And the crime is that I am a Filipino in America" (1995b, 173). And second, Bulosan's essay about "Freedom from Want" published in the *Saturday Evening Post* (March 6, 1943) and displayed in a federal building in San Francisco. The lesson seems unambiguous: despite the suffering and disillusionment, Bulosan was a success story. He personified the platitudinous tale of the migrant quasi-sojourner/exile-become-famous public personality. However, there was an unexpected turn: we are told that "his star faded, he returned to Seattle to do organizing and publicity work for Local 37 of the International Longshoremen's and Warehousemen's Union (ILWU)." So how the twist of the plot happened, what accident intervened in complicating the web of necessity, needs to be spelled out.

As in any news report, the gaps and lacunae shape the form and substance of what we read. What is puzzling to me is surely of interest to many: up to now, no one, least of all our highly credentialed ethnic-studies experts, seems to have asked the simple, obvious but seemingly intractable question: why and how did Bulosan become a writer, specifically the producer of such texts as *The Laughter, AIH,* stories such as "As Long as the Grass Shall Grow," *The Cry*—(as for the recently found *All the Conspirators,* I am doubtful that this is a genuine Bulosan text, so discrepant is the style, tone, and structuring of the materials). And, by extrapolation, of all the critical glosses and inquiries occasioned by Bulosan's "name" as author of poems, essays, stories, novels, letters, and so on.

Allos (short for "Carlos")—let us call him by the name of the protagonist in the sketch "Passage Into Life"—became a writer by accident, by force of circumstance and necessity. In the middle of *AIH,* after surviving blows of adversity fighting racist white men, Allos stops at a hotel in San Luis Obispo, California, and composes a letter to his brother Macario: "Then it came to me, like a revelation, that I could actually write understandable English. I was seized with happiness. . . . When the long letter was finished, a letter which was actually a story of my life, I jumped to my feet and shouted through my tears: 'They can't silence me any more! I'll tell the world what they have done to me!'" (180). Two motives are intertwined here: the need to communicate with kin, a part of the family, becomes also the means to break the silence of subalternity, to act and strike back. It is a mode of decolonizing body and psyche. Achieving solidarity, fraternal communication, is part of the process of liberating oneself from the necessity imposed by a complex conjuncture of political and economic forces, by the deterritorializing vectors of history. It embodies the dialectic of the personal and the collective, the punctual and the epochal. In short, Allos began writing as an act of rebellion against the condition he was born into, against the circumstances and exigencies he shared with others.

One cannot understand this encounter of forces by refusing to read the narrative of *AIH* integrally, in its composite whole. Most commentators of this synoptic life history, disturbed by the masochistic irony of the narrator proclaiming faith in America while being beaten up and mutilated, focus on this dissonance and allied incongruities. They usually set aside part I, chapters 1–12, unable to connect the colonial subordination of the peasant, the forcible maintenance of feudal/patriarchal despotism, with the landscape of isolation, violence, and solidarity leading to an affirmation of democratic ideals in the face of fascism and imperial aggression in the Philippines (San

Juan 1995b). This failure is a symptom of either academic ignorance or, most likely, a cultivated blindness: ignorance of U.S. racial supremacy hidden behind American exceptionalism, blindness to Filipino aspiration for freedom and national independence. This viewpoint detaches U.S. racialist expansionism from the colonial subjugation of Filipinos by the whole machinery of Anglo-Saxon white supremacy. The long and durable history of Filipino resistance to three hundred years of Spanish domination and then to U.S. aggression from 1899 to 1915, and thereafter—the Tayug uprising described by Allos is an insurrection against U.S. rule and its local agents, the quasi-feudal landlords—underwrites in a profound, intimate way the subterranean currents of revolt in Allos and his compatriots. These same currents motivated union organizing with the Congress of Industrial Organizations (CIO) in the mid-thirties, heightening the worldwide solidarity movement for Spanish republican forces combating fascism, and feeding the passionate drive to free the homeland from the savage terror of Japanese imperialism.

We can no longer shirk the imperative of an integrative or synthesizing mode of critical evaluation and ethical judgment. I hazard to state here that any scholarly comment on Bulosan, or any Filipino writer for that matter, that elides the enduring impact—the forcible subjugation and the resistance to it—of U.S. colonial domination of the Philippines is bound to be partial, inadequate, and ultimately useless. And so I am constantly surprised at the recurrent mistake of scholars equating the repressed "nationalism" of subordinated Filipino "wards" (voiced by the chief protagonist of *AIH*) with American nationalism, or imperial chauvinism; these two are worlds apart. It seems an unforgivable error, at this late date, to confuse superpower nationalist jingoism with the "nationalist" impulses of the subjugated natives. Even though they throw around words such as "capitalism" or "colonialism," these latter-day cosmopolitanists cannot distinguish the disparity, or really appreciate the flagrant parasitic relation, between colonial master and subjugated nationality. Of course, for hegemonic reasons, that is what we habitually get; and rare are the exceptions, depending on the climate of dissent and critical awareness of the systemic crisis we are all at present laboring under.

Allos's plight was part of a collective predicament. All the known evidence indicates that Allos left the subjugated territory as part of the recruitment of Filipino labor for the sugar plantations of Hawaii and, later, for agribusiness on the West Coast and in the Alaskan canneries. Most of those permitted "nationals" under indefinite tutelage, neither aliens nor citizens, were in search of an opportunity to work and earn enough to support themselves and help their parents, brothers, and sisters back home. Although the "push" factor (to use the cliché of official discourse) was compelling—namely, the extreme poverty and brutalization of peasants in the administered possession (for a long time, the Philippines was under the Bureau of Insular Affairs)—the "pull" factor that America was the land of promise, prosperity, and easy success exercised its seductive power on most natives, especially desperate peasants. This myth, of course, was exploded by the reality of experience and a belated "shock of recognition."

And so it was neither personal ambition nor dire want that made Allos a writer. Rather, it was history and a body configured by the colonial milieu that converged to lead him by a circuitous or "rhizomatic" line of flight (to use Deleuze and Guattari's term) to his peculiar vocation. Consider this history: his arrival in 1930 in the depths of the Great Depression, when 13 million people were out of work, with thousands of homeless workers and their families foraging in garbage for food. This was punctuated by the brutal Watsonville anti-Filipino riot of January 19–22, 1930, when "Flips" were beaten up and driven out of town (Bogardus 1976). It was the climax of years of racist scapegoating and vigilante atrocities against immigrant and colonized minorities. Exposure to these incidents quickly dissolved all youthful illusions in Allos whose search for his brothers to reconstitute the semblance of family life gave a stabilizing purpose to his nomadic existence. Consider next the breakdown of the body: in 1936 he was diagnosed with tuberculosis and spent two years at the Los Angeles County Hospital. He had several lung operations, lost the ribs on his right side—later, in the fifties, a cancerous kidney had to be removed. It was this physical infirmity that prevented Allos from full-time continuous work in the fields thereafter; his period of convalescence (for two years, at least) allowed him to read and educate himself, thanks to the Los Angeles Public Library, but more to the love of two sisters: the socialist writer Sanora Babb and her indefatigable sister, Dorothy Babb (Alice and Eileen Odell, in *AIH*). This was a fortuitous encounter, equivalent to Allos's friendship with Josephine Patrick when he moved to Seattle, Washington, in the fifties. Deterritorialized and dispossessed, the uprooted native tried to reconstitute home and family in the network of communing minds, interethnic praxis, and collaborating affections.

To be sure, Allos did not journey to the United States to "complete his education and become a writer" (Campomanes 1998, 113), or even to support his parents financially. He could not do it. That might have been the result of a felicitous conjunction of multiple causes. It was mainly the friendship of the Babb sisters that functioned as the enabling condition for Allos becoming a writer with a radical, progressive orientation. The cultural-political setting of Los Angeles reinforced the personal liaison between Allos and the Babb sisters, especially Dorothy (Feria 1957), as well as with other intellectual fellow-travelers. We do not know exactly when this friendship with the sisters began, but I surmise that he made their acquaintance when he moved within the circle of left-wing CIO labor organizers, as well as

Communist Party writers and cinema cultural producers, in Los Angeles between 1930 and 1936. Allos's contact with dissident intellectuals such as Carey McWilliams, John Fante, and Louis Adamic, together with his involvement in the nationwide American Committee for the Protection of the Foreign-Born, a popular front organization campaigning for U.S. citizenship for Filipinos, eased his way into the sites of East Coast publications such as the *New Yorker*, *Town & Country*, and *Harper's Bazaar*, aside from leftist periodicals such as *The Masses*. In addition, Harriet Monroe, editor of *Poetry* magazine, may have inspired Allos to produce eventually *Letter from America* (1942), *Chorus from America* (1942), and *Voice of Bataan* (1943).

## II

We learn that in the summer of 1934 Allos was involved in the Filipino Labor Union strikes in Salinas, El Centro, Vacaville, and Lompoc. Collaborating with Chris Mensalvas, the legendary organizer who arrived in the United States in 1927, Allos and Mensalvas edited a short-lived proletarian literary magazine, *The New Tide*, which would "interpret the struggles and aspirations of the workers, the fight of sincere intellectuals against fascism and racial oppression in concrete national terms" (Bulosan 1973, 199). Affiliated with Mensalvas, Allos participated in the unprecedented Stockton strike in 1949–50, as well as in the activities of the United Cannery, Agricultural, Packing and Allied Workers of America and the Committee for the Protection of Filipino Rights. Anchored to these collective struggles, the Bulosan Imaginary acquired "a local habitation and a name."

We can cite Filipinos who resembled Allos but whose lives followed a different trajectory. Other possible extrapolations of his life can be drawn. If Allos did not enjoy the nurturing friendship of Dorothy Babb and was healthier, he could have pursued the path of Chris Mensalvas and become a charismatic union organizer. If he attempted to get a college degree and devoted himself to supporting his family back home and also entered the petite-bourgeois circle of Filipinos in Chicago, as did Philip Vera Cruz, he probably would not have written *AIH*, *The Laughter*, *The Cry*, and other artistic works whose frame of intelligibility springs from the transcendence of kinship/blood filiation by the exercise of a popular-democratic will to emancipate the colony. Both Mensalvas and Vera Cruz, of course, carved out their own distinguished niches in the history of Filipinos and the multiethnic proletariat in the United States. Both are Filipinos with singular vocations, but they did not write *AIH*, *The Laughter*, or *The Cry*.

Summing up, then, Allos became a writer not through any single act of choice, as may be illustrated in certain episodes of *AIH*. Rather, it came about through his being inscribed within what (to use Friedrich Engels's term) a "parallelogram" or constellation of forces: the physical dis-location of Allos from colonial Pangasinan, Philippines, to the metropole's West Coast; his initiation into the labor-capital arena of conflict (initially through his brothers, but more effectively through Mensalvas) and, eventually, into the intellectual-cultural milieu of Popular Front politics (through the Babb sisters); the breakdown of his health as a result of years of malnutrition and neglect that he shared with the Filipino peasant/working class; and so on. In effect, the historical process of U.S. colonial domination of a people with a vital revolutionary tradition and the emerging resistance of citizens and ethnic workers in the metropolitan center made Allos the kind of writer that he was in that particular and unrepeatable conjuncture of the thirties Depression, leftist resurgence, united front internationalism during World War II, the Huk rebellion, and the McCarthy period of the Cold War in the last century. In brief, he was not a hybrid but an organic product both of his times and his creative interventions.

Does this mean Allos had no agency, or freedom of choice? On the contrary. The paradoxical truth stems from the proposition that the individual is really defined by the totality of social relations in which she or he operates. Thus Allos's personal decisions acquired value, meaning, and efficacy in consonance with the play of those historical forces that I have enumerated, in particular the political and cultural pressures and tendencies symbolized by organizations, discourses, and institutional figures that allowed Allos's contribution to register its distinctive signature. The dialectical principle of self-transformation sprung from the unity of opposites (the fusion of chance and necessity) explains Allos's singular evolution as a Filipino bachelor, artist, racialized scapegoat, union militant, and socialist intellectual. No individual makes history alone, it goes without saying, except as a part of the contradictory social groups and forces of "elective affinities" that constitute the map of humankind's struggle for freedom against natural and man-made necessity. This explains Allos's continuing relevance.

Alone among contemporary Anglo-Americanists, Michael Denning, in his wide-ranging *The Cultural Front*, deploys a historical-materialist analytic to chart and assay the exact placing of Allos's *AIH* in the precarious, ever-shifting field of hegemonic contestation. Denning's genealogy of literary forms is highly instructive; however, he has needlessly limited himself by concentrating on *AIH* to the neglect of Bulosan's other writings. In this he shares the prevailing tendency of current scholarship to virtually equate *AIH* with all of Bulosan and thus prejudice any larger, more informed aesthetic or moral judgment. No wonder young Pinays sometimes say that Bulosan is passé, obsolete; that he no longer speaks to the hip-hop, rapping gangs in Daly City, Manhattan, or elsewhere. He no longer speaks to the volatile and ludic desire of Pinays dreaming of becoming postmodern *babaylan*s. Everyone knows that the few surviving "Manongs" are today an object of sanctimonious nostalgia, or exoticizing charity. Even before Vera Cruz's resignation from the Mexican-dominated United Farm Workers of America, Filipinos have already moved from the farms to service and care industries, some to professional-managerial occupations, a few to bureaucratic niches. Some have been deported as suspected terrorists (Beltran 2004); others as victims of the USA PATRIOT Act (witness the fate of the Cuevas family of Fremont, California) and the racialized war of the "civilized" on fundamentalist Islamic extremism.

We need a renewal of critical practice to address the changes bifurcating Allos's time and the present. The obsession with the melodramatic aporias and the populist Americanism of *AIH* needs to be rectified; the clichés and banalities are accumulating. In this light, I submit that the entire body of Bulosan criticism needs to be "decentered" if we are to free ourselves from stifling scholastic orthodoxies and "model-minority" pieties. Official protocols, concepts, and tropes need to be reassessed and altered. There are various strategies for renewing our critical spirits; my suggestion is only one among many. What would our assessment look like if we took *The Cry* as the pivotal center of the still-evolving Bulosan corpus, or *The Laughter* as the organon of interpretive strategies, or even the short fiction and letters as providing the foundational criteria of judgment? Or even the allegorical fables and pedagogical instruments such as "As Long as the Grass Shall Grow," "Story of a Letter," or "Homecoming," and the substantial number of stories gathered in *The Philippines Is in the Heart*? We could try this experiment of paradigm shifting and pedagogical makeover. I am quite sure we will wake up from our dogmatic slumber and breathe anew redemptive winds from a newly discovered horizon of thought and moral economy of feeling, action, and hope.

We can learn much from Denning's historical triangulation of the "sentimental education" of the writer caught between the old world of tribal jealousies and the new world of international solidarity against fascism. This is, indeed, a genuinely internationalist mode of transcultural inventory. *AIH* certainly makes sense as a typical Popular Front expression with a "sentimental, populist, and humanist nationalism" that is qualified by its ethnic particularity, manifesting generic affinities with Woody Guthrie's *Bound for Glory* and Ernesto Galarza's *Barrio Boy*. But is it valid to consider the Manongs as immigrants similar to the Irish, Italians, and so on? In becoming a positive image, the power of the Negative has been annulled. Denning's Popular Front optic assuredly invests *AIH* with larger political resonance. But its fixation on the inadequate immigrant paradigm prevents a grasp of the subversive impulses born from the condition of exile and colonial statelessness, emancipatory impulses that transgress the vertigo-inducing play of differences in their drive for contacts, linkages, affiliations, and connections. This is a recurrent mistake of numerous ethnic-studies scholars.

*AIH*'s narrative's political vision, Denning suggests, is "embodied in the figure of the itinerant organizer" (1997, 276–77). Let us review the background of this mediating figure. The Filipino worker in the United States up to 1934 was considered a "national," a nomadic subaltern without citizenship rights, almost a refugee. We need to emphasize that between the defeat of the Aguinaldo Republic (1901) and the establishment of the Philippine Commonwealth (1935), Filipinos in the United States were, strictly speaking, not immigrants but exiles, deracinated subjects, displaced colonials, sojourners not settlers. Their textbook label was "colonial wards." Their quasi-national sovereignty was wrested from them by U.S. military-economic aggression and territorial annexation. About 1.4 million Filipinos died in this extension of messianic "Manifest Destiny" through President William McKinley's policy of "Benevolent Assimilation." This is a requisite, even ineluctable, distinction. After 1935, they became full-fledged aliens and were subject to repatriation or deportation (McWilliams 1997); immigration from the Philippines was restricted to fifty persons annually (Takaki 1989). These are the historical parameters for Filipino subject-position or citizenship identification in the decades between colonial annexation in 1898 and formal independence of the country in 1946.

What is the consequence? Failure to recognize the colonial relationship between the Philippines and the United States (and the neocolonial tie-up after 1946) and the racial-national subordination of Filipinos leads to marginalizing the first part of *AIH*, that is, the democratic struggle of peasants against feudal exploitation, and the nationalist demand of the popular masses for sovereignty and the right of self-determination (Chung 1996). This is what a U.S.-centered, liberal framework expunges from sight: the national-popular vision that informs Allos's work, given that the Filipino proletariat still remains inchoate, without national cohesion or autonomy, unable to realize its ethicopolitical hegemony in a specific social formation. The problem is not one of representation, but one of presentation, of recognition and respect for individual Filipino worth affiliated to a sovereign collectivity. Dispossessed and dispersed, Filipinos (from Allos's time to the present) are still in the process of becoming—in search of a true sovereign homeland.

There is no denying that Allos was a product of his time and place. Critics have charged him for the sexism of his fictional characters (Koshy 2004; Lee 1999;). Yet it is imperative to make the elementary discrimination between Allos the author and the fictional construct, the "Allos" of *AIH*, who, as everyone knows, is a composite portrait of numerous Filipinos who embody varying attitudes, thoughts, patterns of behavior, and so forth. Unless proof is offered, it is wise not to fuse the narrative persona, the invented character, with the author. Trust the tale, not the author, D. H. Lawrence counseled his readers. Allos, unfortunately, did not always anticipate this possible confusion and its damaging consequences.

Is sexism found in the characters' actions and thoughts? Of course. But the heterosexism and the homosociality discerned in the narrative needs to be plausibly grounded in their concrete historical environment, just as the close fraternal intimacy of African slaves in the Southern plantations, or of colonized subjects in Puerto Rico, Hawaii, or Cuba, needs to be inscribed in situations of extreme deprivation. While it is true that in Allos's time, what Koshy calls "commodification of desire" has become the regulatory principle of capitalism, it is necessary to pay close attention to the tributary or feudal social entanglements in the Philippines and the distortion or exacerbation of these feudal bonds by the colonial U.S. regime. Sexuality of the Filipino colonial subject is much more complex because of the mixture of several modes of production and their manifold layering in the fractured social formation. Clearly, the historically derived category of "biopower" and corollary notions appropriate for developed industrial capitalism cannot be superimposed on a backward, uneven, feudal/comprador setting. Capitalist biopower by definition cannot function at all inserted into a tributary kin-centered social order complicated with archaic survivals incorporated in a distorted Christian bureaucratic setup. It is a serious failure of judgment to impose the capitalist binary male/female sexuality on an archaic, feudal formation such as the U.S.-dominated Philippines then and now.

What postmodernist critics privilege as the valorization of semiotic differences turns out, ironically, to be a mandate for monolithic vision and straitjacket pronouncements. This mandate is often announced in a theater of consumption where hedonistic lifestyle and consumerist pleasure conceals the labor that produces the occasions and means of pleasure. Allos's predicament lies not chiefly in his perverted sexuality, but in the control of his labor-power (organically tied to the dynamics of his psyche and bodily functions) by the colonial bureaucracy and later by U.S. monopoly capital. Representations of intimacy, affect, libidinal fantasies, and so on, cannot be properly assessed unless the mechanisms of reification that sustain the imperialist order are clarified; but they cannot be clarified if the concept of class and the exploitation of labor are dismissed or marginalized as useless in discussing sexuality, difference, and so forth, because "class" is allegedly totalizing or homogenizing. Instead of "class," an abstract conception of particularity or singularity operates in its place, which prevents the understanding and appreciation of Allos's perennial search for community, the "concrete universal" of social justice and national-popular sovereignty.

In contrast to mainstream prejudice, I would argue the unorthodox position. What *AIH* foregrounds, after muddling through undecidables and disorienting indeterminacies fostered by a system in which "all that is solid melts into air" (as Marx lauded capitalism), is the centrality of class as a social category that Filipinos and other oppressed groups can use to understand how they can transform their condition decisively. The notion of class exploitation is more decisive than race or sexuality because it challenges directly the power of capital. Without a change in the mode of production, no significant change in social relations, including practices of sexuality and ethnic interactions, can be realized. Engagement with social class (not to be construed in terms of income or status), including the colonial condition of the Filipino workers and peasants condemned to labor in occupied territory, leads us directly to confront the processes of material production and the unequal division of labor, the sociohistorical reality to which the oppressive hierarchies of gender, race, and sexual preference are anchored and legitimized, made normal and commonsensical. Bulosan concurs with this stance in his conception of the writer as citizen and worker, eloquently inscribed, for example, in a letter of January 17, 1955, published as "The Writer as Worker" (*Midweek*, July 17, 1988) as well as in his programmatic autobiographical sketch in the standard reference work, *Twentieth Century Authors*.

This is not to privilege the past, or glorify descent, lineage, ancestral origin. Because Filipinos are united in their shared condition of being colonized, and in the process racialized and inferiorized across the public/private divide, the key to their liberation is the destruction of the colonizing system, its institutions and practices, which still prevail in diverse altered forms. This is the goal of the project of "becoming Filipino" in *AIH*, since—amid the ruins of the homeland and the barbaric reign of white supremacy in the metropole—the chief basis on which Filipinos can unite, given the multiplicity of their languages and ethnic differences, is the political project of national self-determination, the collective project of popular, democratic sovereignty. This project (practiced, for example, by the National Democratic Front of the Philippines and the New People's Army) has been stigmatized and denounced today by the high priests of the globalizing power bloc as "terrorist."

We are Filipinos not so much because of ethnic markers, common origin, or shared memories—they do play their integral part—but primarily because of being united in a political project: that of liberating the Philippines (in its geographical locus and in the diaspora) from class inequality and national bondage. A redeemed future, what Ernst Bloch (1970) calls the reality of the "not-yet," does not exist separate from the actual movement of our minds and bodies. Allos tried to assay in the motion of events the shape of an emerging future. This is the project of actualizing a "concrete universal" in which particulars find their effective place within a determinate and differentiated totality. Frankly I do not think that postmodernist critics, trapped in the fetishism of hybridity, infinite substitution of signs in a "third space," hyperreal simulations, and other "morbid symptoms" (to use Gramsci's phrase) of reification, can really grasp and appreciate the value of this project as a "concrete universal," a totality that embraces multiplicity and individuality in a way that can only be posited by the mystified Allos as "America," with all its unfortunate essentializing, pejoratively utopian connotations.

# III

This leads me to the task I mentioned earlier, that of shifting the center of gravity, the Archimedean point of critique, to the post–World War II period of Allos's career, from 1946 to September 11, 1956, our 9/11 benchmark. This is an attempt to define what Felix Guattari calls "a transversalist conception of subjectivity" conceived as a collective "assemblage" of enunciations (1995, 4, 127). Let us review the historical-empirical coordinates of this career that would constitute the field of conditions from which certain inferences about the temper of his life and the qualities of his art can be drawn:

1. *Gestation*: from 1911 to 1930, the period of youth and adolescence, coinciding with the pacification of the islands; the massacre of recalcitrant Moros (inhabitants of Islamic faith); the passage of the Jones Law in 1916 (following the Payne-Aldrich Tariff Act) which imposed "free trade" and confined the Philippines to feudal-agricultural status.
2. *Emergence*: from 1930 to 1946, the period of apprenticeship and maturity, ushering Allos into the Depression metropole; a series of anti-Filipino riots; the June 1932 "Bonus March" in Washington, DC; the passage of the 1934 Tydings-McDuffie Act and the ten-year Commonwealth interregnum, which installed neocolonialism; CIO organizing (1934–37) and the July 1934 General Strike in San Francisco; World War II, the Japanese occupation of the Philippines, and the return of General Douglas McArthur. This period also saw the beginning of the New Deal in 1933 with Franklin D. Roosevelt's administration, and the publication of key modernist works by Ezra Pound, John Dos Passos, John Steinbeck, and William Carlos Williams, as well as Orson Welles's *Citizen Kane*. From 1938 (when he was released from the hospital) to 1941, Allos reached the point of disenchantment and rupture; he confessed in his

autobiographical testament that "it took me another five years before I was able to put my grand dream on paper in a literate form" (1995b, 216).

3. *Breakthrough*: from 1946 to 1956, Allos's return to labor-union activism as editor of the ILWU 1952 *Yearbook*. He was invited to undertake this editorial job in 1950 by his old friend Chris Mensalvas who was president of ILWU, Local 37, the Filipino cannery workers' union, from 1949 to 1959. FBI surveillance of Allos, dormant since his days with the leftist Hollywood circle, heated up during the attempt to deport Mensalvas and Ernesto Mangaoang, ILWU official, branded as "communists." The year 1948 may be a pivotal year for Allos, as intimated by two letters in which the theme of individual sacrifice for the good of the community is an obsessive leitmotif: one in which he wrote to his nephew Arthur the following lines: "Every man dreams to make something of himself, but sometimes he gives up these dreams for others. And that is the greatest decision of all for a man to make"; and another letter to his nephew Fred in which he urges Fred to apply his intellectual gifts "toward the safeguarding of our great heritage, the grandeur of our history, the realization of our great men's dream for a free and good Philippines. That is real genius; it is not selfish; it sacrifices itself for a free and good Philippines" (Campomanes and Gernes 1988, 33, 36).

While the Philippines was granted formal independence in 1946, it remained economically, politically, and militarily dependent on Washington through the infamous "parity" amendment to the Philippine Constitution; the Huks ("Huk" is the acronym for "Army Against the Japanese"), organized in 1942 to fight the Japanese occupiers, was declared illegal in 1948; its leftist representatives were ousted from the Philippine Congress in 1946. Gradually the Huk rebellion declined beginning in 1951 with the arrest of many nationalists, including the poet and trade unionist Amado V. Hernandez (whose arrest Bulosan denounced in the 1951 ILWU *Yearbook*). The key document for this period is Bulosan's article "Terrorism Rides the Philippines" (1952), deeply prophetic in this period when state terrorism (implemented by President Macapagal-Arroyo backed by Washington/Pentagon) is inflicting havoc and untold suffering. When Bulosan died, fascist repression eased the way for the signing of the U.S. Mutual Defense Treaty; the replacement of the Bell Trade Act with the Laurel-Langley Agreement reinforcing Philippine dependency; the U.S. National Security Council authorized expenditures to suppress the Huk insurgency. This period of the Cold War includes the Taft-Hartley Act restricting trade union power, the Korean War, McCarthy's anticommunist crusade, the advent of mass television, and major works by Norman Mailer, Tennessee Williams, Arthur Miller, J. D. Salinger, and James Baldwin.

# IV

Calibrated within a historical-materialist perspective, the aforementioned parameters are pedagogical indicators or guides for further biographical and sociocultural investigations. They are not meant to replace analytic inquiries of specific texts or of sequences of expressive practices alongside, or coeval with, the written word. Within this synchronic and diachronic field of conditions, we can infer the mediating factors of culture and nature that would allow us to elucidate the complex interactions between the individual and his world. I propose that this schematic periodizing of Allos's itinerary as an exiled native endeavoring some kind of "homecoming" be considered as a heuristic point of departure for the project of decentering the multiethnic archive and a metropole-centered, hegemonic criticism. In the process, it might also serve to renew the submerged liberatory energies of Bulosan's works for the next generation of Filipino Americans (not all of whom, I trust, will be sucked into the abyss of cyberinformation and commodified simulacra) in what is now a planetary diaspora of ten million overseas *kababayan* (compatriots). This will also be a means of foregrounding the theme of exile and return that underlies and to some extent makes coherent the fragmentary, unraveled strands of Allos's life.

During this last decade of his life, Allos wrote *The Cry* as well as numerous essays, poems, and still-unpublished stories and articles. Notable is an unsigned protest (already noted earlier) against McCarthyite repression in the Philippines entitled "Terrorism Rides the Philippines" in the *1951 International Longshoreman's and Warehouseman's Union Yearbook*. The value of this essay cannot be overemphasized. It shows Allos in the thick of the motion of events, the "not-yet" moving to the "concrete universal." Contrary to the rumor, Allos did not lapse into despair despite being blacklisted, ostracized from Establishment media, reviled and calumniated by reactionary Filipino journalists. Apart from the ILWU, he affiliated with the progressive group surrounding Josephine Patrick, his comrade in Seattle, who was active in the Committee for the Protection of the Foreign-Born and in the Communist Party USA with its Popular Front program. At this time, together with novelist Howard Fast and black educator W. E. B. Du Bois, Allos supported an effort to publish the autobiography of Luis Taruc, one of the leaders of the Huk rebellion in the Philippines (De Leon 1999). Taruc's *Born of the People* (actually authored by William J. Pomeroy) was first published in 1953 by International Publishers in New York (Pomeroy 1992).

A catalyzing encounter of visions and sensibilities occurred at this point in history. I suggest that it is Allos's acquaintance with the poet-unionist Amado V. Hernandez's work and encounter with Taruc's biography that afforded the condition of possibility for the construction of what can be called "national allegory" (to use Fredric Jameson's controversial notion [2000]), by no means a photographic documentary or "realistic" description of the Huk insurgency in the Philippines. (Bulosan never became a U.S. citizen and never visited the Philippines.) Now a cursory examination of the essay "Terrorism Rides the Philippines," together with selected letters to friends during this period, will easily demonstrate Allos's sufficient understanding of the political, cultural, and economic situation in the Philippines. He followed events closely, tracking the nuances and innuendoes in the news reports and communication from friends. But he was more interested in how his situation was refracted and elaborated by events happening in the Philippines, how he could make sense of his life in relation to the situation of his compatriots, than in compiling raw facts and inventorying incidents for their own sake.

*The Cry* invents an example of an exceptional genre called "minor literature" by Gilles Deleuze and Felix Guattari (1986). Like *AIH*, it is not the stereotypical autobiography of the individual hero confronting the problems of a "godless" cosmos, nor a psychological novel in the manner of Dostoevsky or Faulkner, but a synthesis of typical individuals and representative situations. *The Cry* does not claim by any means to simply document experience because "it was there." That notion is at best a "mimetic fallacy," at worst just a mistaken view of the concept of realism. Realism—specifically, a critical one in which verisimilitude functions to render the determinately typical, not the statistical average (Lukacs 1972)—is not a mechanical reproduction of sensory data, or unmediated transcript of impressions; rather, it is a sophisticated aesthetic convention with a code of rules and protocols. It is ludicrous to oppose imagination to experience (Teodoro 1985) since the raw materials of experience are already mediated through the imagination, through the transfiguring aesthetics of novelistic invention. A "minor" literature seeks to fulfill the responsibility to the Other; the Other here conceived as the realm of possibilities, as the negative Alterity that interrogates the Modernity inaugurated by Hobbesian individualism and Lockean liberalism—to use Enrique Dussel's (2007) articulation of the difference.

This is the moment to return to my thesis whose import may now be obvious but still needs specification: Allos's body of writing cannot be fully understood and appreciated without respecting his ethico-artistic motivations (which may or may not be realized in practice) and its ideological, philosophical grounding. This can be found, among other texts, in "The Writer as Worker" (noted earlier), or in the letters in which axiomatic principles and thought experiments may be found. In one letter dated April 8, 1955, Allos reflects on his own work:

> My politico-economic ideas are embodied in all my writings, but more concretely in my poetry. Here let me remind you that *The Laughter* is not humor: it is satire; it is indictment against an economic system that stifled the growth of the primitive, making him decadent overnight without passing through the various stages of growth and decay. The hidden bitterness in this book is so pronounced in another series of short stories [now collected in *The Philippines Is in the Heart*], that the publishers refrained from publishing it for the time being. (1995b, 184)

Allos is more teleological and reflexive in the 1955 autobiographical sketch for *Twentieth Century Authors*. Notice that after recounting his life history, the "voyage in and out," he returns to the traumatic moment of illness—his first one in 1936–1938 precipitated the discovery of his artistic vocation, as I have described earlier—against the background of a seemingly irretrievable past, a loss that cannot be healed by elegiac reiteration and memorializing prayer, against which the compulsion to launch forward erupts in this agonistic, prophetic confession of faith:

> I am sick again. I know I will be here (Firland Sanitarium, Seattle, Washington) for a long time. And the grass hut where I was born is gone, and the village of Mangusmana is gone, and my father and his one hectare of land are gone, too. And the palm-leaf house in Binalonan is gone, and two brothers and a sister are gone forever.
>
> But what does it matter to me? The question is—what impelled me to write?
>
> The answer is—my grand dream of equality among men and freedom for all. To give a literate voice to the voiceless one hundred thousand Filipinos in the United States, Hawaii, and Alaska. Above all and ultimately, to translate the desires and aspirations of the whole Filipino people in the Philippines and abroad in terms relevant to contemporary history.
>
> Yes, I have taken unto myself this sole responsibility. (1995b, 216)

This vow reiterates the one made in *AIH* as he recalls the Tayug peasant uprising near his hometown: to "give significance to all that was starved and thwarted in my life" (1973, 62), the kernel of the lifelong project for which he became a writer, not just any writer but an "organic intellectual" of the Filipino masses (San Juan 2000). Because of this overriding commitment, Allos's portrayal of all "the wretched of the earth" departed from the code of classic realism and adopted a more tendentious cast, a Brechtian teaching/learning rationale aimed at "conscienticization." This defines more precisely the allegorical/didactic style and dialogic norm of his texts, qualities that display affinities with the "rhizomatic" poetics of Kafka and other decolonizing "third world" writers. Indeed, Allos's texts show characteristics of "minor" (employed in a special sense) writing formulated by Deleuze and Guattari—"deterritorialization of language, the connection of the individual to a political immediacy, and the collective assemblage of enunciation" (1986, 18)—aspects of which I have touched on here and elsewhere.

There is, to be sure, nothing minor in Allos's intervention in counter-hegemonic revolutions. When Allos's novel first appeared in the Philippines as *The Power of the People* just after the February 1986 "People Power" revolt, I argued that the work can be viewed as a kind of "national allegory" in the sense that the Chinese Lu Hsun's or the Senegalese Ousmane Sembene's works functioned as polysemic indices and symbolic fables of their distinctive social formations. It addressed in an oblique way the crisis of that specific conjuncture in U.S.–Philippines history, the persecution of Filipino militants Mensalvas and Mangaong figuring as a synecdoche of the repression of the Huks by the Magsaysay puppet regime in the Philippines (De Vera 1994).

Uncannily, the Huk uprising brought back images of the Tayug insurrection—an image compulsively repeated in national-democratic narrativization of Philippine history. This episode spanned the early years of the Cold War era prior to the explosion of the Civil Rights struggles in the sixties and the resurgence of "third world" liberation movements from Algeria and Cuba to Vietnam and Nicaragua. The threat of deportation for Filipino activists (recall the earlier fates of Pedro Calosa and Pablo Manlapit) foreclosed Allos's dream of returning to the land of his birth. He never applied for U.S. citizenship (Guyotte 1997), fearing perhaps that he would be turned down since the FBI had already been on his trail since his days with the Hollywood prime suspects (one wonders if he ever met Bertolt Brecht, Theodor Adorno, or Thomas Mann, all exiles from Nazi Germany, in Los Angeles). In any case, for Allos (ca. 1955), the stakes were no longer the urge to belong to a utopian "America" or return to a pastoral refuge in Pangasinan; it was now writing "for or against war, for or against life" (1995b, 184). In doing so, he reclaimed for the Filipino diaspora the proletarian incarnation of a critical universality first fully announced in Marx and Engels's 1848 *Communist Manifesto*.

Can we not consider *The Cry* as a sublimated sequel to *AIH*? Again, from a dialectical viewpoint, there was negation and affirmation across the terrain of thought and lived experience. Clearly the search for community across race, gender, and class persisted, but sublated into another level: now, the guerilla contingent becomes the site of the unfolding of a concrete and critical universal, the unwinding of a unity of opposites, the stratified totality of a nation in the process of becoming. It was an allegory of the people's self-movement, a spontaneous but also necessary internal self-transformation, with all the inconsistencies, excesses, and contradictions that characterize such beginnings in history. It could not be just a repetition of the Manongs driven by an alienated and alienating environment until the war against fascist capital unites everyone. His letters to Dorothy Babb (the person most intimately attached to Allos) from 1937 to 1942 closes that period of beleaguered self-examination and familial anxieties. Allos's tried-and-tested sensibility had to wrestle with the new forms of barbarism, including the vagaries of self-indulgent petite-bourgeois desire, and explore new forms of popular resistance and class-sectoral alliance.

A historic rupture occurred in Allos's journey, as well as in the itinerary of the Filipino community in the United States, marked by the Huk insurrection from 1946 to 1952. It was heightened by the anticommunist panic surrounding the Korean War and the confrontation with Communist China. Allos's possible meeting with Amado V. Hernandez may have rekindled memories of his impassioned solidarity with the Spanish Republican forces expressed in poems such as "Biography Between Wars," "Meeting with a Discoverer," and others. One letter confessed his "secret dream of writing here [in the United States] a 1,500 page novel covering thirty-five years of Philippine history," with the fourth one covering 1951–1961, which I consider will be a great crisis in Philippine history" (1995b, 180). This "crisis" was fully dramatized in the bloody sacrificial encounters of the insurgents in *The Cry*.

Allos would not traverse that ten-year crucial passage, uncannily prophesied in November 1949, foiled by the combined weight of the past and the burden of the present. Had he lived a few more years, his involvement with the ILWU would have eventually connected him with Philip Vera Cruz, Larry Itliong, and the vanguard of the California farmworkers' strike then training in the fields of Delano and Coachella in the early sixties. The Manongs rediscovered, or more precisely reinvented, themselves in reaffirming the right to strike. But FBI harassment and racial exclusion would not prolong his life to the time of another renaissance of popular-democratic faith, the Civil Rights and antiwar movement of the sixties. Refracting the leitmotif of homecoming that sutures the solitude of his stories, poems, and letters, *The Cry* enacts the return— one traumatized character (Dante) already home from the United States awaits the coming of another one, the "wounded" messenger (Felix

Rivas) who never appears, suspending the denouement, converting this expectation of the advent of the legendary bearer of "Good News" into a permanent condition. Is this Allos's metaphor for hope, the "Not-Yet" pregnant in the womb of the present, realizing his responsibility for Others?

Cultural practices and artistic representations, of course, are products of history and the interpellations of group consciousness. And though not directly caused by practical necessities, they register both the pressure of the moment and the exigencies of the embattled artist. Suffice it here to assert, again, that the central theme of exile and tortuous return in all of Bulosan's works can be rearticulated as the project of liberating the homeland from feudal and colonial oppression, a collective project of national, democratic self-determination. This desire to complete the "unfinished revolution" of 1898 amid the self-alienation and deracination of the colonized subject transplanted to the "belly of the beast" is one that, in varying historical arenas, resonates in the life and deeds of such revolutionary militants and thinkers as Jose Marti, Aime Cesaire, C. L. R. James, Frantz Fanon, Edward Said, and others. I cite two reviewers who elaborate on this theme in their own way. This is a topic that, to my knowledge, only one scholar, Tim Libretti (1998), has so far explored in-depth. From a sympathetic perspective, Viet Thanh Nguyen writes:

> Poverty, shame, and shattered dreams prevented the [Filipino] migrants from going back to the Philippines. Many died in the United States, old, alone, and broken in body.
>
> Bulosan shared that fate, but in *The Cry* he revisits his native land the only way he can. The anguish of the novel is not only the anguish of its characters, but of its author as well; the book represents the act of an imagination in exile attempting to carve out a space away from the confusions of America, and attempting to return home with a starkness of clarity that life in America did not allow. Bulosan saw himself in those revolutionary seven, hampered by deep physical and emotional pain, but striving for a distant yet definite goal. (1996, 6)

While Nguyen wonders how the novel "feels contemporary in that the situation today is not any different than in 1950" so that the work of writing for the sake of justice and social change proves even more imperative, Tomio Geron reaffirms the need to move away from Popular Front categories to confront the historical necessities, both personal and collective, that transformed the naive and trusting peasant boy from the village of Mangusamana, Philippines, to the prophetic visionary forging the "conscience of his race":

Bulosan writes from the perspective of "exile" rather than the traditional Asian American "immigrant." He saw American imperialism in the Philippines as the cause of his family's dismemberment and dislocation, and connected it directly to the exploitation he suffered at the hands of capitalists in the United States. These appraisals argue against cultural-pluralist and assimilationist notions of "multiculturalism," examining power relations in the Filipino experience in America and the Philippines. (1995, 13)

These varying testimonies argue that it is possible to offset the hegemonic doxa that endorses the immigrant story of hard work and success implicit, if somewhat parodied and undercut, in *AIH*. But it will need a massive consensus to offset that view, one premised on the argument that Allos's role as exiled writer-activist cannot be fixated and reified to the early period of his struggle in the United States, the thirties and the Popular Front agenda. When *AIH* ends with the united-front campaign against German and Japanese imperialism, we do not pack up our bags and go back to the disenfranchised communities to enjoy the rewards of pax Americana. Allos himself did not settle back to bask in the glories of American Exceptionalism; his utopianism, however much romanticized or displaced by a yearning for "roots" in the past growing into the future, proved resilient to compel him to reengage with his newfound "brothers" in the ILWU as well as in the homeland where the survivors of Luis Taruc's guerillas would soon evolve into the embryonic avatars of the Communist Party of the Philippines' New People's Army.

# VI

We owe it to Lane Hirabayashi and Marilyn Alquizola that finally, after five years of waiting, the FBI records of the surveillance of Allos have been released to the public by virtue of the Freedom of Information Act. This, I hope, will spur the decentering of the Bulosan canon to liberate its emancipatory energies in a world-systemic critique. We need to undertake the task that Pascale Casanova recently reminded us of, the task of reestablishing "the lost bond between literature, history and the world, while still maintaining a full sense of the irreducible singularity of literary texts" (2005, 71). It is analogous to recognizing the dialectical reciprocity of Allos, the singular individual, and Bulosan as representative of the Filipino collectivity, the emergent provocative voice not only of the Filipino masses of workers and peasants, but also of all the dispossessed and disinherited of the earth. This is the concrete universal we need to theorize and achieve against the temptation of model-minority success and postcolonial mimicry.

At about the time Allos wrote "Terrorism Rides the Philippines," two labor-union militants were born as prophetic signifiers of the future: Gene Viernes in 1951 and Silme Domingo in 1952. Both young men matured in Seattle during the social ferment of the sixties and the anti-Marcos mobilization from 1972 to 1986. They also became involved early in their life with the ILWU, Local 37, Bulosan's and Mensalvas's union. In 1981, both were murdered by pro-Marcos thugs supported by reactionary elements of the Filipino American community in Seattle. Domingo was a key militant of the leftist Union of Democratic Filipinos leading the resistance against the U.S.–Marcos dictatorship; the trial of the murderers revealed the complicity of local Filipino leaders with the brutal gangster tactics of the Marcos regime to suppress dissent in the United States. This is unequivocal proof of Allos's belief that one cannot divorce the struggle back home against feudal-comprador barbarism supported politically and militarily by the imperialist bloc (see Schirmer and Shalom 1987, 143–52) from the fight for social justice and equality in the metropole of finance capital. Both fronts in the popular-democratic struggle are linked dialectically, as dramatized by the character Dante in *The Cry*—a shadowy double or hypothetical surrogate for Allos—whose "wounds" inflicted by his ordeal in the United States must be cauterized and cured by facing the same enemies he fled from in the guise of the local landlords, bureaucrats, and predatory warlords who safeguarded their masters' interests. This is also what Philip Vera Cruz found when, despite his public protest, he witnessed Cesar Chavez endorsing the vicious Marcos dictatorship in the seventies. Vera Cruz had no alternative but to resign from the very union that he, Larry Itliong, and other Filipinos helped organize with the historic Delano Grape Strike in 1965 nine years after Bulosan's death.

In April 2006 the Library of Congress held a symposium honoring Carlos Bulosan and his still-unassayed contribution to U.S. multicultural democracy in the light of the one hundred year anniversary of the Filipino arrival in U.S. territory. This is an unprecedented and salutary event. The Philippines is currently experiencing a political crisis reminiscent of the imposition of brutal military rule by Ferdinand Marcos in 1972. Were he alive, Bulosan would be the first to rally Filipinos against the unprecedented extrajudicial political killings and abductions by the fascist terrorist Arroyo regime of lawyers, journalists, parliamentarians, and other citizens in their country of origin. Amid the "war against terrorism," with the Philippines declared as the "second battlefront" after the 9/11 attack on the World Trade Center and the Pentagon, it is an opportune time to reappraise Bulosan's works, its resonance and incalculable influence on the contingents of young Filipino migrants (called OFWs, Overseas Filipino Workers) in the United States, Europe, and elsewhere.

There are signs that, despite the apathy I noted earlier, Bulosan's writings are finally being rediscovered and renewed at the same time, by a new generation of readers here, in the Philippines, and in the unprecedented Filipino diaspora around the planet. One example of renewal is the prodigiously resourceful staging of the short story "The Romance of Magno Rubio," directed by Loy Arenas. There is no doubt the beneficiaries (mentioned by Mensalvas in his obituary in which he inventoried Allos's estate as "one old typewriter, wornout socks, old suit" and "Beneficiaries" as "His people" will now exceed the number of those heroic Manongs whom Bulosan—as Dolores Feria, his devoted friend reported a year after he died— cherished in his shy and gentle way; the *kababayan* whom he initially addressed and paid homage to a century ago (Cimatu 2002; Feria 1956).

# 5

# Emergency Signals from the Shipwreck

Ang hindi lumingon sa pinanggalingan ay hindi makararating sa paroroonan.

[One who does not look back to where he came from will not reach his destination.]

—Ancient Tagalog proverb

## By Way of Prologue

"Inside and outside my country, tyranny reigns." Thus began the unforgettable 1838 narrative of *Florante at Laura* by Francisco Balagtas (1978), a poem recognized as the inaugural discourse of Filipino nationalism. It inspired popular and *ilustrado* agitation, including the Cavite Mutiny of 1872 that led to the execution of the three martyr priests Jose Burgos, Mariano Gomez, and Jacinto Zamora. In his travels in Europe, Jose Rizal, the national hero, constantly read Balagtas's *awit* (ballad) that inspired his novels *Noli me tangere* and *El Filibusterismo*; smuggled into the islands, Rizal's writings acted as "emergency signals" that sparked the Katipunan revolt of 1896. Charged for being *filibusteros* in the wake of the Cavite Mutiny, influential Filipino intellectuals were deported by the Spanish colonial government to Marianas Islands. Rizal was exiled to Dapitan, Mindanao, in 1892, four years before being shot on December 29, 1896, in Manila.

During Spanish rule, the physical movement of the Indios was tightly regulated, under strict surveillance by both secular and spiritual authorities. Outside and inside the colony, the Filipino subaltern was a marked man. Women, of course, were confined to domestic and institutional

"prisons" and their disciplinary regimes. Space was systematically policed, monitored, and demarcated. After Marianas Islands, Guam (not
counting the prison of Montjuich in Barcelona, Spain, where Rizal and Isabelo de los Reyes were once interned) became the next destination for insurgents. After the United States crushed the revolutionary forces of the
first Philippine Republic, it sent the most distinguished Filipino insurgent
Apolinario Mabini to Guam for refusing to sign a loyalty oath. Others
chose Hong Kong, Japan, or recalcitrant solipsism as alternative surrogates for the occupied homeland.

In the period of direct U.S. imperial domination, space came under the
rule of market capital and commodity exchange. The practice of removal
or transporting Filipinos from their regional habitat to other parts of the
empire would no longer be called deportation or exile but recruitment or
migrant passage—mainly to the Hawaii sugar plantations. Although Filipinos were now U.S. "wards," still Pedro Calosa, leader of the Tayug revolt, was banished from Hawaii to the Philippine Islands territory for the
"crime" of union organizing. In the next decades, the generation of Carlos Bulosan and Philip Vera Cruz—thousands of dispossessed peasants
and workers—shifted their port of entry to San Francisco, Los Angeles,
and Seattle to become the migrant farmworkers and cannery workers who
would pioneer the heroic project of mobilizing the multiethnic U.S. proletariat from the thirties to the sixties, ending with the formation of the
United Farm Workers of America.

Meanwhile, subaltern *pensionados*, some schooled by the soldiers who
defeated General Emilio Aguinaldo, traveled to U.S. universities under contract. They returned to serve as bureaucrats and propagandists in the U.S.
colonial administration and, afterwards, in the Commonwealth experiment of neocolonialism under Manuel Quezon and in the successive post–
World War II neocolonial regimes. A lonely deviant was Jose Garcia Villa.
His revolt against hypocritical bourgeois morality (which the *pensionados*
symbolized) and surviving feudal mores led to his self-exile, first in Albuquerque, New Mexico, as a melancholy soul, and then to New York City
as a kind of hybrid denizen of the "internal colonies" of the metropole. Although celebrated today by a few isolated Filipino writers, Villa has never
really been admitted to the mainstream canon of American literature, so
that no country or people can really grant him any credential or status of
belonging to a distinct cultural heritage except the Philippine nation-state
and the handful of Filipinos who care about an emergent self-determined
national culture. Cosmopolitanism or the universal citizenship of globalization is still a mirage, a seductive alibi, for neocolonials.

Today, Filipinos count unofficially as the largest Asian American
group—more than three million—in the United States. No longer dominant
in the agribusiness of the West Coast, they now supply hands to the service

industries (housework, health care, tourist enterprises) throughout the metropolis. Some argue that General Cesar Taguba of recent fame as investigator of the Abu Ghraib prison scandals (notwithstanding the shocking revelation of his "real" experience in the military) may testify to the distance Filipinos have come from being cooks in the White House or stewards in the U.S. Navy. As most census studies indicate, however, the community is more scattered and divided politically, certainly economically (social class), than other nationalities, owing chiefly to the impoverished, subordinated plight of their country of origin. What is more ominous is that after September 11, 2001, several hundred Filipinos were summarily deported, and many more were threatened by exclusion or expulsion, under the controversial USA PATRIOT Act and other State terrorist measures. We seem to be returning to the time when Filipinos were hunted and lynched by white vigilantes in Washington and California, or else exhibited as exotic specimens in various industrial exposition sites or safely policed shopping bazaars. We are again considered an important target population.

Of more consequence today is the unprecedented "diaspora" of ten million Filipinos around the world, mainly as domestics, semiskilled workers, caregivers, entertainers, and professionals—the Philippines has surpassed other countries in becoming the largest supplier of contract labor (the infamous Guantanamo detention cells were built by Filipino workers). However, this has also meant that the image of the Filipino has become that of "servants of globalization," as one textbook puts it.

The following reflections—in truth, fragments from an exile's journals—were written in the mid-nineties to address this altered situation of the Filipino abroad, at the end of the Cold War and the beginning of the era of what is now labeled the "clash of civilizations" with the "war on terrorism" as its offshoot. It is coincidentally the era of the homeless, the displaced, the refugee of genocidal wars. It is the era of the Overseas Filipino Worker, of Flor Contemplacion, and the contrived scourge of the Abu Sayyaf. Individual or personal cases of Filipino exile have metamorphosed into the generalized plight of economic refugees or of political asylum cases (like Benigno Aquino Jr. in the period of the Marcos dictatorship), émigrés, expatriates, and into some kind of diaspora sponsored by the World Bank/International Monetary Fund—of course, a diaspora with Filipino specific characteristics, not to be confused with the prototypical Jewish Diaspora, or subsequent replicas (Chinese, Indian, African).

Exile has now assumed multiple masks. Victim of Zionism and Western imperialism, the late Palestinian scholar Edward Said (2000) describes exile as "the unhealable rift forced between a human being and a native place, between the self and its true home: its essential sadness can never be surmounted." He is echoing the great Dante's elegy of the exile in *Divina Commedia*: "You will leave everything loved most dearly; and this is the

arrow that the bow of exile shoots first." Bewailing the predicament of
millions of Palestinians, and by extension, millions of refugees all over the
world (now including Filipinos), Said attests to the pathos of exile in "the
loss of contact with the solidity and the satisfaction of earth." This pathos
of alienation does not, I think, befit the examples offered by Rizal, Mabini,
or sacrificed representatives of the Filipino nation/people-in-the-making.
Nonetheless, my "untimely" intervention in my book *From Exile to Diaspora* (1998b) can be considered an attempt to recover the palpability of
Filipino "earth" via the route of the Filipino proverb cited as epigraph and
its allusion to the nascent reality of beleaguered but liberated zones in the
homeland (homecoming is thus always a permanent possibility wherever
and whenever we commit ourselves to the principles of social justice and
communal-democratic sovereignty), which are the places of hope and eventual reunion. Despite local differences and multiple languages, the submerged rallying cry of all Filipinos abroad, of all Filipinos overseas, is
"Tomorrow, see you in Manila!"

---

It has been almost forty years now, to this longest day, June 21, 1996, of
my sojourn here in the United States ever since we left Manila. The time
of departure can no longer be read in the number of passports discarded,
visas stamped over and over again. A palimpsest to be deciphered, to be
sure. But you can always foretell and anticipate certain things. For example, when someone meets you for the first time, this Caucasian—in general,
Western—stranger would irresistibly and perhaps innocently (a reflex of
commonsensical wisdom) always ask: "And where are you from?" Alas,
from the red planet Mars, from the volcanic terra of the as yet undiscov-
ered satellite of Andromeda, from the alleys of Tondo and the labyrinths
of Avenida Rizal. . . .

The sociologist Zygmunt Bauman (1996) delineates the possible life
strategies that denizens of the postmodern era can choose: stroller,
vagabond, tourist, player. In a world inhospitable to pilgrims, I opt for the
now obsolete persona of the exile disguised as itinerant and peripatetic
student without credentials or references, sojourning in places where new
experiences may occur. No destination or destiny, only a succession of
detours and displacements.

Apropos of the sojourner, Cesar Vallejo (1976) writes during his exile
in Paris, November 12, 1937: *Acaba de pasar sin haber venido* ("He just
passed without having come"). A cryptic and gnomic utterance. One can
interpret this economy of the psyche thus: for the sake of a sustained bliss
of journeying, the "passenger" (the heroine of the passage) forfeits the
grace or climax of homecoming. But where is home? Home is neither on

the range nor valley nor distant shores—it is no longer a "place," but rather a site, or locus, to which you can return no more, as Thomas Wolfe once elegized. We have not yet reached this stage, the desperate act of switching identities (as in Michaelangelo Antonioni's *The Passenger*, in which the protagonist's itinerary ends in the ad hoc, repetitious, inconsequential passage into anonymous death) so as to claim the spurious originality of an "I," the monadic ego, a.k.a. the foundation of all Western metaphysics. Our postdeconstructionist malaise forbids this detour, this escape. Antonioni's existential "stranger" forswears the loved one's offer of trust, finding danger even boring and trivial. After all, you are only the creature—not yet a cyborg—shunted from one terminus to another, bracketed by an a-methodical doubt and aleatory suspicion.

So here we are, "here" being merely a trope, a figure without referent or denotation. To such a denouement has Western consumerized technological society come, trivializing even third world revolutions and violence as hackneyed cinematic fare, a quotidian banality.

*Beyond Rangoon* is the latest of such commodities in the high-cultural supermarket of the Western metropolis. The setting is no longer Burma but Myanmar. The names don't matter; what is needed is some exotic location on which to transplant a white American woman's psyche suffering a horrendous trauma: discovering the murdered bodies of her husband and son upon coming home from work. Desperate to put this horror behind her, she and her sister then join a tour to Myanmar. Soon she gets involved in the popular resistance against a ruthless military dictatorship. So what happens? Carnage, melodramatic escapades, incredible violence, and slaughter, until our heroine begins to empathize with the unruly folk and arguably finds her identity by rediscovering her vocation; as physician, at the end of the film, without much ado she begins to attend to the victims without thought of her own safety or pleasure. She is reconciled with the past, finding substitutes for the dead in "third world" mutilated bodies. And so white humanity redeems itself again in the person of this caring, brave, daring woman whose "rite of passage" is the thematic burden of the film. It is a passage from death to life, not exactly a transmigration from scenes of bloodletting to moments of peace and harmony; nonetheless, strange "third world" peoples remain transfixed in the background, waiting for rescue and redemption. So for the other part of humanity, there is no movement but simply a varying of intensity of suffering, punctuated by resigned smiles or bitter tears.

So the "beyond" is staged here as the realization of hope for the West. However, what is in it for us who are inhabiting (to use a cliché) the "belly of the beast"? But let us go back to Vallejo, or to wherever his imagination has been translocated. Come to think of it, even the translation of Vallejo's line is an escape: there is no pronoun there. Precisely the absence of the phallus (if we follow our Lacanian guides) guarantees its infinite circulation as the wandering, nomadic signifier. Unsettled, traveling, the intractable vagrant. . . .

Lost in the desert or in some wilderness, are we looking for a city of which we are unacknowledged citizens? Which city, Babylon or Jerusalem? St. Augustine reminds us: "Because of our desire we are already there, we have already cast our hope like an anchor on these shores." By the logic of desire, the separation of our souls from our bodies is finally healed by identification with a figurelike Christ who, in Pauline theology, symbolizes the transit to liberation from within the concrete, suffering body. What is foreign or alien becomes transubstantiated into a world-encompassing Ecclesia, a new polis in which we, you and I, find ourselves embedded.

---

Stranger no more, I am recognized by others whom I have yet to identify and know. Instead of Albert Camus's *L'Etranger* (which in my youth served as a fetish for our bohemian revolt against the provincial Cold War milieu of the Manila of the fifties), Georg Simmel's "The Stranger" (1950) has become of late the focus of my meditation. It is an enigmatic text whose profound implications cannot really be spelled out in words, only in lived experiences, in praxis.

Simmel conceives "the stranger" as the unity of two opposites: mutating between "the liberation from every given point in space" and "the conceptual opposite to fixation at such a point," hence the wanderer defined as "the person who comes today and stays tomorrow." Note that the staying is indefinite, almost a promise, not a certainty. But where is the space of staying, or maybe of malingering?

Simmel's notion of space tries to bridge potentiality and actuality: "although he has not moved on, he has not quite overcome the freedom of coming and going. He is fixed within a particular spatial group, or within a group whose boundaries are similar to spatial boundaries" (1950, 505). The wanderer is an outsider, not originally belonging to this group, importing something into it. Simmel's dialectic of inside/outside spheres is tricky here; it may be an instance of wanting to have one's cake and also eat it:

> The unity of nearness and remoteness involved in every human relation is organized, in the phenomenon of the stranger, in a way which may be most briefly formulated by saying that in the relationship to him, distance means that he, who is close by, is far, and strangeness means that he, who also is far, is actually near. For, to be a stranger is naturally a very positive relation; it is a specific form of interaction. The inhabitants of Sirius are not really

strangers to us, at least not in any sociologically relevant sense: they do not exist at all; they are beyond far and near. The stranger, like the poor and like sundry "inner enemies," is an element of the group itself. His position as a full-fledged member involves both being outside it and confronting it. (1950, 506–507)

And so, following this line of speculation, the query "Where are you from?" is in effect a token of intimacy. For the element that increases distance and repels, according to Simmel, is the one that establishes the pattern of coordination and consistent interaction that is the foundation of coherent sociality. Neither paradox nor aporia, this theme needs pursuing up to its logical or illogical end.

Between the essentialist mystique of the Volk/nation and the libertarian utopia of laissez-faire capitalism, the "stranger" subsists as a catalyzing agent of change. In other words, the subversive function of the stranger inheres in his being a mediator of two or more worlds. Is this the hybrid and in-between diasporic character of postcoloniality? Is this the indeterminate species bridging multiple worlds? Or is it more like the morbid specimens of the twilight world that Antonio Gramsci, languishing in prison, once alluded to, creatures caught between the ancien régime slowly dying and a social order that has not yet fully emerged from the womb of the old?

We are brought back to the milieu of transition, of vicissitudes, suspended in the proverbial conundrum of the tortoise overtaking the hare in Zeno's paradox. This may be the site where space is transcended by time. The stranger's emblematic message may be what one black musician has already captured in this memorable manifesto by Paul Gilroy (1993): "It ain't where you're from, it's where you're at."

Historically, the stranger in Simmel's discourse emerged first as the trader. When a society needs products from outside its borders, a middleman is then summoned who will mediate the exchange. (If a god is needed, as the old adage goes, there will always be someone to invent him.) Yet what happens when those products coming from outside its territory begin to be produced inside, when a middleman role is no longer required, that is, when the economy is closed, land divided up, and handicraft guilds formed to ensure some kind of autarky? Then the stranger, who is the supernumerary (Simmel cites European Jews as the classic example), becomes the settler whose protean talent or sensibility distinguishes him. This sensibility springs from the *habitus* (to use Pierre Bourdieu's term) of trading "which alone makes possible unlimited combinations," where "intelligence always finds expansions and new territories," because the trader is not fixed or tied to a particular location; he doesn't own land or soil or any ideal point in the social environment. Whence originates his mystery? From the medium of money, the instrument of exchange:

Restriction to intermediary trade, and often (as though sublimated from it) to pure finance, gives him the specific character of mobility. If mobility takes place within a closed group, it embodies that synthesis of nearness and distance which constitutes the formal position of the stranger. For the fundamentally mobile person comes in contact, at one time or another, with every individual, but is not organically connected, through established ties of kinship, locality, and occupation, with any single one. (Simmel 1950, 509)

From this paradoxical site of intimacy and detachment, estrangement and communion, is born the quality of "objectivity" that allows the fashioning of superior knowledge. This does not imply passivity or indifference, Simmel argues: "it is a particular structure composed of distance and nearness, indifference and involvement." For instance, the dominant position of the stranger is exemplified in the practice of those Italian cities that chose judges from outside the city because "no native was free from entanglement in family and party interests." Can the court system in the Philippines ever contemplate this practice, courts that are literally family sinecures, nests of clan patronage and patriarchal gratuities? Only, I suppose, when there is a threat of interminable feuds, a cycle of vindictive retribution. Otherwise, legitimacy is always based on force underwritten by custom, tradition, the inertia of what's familiar. So strangeness is subversive when it challenges the familiar and normal, the ineluctable pathos of sameness.

On the other hand, it may also be conservative. The stranger then, like Prince Myshkin in Dostoevsky's *The Idiot* (1971), becomes the occasion for a public display of intimacies. He becomes the hieratic vessel or receiver of confessions performed in public, of confidential information, secrets, rumors, and others. He is the bearer of guilt and purgation, the stigmata of communal responsibility and its catharsis. His objectivity is then a full-blown participation that, obeying its own laws, thus eliminates—Simmel theorizes—"accidental dislocations and emphases, whose individual and subjective differences would produce different pictures of the same object." From this standpoint, the prince is a stranger not because he is not Russian but because he "idiotically" or naively bares whatever he thinks—he says it like it is. Which doesn't mean he doesn't hesitate or entertain reservations, judgments, and so on. Dostoevsky invents his escape hatch in the prince's epileptic seizures that become symptomatic of the whole society's disintegrated totality.

---

We begin to become more acquainted with this stranger as the spiritual ideal embedded in contingent reality. Part of the stranger's objectivity is his freedom: "the objective individual is bound by no commitments which could prejudice his perception, understanding, and evaluation of the given." Is this possible: a person without commitments, open to every passing opportunity? Baruch Spinoza, G. E. Moore, and Mikhail Bakhtin are not wanted here. Ethics be damned.

At this juncture I think Simmel is conjuring up the image of the value-free sociologist who has completely deceived himself even of the historical inscription of his discipline, finally succumbing to the wish-fulfillment of becoming the all-knowing scientist of historical laws and social processes. Simmel is quick to exonerate the stranger, the middleman-trader, from charges of being a fifth columnist, an instigator or provocateur paid by outsiders. On the other hand, Simmel insists that the stranger "is freer, practically and theoretically; he surveys conditions with less prejudice; his criteria for them are more general and more objective ideals; he is not tied down in his action by habit, piety, and precedent." The stranger has become some kind of omniscient deity, someone like the god of Flaubert and Joyce paring his fingernails behind the clouds while humanity agonizes down below.

Finally, Simmel points out the abstract nature of the relation of others to the stranger. This is because "one has only certain more general qualities in common," not organic ties that are empirically specific to inhabitants sharing a common historical past, culture, kinship, and others. The humanity that connects stranger and host is precisely the one that separates, the element that cannot be invoked to unify the stranger with the group of which he is an integral part. So nearness and distance coalesce again: "To the extent to which the common features are general, they add, to the warmth of the relation founded on them, an element of coolness, a feeling of the contingency of precisely this relation—the connecting forces have lost their specific and centripetal character" (1950, 509).

One may interpose at this point: Why is Simmel formulating the predicament of the stranger as a paradox that too rapidly resolves the contradictions inherent in it? The dialectic is short-circuited, the tension evaporated, by this poetic reflection: "The stranger is close to us, insofar as we feel between him and ourselves common features of a national, social, occupational, or generally human, nature. He is far from us, insofar as these common features extend beyond him or us, and connect us only because they cannot connect a great many people." What generalizes, estranges; what binds us together, individualizes each one. A symmetrical truism, or another liberal platitude?

We witness an immanent dialectical configuration shaping up here. Every intimate relationship then harbors the seeds of its own disintegration. The aborigine and the settler are wed in their contradictions and interdependencies. For what is common to two, Simmel continues to insist, "is never common to them alone but is subsumed under a general idea which includes much else besides, many possibilities of commonness." This, I think, applies to any erotic relationship which, in the beginning, compels the lovers to make their relationship unique, unrepeatable, even idiosyncratic. Then estrangement ensues; the feeling of uniqueness is replaced by skepticism and indifference, by the thought that the lovers are only instances of a general human destiny. In short, the lovers graduate into philosophers reflecting on themselves as only one of the infinite series of lovers in all of history. These possibilities act like a corrosive agent that destroys nearness, intimacy, communal togetherness:

> No matter how little these possibilities become real and how often we forget them, here and there, nevertheless, they thrust themselves between like shadows, like a mist which escapes every word noted, but which must coagulate into a solid bodily form before it can be called jealousy . . . similarity, harmony, and nearness are accompanied by the feeling that they are not really the unique property of this particular relationship. They are something more general, something which potentially prevails between the partners and an indeterminate number of others, and therefore gives the relation, which alone was realized, no inner and exclusive necessity. (Simmel 1950, 510)

Perhaps in Gunnar Myrdal's "America" (1974), in which a universalistic creed, once apostrophized by that wandering French *philosophe* De Tocqueville, prevails, this privileging of the general and the common obtains. However, this "perhaps" dissolves because we see, in the history of the last five decades, that cultural pluralism is merely the mask of a "common culture" of market individualism, of class war inflected into the routine of racial politics. Witness the victims of the Civil Rights struggles, the assassination of Black Panther Party members, lethal violence and psychic injury inflicted on Vincent Chin, Leonard Peltier, Mumia Abu-jamal, and so on.

As antidote to the mystification of hybridity and in-betweenness, we need therefore to historicize, to come down to the ground of economic and political reality. What collectivities of power/knowledge are intersecting and colliding? In a political economy where racial differentiation is the fundamental principle of accumulation, where profit or the private extraction of surplus value is the generalizing principle, it is difficult to accept Simmel's concept of strangeness as premised on an initial condition of intimacy and mutual reciprocity in a mythical level playing field. Simmel is caught in a bind. He says that the Greek attitude to the barbarians illustrates a mind frame that denies to the Other attributes that are specifically human. However, in that case the barbarians are not strangers; the relation to them is a nonrelation. Whereas the stranger is "a member of the group," not an outsider. Simmel arrives at this concluding insight:

> As a group member, the stranger is near and far at the same time as is characteristic of relations founded only on general human commonness. But between nearness and distance, there arises a specific tension when the consciousness that only the quite general is common stresses that which is not common. [Here is the kernel of Simmel's thesis.] In the case of the person who is a stranger to the country, the city, the race, etc., however, this non-common element is once more nothing individual, but merely the strangeness of origin, which is or could be common to many strangers. For this reason, strangers are not really conceived as individuals, but as strangers of a particular type: the element of distance is no less general in regard to them than the element of nearness. (1950, 511–12)

Examples might illuminate these refined distinctions. Simmel cites the case of the categorization of the Jew in medieval times that remained permanent despite the changes in the laws of taxation: the Jew was always taxed as a Jew, his ethnic identity fixed his social position, whereas the Christian was "the bearer of certain objective contents" that changed in accordance with the fluctuation of his fortune (ownership of property, wealth). If this invariant element disappeared, then all strangers by virtue of being strangers would pay "an equal head tax." In spite of this, the stranger is "an organic member of the group which dictates the conditions of his existence"—except that this membership is precisely different in that while it shares some similarities with all human relationships, a special proportion and reciprocal tension produce the particular, formal relation to the "stranger."

An alternative to Simmel's hypothesis is the historical case of Baruch Spinoza, the archetypal exile. A child of the Marrano community of Jews in Amsterdam, Holland, who were driven from Portugal and Spain in the fourteenth and fifteenth centuries, Spinoza was eventually excommunicated and expelled by the elders of the community. Banned as a heretic, Spinoza became an "exile within an exile." It was, however, a *felix culpa* since that became the condition of possibility for the composition of the magnificent *Ethics*, a space of redemption in which *deus/natura* becomes accessible to ordinary mortals provided they can cultivate a special form of rationality called *scientia intuitiva*. The "impure blood" of this "Marrano of Reason" affords a created world of secular reason that, if we so choose, can become a permanent home for the diasporic intellect. Unfortunately, except for a handful of recalcitrant spirits, Filipinos have not yet discovered Spinoza's *Ethics*. I suspect, however, that Rizal and the Propagandists, Isabelo de Los Reyes, Apolinario Mabini, S. P. Lopez, and Angel Baking, were not unaware of its dissemination in the radical anarchist and socialist tradition of the Enlightenment.

---

You will leave everything loved most dearly;
And this is the arrow
That the bow of exile shoots first. . . .

—Dante Alighieri, *The Divine Comedy*

So where are we now in mapping this terra incognita of the nomadic monster, the deviant, the alien, the stranger, the Filipino subaltern?

We are unquestionably in the borderline, the hymen, the margin of difference constituted by that simultaneous absence and presence that Jacques Derrida was the first to theorize in his strategy of suspicion. It is, one might suggest, an epileptic seizure that is regularized, as the character of Prince Myshkin in Dostoevsky's *The Idiot* demonstrates. When asked by that unforgettable mother, Mrs. Yepanchin, what he wrote to her daughter Aglaya—a confession of need of the other person, a communication of desire for the other to be happy as the gist of the message, Prince Myshkin replied that when he wrote it, he had "great hopes." He explains: "Hopes—well, in short, hopes of the future and perhaps a feeling of joy that I was not a stranger, not a foreigner, there. I was suddenly very pleased to be back in my own country. One sunny morning I took up a pen and wrote a letter to her. Why to her, I don't know. Sometimes, you know, one feels like having a friend at one's side" (1971, 105).

Dear friend, where are you?

\*   \*   \*   \*   \*

Since we are in the mode of a "rectification of names," a semantic interlude is appropriate here. Just as our current hermeneutic trend seeks etymologies for traces of the itinerary of meanings, let us look at what Webster offers us for the word "exile": it means banished or expelled from one's native country or place of residence by authority, and forbidden to return, either for a limited time or for life; abandonment of one's country by choice or necessity. "The Exile" originally refers to the Babylonian captivity of the Jews in the sixth century B.C.

The Latin *exilium* denotes banishment; the Latin *exilis* denotes slender, fine, thin; "exilition," now obsolete, "a sudden springing or leaping out." This "sudden springing or leaping out" offers room for all kinds of speculation on wandering strangers inhabiting borderlines, boundaries, frontiers, all manner of refusals and evasions. Yet the movement involved in exile is not accidental or happenstance; it has a telos underlying it. It implicates wills and purposes demarcating the beginning and end of movement. As Spinoza teaches us, everything can be grasped as modalities of rest and motion, of varying speed. Even here ambiguity pursues us: rest is relative to motion, motion to rest. If everyone is migrating, then who is the native and who the settler?

Another word should supplement "exile," and that word is "migration." The movement from place to place that this word signifies in one epoch is quite circumscribed: it is the movement from one region to another with the change in seasons, as many birds and some fishes follow, for instance, "migratory locust," "migratory" worker: "one who travels from harvest to harvest, working until each crop is gathered or processed," to wit, the Filipino "Manongs" and their Mexican counterparts. The species of Homo sapiens pursues the line of flight instinctively followed by bird and fish, but this calibration of the instinct itself is drawn by the rhythm of the seasons, by Earth's ecological mutation. So exile betrays political will, while migration still obscures or occludes the play of secular forces by the halo of naturalness, the aura of cosmic fate and divine decree. The fate of Bulosan and compatriots of the "warm body export" trade today—all ten million bodies, with at least five of them returning daily at the Ninoy Aquino International Airport as cadavers—offers the *kairos* of an exemplum. The "disappeared" in the era of martial law has now been replaced by the "returned" in the era of transnational corporate globalization.

* * * * *

The life history of the national hero Jose Rizal offers one heuristic paradigm for Filipino intellectuals in self-exile.

When this leading anticolonial propagandist-agitator was banished to Dapitan, in the southern island of Mindanao, in 1892, he assured his family that "wherever I might go I should always be in the hands of God who holds in them the destinies of men." Despite this unabashed deistic faith, Rizal immediately applied himself to diverse preoccupations: horticulture, eye surgery, collecting butterflies for study, teaching, civic construction, composing a multilingual dictionary, and trying out a liaison with an "alien" woman, a "sweet" stranger (*dulce extranjera*). He also maintained a voluminous correspondence with scientists and scholars in Europe and Manila. Even though the Spanish authorities were lenient, Rizal had no utopian illusions: "To live is to be among men, and to be among men is to struggle. . . . It is a struggle with them but also with one's self, with their passions, but also with one's own, with errors and with anxieties" (1976, 30).

The anguish of Rizal's exile was assuaged somewhat by his female companion, Josephine Bracken, an Irish Catholic from Hong Kong.

Nevertheless, he could not deny that his being transported to Dapitan was demoralizing, unsettling, given "the uncertainty of the future." This is why he seized the opportunity to volunteer his medical skills to the Spanish army engaged in suppressing the revolution in Cuba. Amplifying distance and alienation, he could resign himself to the demands of duty, of the necessity "to make progress through suffering." Fatalism and service to the cause of humanity coalesced to distinguish the ethos of this deportation at a time when rumblings of popular discontent had not yet climaxed in irreversible rupture. When Rizal was executed in December 1896, the revolution had already exploded, concentrating scattered energies in the fight against a common enemy, first Spain and then the United States. Homecoming was near, the return a challenging task or impending necessity.

*     *     *     *     *

In the context of globalized capitalism today, the Filipino diaspora acquires a distinctive physiognomy and temper. We can exercise a thought experiment of syncretism and cross-fertilization. The Pinoy diaspora is a fusion of exile and migration: the scattering of a people, not yet a fully synthesized nation, to the ends of the earth, across the planet throughout the sixties and seventies, continuing up to the present. We are now a quasi-wandering people, pilgrims or prospectors staking our lives and futures all over the world—in the Middle East, Africa, Europe, North and South America, in Australia and all of Asia, in every nook and cranny of this seemingly godforsaken Earth. Explorers and adventurers all. No one yet has performed a "cognitive mapping" of these movements, their geometry and velocity, across national boundaries, mocking the carnivalesque borderland hallucinations glorified by postmodernist academics of color.

Who cares for the Filipino anyway? Not even the Philippine government and its otiose consulates—unless compelled by massive demonstrations of anger such as the one that followed the execution of Flor Contemplacion in Singapore. What can you expect from parasitic oligarchs and government flunkies of finance-capital? We are a nation in search of a national-democratic sovereign state that will care for the welfare of every citizen, particularly those historically oppressed (peasants, workers, Moros, women, indigenous communities, children). When Benigno Aquino was killed, the slogan "the Filipino is worth dying for" became fashionable for a brief interval between the calamity of the Marcos dictatorship and the mendacity of Corazon Aquino's rule and her even more bloody unconscionable successors. Yet today Filipinos are dying—for what? For the status quo? For more self-sacrifices for parasites? For Bush's obscene "war of terror" for oil, white supremacy, and corporate superprofits?

In 1983 alone, there were three hundred thousand Filipinos in the Middle East and close to one hundred thousand in Europe. I met hundreds of Filipinos, men and women, in the city park in Rome, in front of the train station, during their days off as domestics and semiskilled workers. I met Filipinos hanging around the post office in Tripoli, Libya, in 1980. And in trips back and forth I've met them in London, Amsterdam, Madrid, Barcelona, Hong Kong, Taipei, Montreal, and, of course, everywhere in the United States—a dispersed nationality, perhaps a little better than Bulosan and Philip Vera Cruz and his compatriots during the thirties and forties, field hands and laborers migrating from harvest to harvest from Hawaii and California through Oregon to Washington and Alaska. A whole people dispersed, displaced, dislocated. A woman from Negros watched her husband flying to Saudi Arabia in 1981: "Even the men cry on leaving and cling to their children at the airport. When the airplane lifted off, I felt as though my own body was being dislocated." Like birth pangs, the separation of loved ones generates a new experience, a nascent "structure of feeling," for which we have not yet discovered the appropriate plots, rhetorical idioms, discursive registers, and architectonic of representation. Indeed, this late-capitalist diaspora demands a new language and symbolism for rendition. As picaresque fable? Epic saga? Or as tragic-comic spectacle?

The cult hero of eclectic postmodernity, Salman Rushdie, offers us a harvest of ideas on this global phenomenon in his novel, *Shame* (1983). The migrant has conquered the force of gravity, Rushdie writes, the force of belonging; like birds, he has flown. Roots that have trammeled and tied down have been torn. The conservative myth of roots (exile, to my mind, is a problem of mapping routes, not digging for roots or fabricating ethnographic travelogues) and gravity has been displaced by the reality of flight, for now to fly and to flee are ways of seeking individual freedom—a flight of escape for more risky engagements and self-testing provocations?

> When individuals come unstuck from their native land, they are called migrants. When nations do the same thing (Bangladesh), the act is called secession. What is the best thing about migrant peoples and seceded nations? I think it is their hopefulness. Look into the eyes of such folk in old photographs. Hope blazes undimmed through the fading sepia tints. And what's the worst thing? It is the emptiness of one's luggage. I'm speaking of invisible suitcases, not the physical, perhaps cardboard, variety containing a few meaning-drained mementoes: we have come unstuck from more than land. We have floated upwards from history, from memory, from Time. (Rushdie 1983, 91)

Rushdie finds himself caught not only in the no-man's-land between warring territories, but also between different periods of time. He considers Pakistan a palimpsest souvenir dreamed up by immigrants in Britain, its history written and rewritten, insufficiently conjured and extrapolated. Translated into a text, what was once a homeland becomes a product of the imagination. Every exile or deracinated subaltern shares Rushdie's position, or at least his invented habits: "I, too, like all migrants, am a fantasist. I build imaginary countries and try to impose them on the ones that exist. I, too, face the problem of history: what to retain, what to dump, how to hold on to what memory insists on relinquishing, how to deal with change" (1983). We select the construction materials of our salvaging vessel from the driftwoods of memory, shipwrecked souvenirs—emergency signals flashing from flotsam and jetsam, the wreckage of dreams, promises, wagers risked.

And so this is the existential dilemma. For all those forced out of one's homeland—by choice of necessity, it doesn't really make a difference—the vocation of freedom becomes the act of inventing the history of one's life, which is equivalent to founding and inhabiting that terra incognita, which only becomes known, mapped, named as one creates it partly from memory, partly from dream, partly from hope. Therefore the stranger is the discoverer of that region that becomes home in the process the termination of which coincides with the life of the planet Earth, the stranger dissolving the estranging homelessness of our galaxy. You, stranger, my friend. . . .

\* \* \* \* \*

At this crossroad, let us seek pedagogical counsel from the mentor of the Palestinian diaspora, Edward Said, who has poignantly described the "agon" of exile. Said cited the Philippines' colonial dependency in his magisterial study *Culture and Imperialism* (1993). Caught in medias res and deprived of geographical stability or continuity of events, Said elaborates, the Palestinian narrator of the diaspora has to negotiate between the twin perils of fetishism and nostalgia:

> Intimate mementoes of a past irrevocably lost circulate among us, like the genealogies and fables severed from their original locale, the rituals of speech and custom. Much reproduced, enlarged, thematized, embroidered and passed around, they are strands in the web of affiliations we Palestinians use to tie ourselves to our identity and to each other. . . . We endure the difficulties of dispersion without being forced (or able) to struggle to change our circumstances. . . . Whatever the claim may be that we make on the world—and certainly on ourselves as people who have become restless in the fixed place to which we have been

assigned—in fact our truest reality is expressed in the way we cross over from one place to another. We are migrants and perhaps hybrids in, but not of, any situation in which we find ourselves. This is the deepest continuity of our lives as a nation in exile and constantly on the move. (1993, 39)

Said's hermeneutic strives to decipher the condition of exile as the struggle to recover integrity and reestablish community not in any physical location but in the space of cultural production and exchange. Despite its cogency and the eloquence of its truth-bearing signs, Said's discourse can only articulate the pathos of a select few, the elite intelligentsia. Meanwhile, the intifada partisan has indeed gone beyond the irony of Said's humanism and the hubris of Derrida's difference to challenge U.S.-supported Zionist occupation.

\*\*\*\*       \*\*\*\*              \*\*\*\*       \*\*\*\*

We Filipinos need a cartography and a geopolitical project for the masses in diaspora, not for the elite in exile. Many of our fellow expatriates, however, are obsessed with beginnings.

Speaking of who arrived here first on this continent, our "born-again" compatriots are celebrating the first men from the archipelago who landed one foggy morning of October 21, 1587, at Morro Bay, California. These sailors from the Spanish galleon *Nuestra Señora de Buena Esperanza* were colonial subjects, not "Filipinos." "Filipino" is the term that in those days only referred to Spaniards born in the Philippines (in contrast to the Peninsulares, those born in the European metropolis). But no matter, the name has become symbolic of the renewed search for identity. Any relic, whether Creole or bastard, seems useful.

Such "roots" seem to assimilated Filipino Americans a prerequisite for claiming an original, authentic identity as a singular people. After all, how can the organic community grow and multiply without such attachments? Margie Talaugon of the Filipino American Historical National Society points to Morro Bay as the spot "where Filipino American history started" (*Sacramento Bee*, May 19, 1996). If so, then it started with the Spaniards expropriating the land of the Indians for the Cross and the Spanish Crown. Do we want to be part of the gang of bloody conquistadors (whether Spanish, French, or Anglo-Saxon Puritans) guilty of the genocide of Native Americans?

Under the command of Pedro de Unamuno, "a few Luzon Indians" acting as scouts (because of their color) accompanied the exploring party into the California interior. Lo and behold, they were ambushed by the natives who failed to correctly interpret their offerings. In the skirmish born of misrecognition, one Filipino lost his life and Unamuno withdrew. Other expeditions followed—all for the purpose of finding out possible ports along the California coast where galleons sailing from Manila to Acapulco could seek refuge in case of attack from pirates. When the Franciscan missionaries joined the troops from Mexico, mandated to establish missions from San Diego to Monterey that would serve as way stations for the Manila galleons, Indios from *las islas Filipinas* accompanied them as menials in colonizing Indian territory in what is now the state of California. Do we need to cherish this memorial of complicity with bloodthirsty conquest?

*     *     *     *     *

Anxiety underlying the claim to be first in setting foot on the North American continent also accounts for the revival of interest in the fabled "Manillamen." The rubric designates the Malay subjects of the archipelago who allegedly jumped ship off Spanish galleons and found their way into the bayous of Louisiana as early as 1765. In contrast to the early Luzon "Indians," these were rebels protesting the brutal conditions of indenture; they were "not knowing" accomplices or accessories to colonial rampage. There is even a rumor that they signed up with the French buccaneer Jean Baptiste Lafitte; if true, they then took part in the Battle of New Orleans during the War of 1812. These fugitives settled in several villages outside New Orleans, in Manila Village on Barataria Bay. They engaged chiefly in shrimp fishing and hunting.

The most well-known settlement (ca. 1825) was St. Malo that was destroyed by a hurricane in 1915. The Filipino swamp settlers of St. Malo were memorialized by one of the first "Orientalists," Lafcadio Hearn, whose life configuration appears as rhizomatic as the transplanted Malays he sought to romanticize. Hearn loved all things Japanese, and all things that can be exoticized. Following is an excerpt from his article "Saint Malo: A Lacustrine Village in Louisiana," which appeared in *Harper's Weekly* on March 31, 1883:

> For nearly fifty years, there has existed in the southern swamplands of Louisiana a certain strange settlement of Malay fishermen—Tagalas from the Philippine Islands. The place of their lacustrine village is not precisely mentioned upon maps, and the world in general ignored until a few days ago the bare fact of their amphibious existence. Even the United States mail service has never found its way thither, and even the great city of New Orleans, less than a hundred miles distant, the people were far better informed about the Carboniferous Era than concerning the swampy affairs of the Manila village. . . .

Out of the shuddering reeds and grass on either side rise the
fantastic houses of the Malay fishermen, poised upon slender support above the marsh, like cranes watching for scaly prey. . . .
There is no woman in the settlement, nor has the treble of a female
voice been heard along the bayou for many a long year. . . . How,
then, comes it that in spite of the connection with civilized life,
the Malay settlement of Lake Borgne has been so long unknown?
Perhaps because of the natural reticence of the people.

What is curious is that Hearn, in another "take" of this landscape (in
*Times-Democrat*, March 18, 1883), shifts our attention to the mood and
atmosphere of the place to foreground his verbal artistry. The need to
know these strange swamp dwellers is now subsumed into the program of
a self-indulgent aestheticizing drive; the will to defamiliarize turns the inhabitants, the "outlandish colony of Orientals," into performers of fin de
siècle decadence. Voyeurism feeds on invidious contrasts and innuendoes
that recall Baudelaire's posture of worldly ennui:

Louisiana is full of mysteries and surprises. Within fifty miles of
this huge city, in a bee line southwest, lies a place as wild and weird
as the most fervent seekers after the curious could wish to behold—
a lake village constructed in true Oriental style, and equally worthy of prehistoric Switzerland or modern Malacca. . . . The like
isolation of our Malay settlement is due to natural causes alone,
but of a stranger sort. It is situated in a peculiarly chaotic part of
the world, where definition between earth and water ceases—an
amphibious land full of quiverings and quagmires, suited rather to
reptile life than to human existence—a region wan and doubtful
and mutable as that described in "The Passing of Arthur," where
fragments of forgotten peoples dwell . . . a coast of ever shifting
sand, and, far away, the phantom circle of a moaning sea. . . .
    Nature, by day, seems to be afraid to speak in a loud voice
there; she whispers only. And the brown Malays—forever face
to face with her solitude—also talk in low tones as through
sympathy—tones taught by the lapping of sluggish waters, the
whispering of grasses, the murmuring of the vast marsh. Unless an
alligator shows his head—then it is a shout of "Miro! cuidado!"

Since the voices captured were conversing in Spanish, we know that
these brown settlers have been Hispanicized and estranged from their original surroundings. But never mind: the sounds blend with the other creatures of the bayous, a cacophony of organic life orchestrated by Hearn's
precious craft. St. Malo's miasma is domesticated for the elegant French

salons of New Orleans and the adjoining plantations. Unlike the foggy, damp, and rainy Siberia of Chekhov's story "In Exile" (1979; written in 1892), which becomes the site of epiphanic disclosures and cathartic confessions, Hearn's theater affords no such possibility. Old Semyon, Chekhov's choric observer, can demonstrate his toughness and fortitude all at once in the face of Czarist inhumanity: "Even in Siberia people can live—can li-ive!"

The repressed always returns, but in serendipitous disguise. Hearn would be surprised to learn that St. Malo's descendants, now in their eighth generation, are alive and well, telling their stories, musing: "Well, if we don't know where we come from, how do we know where we are going?" The indefatigable filmmaker Renee Tajima interviewed the Burtanog sisters in New Orleans and notes that "there are no mahjongg games and trans-Pacific memories here in the Burtanog household. The defining cultural equation is five-card Stud and six-pack of Bud (Lite). The talk is of former husbands, voodoo curses, and the complicated racial design of New Orleans society."

Out of the mists exuding from Hearn's prose, the Burtanog sisters speak about antimiscegenation and Jim Crow laws, the hierarchical ranking and crossing-over of the races in Louisiana. However, in conformity with the Southern ethos, they consider themselves "white." These exuberant women certainly do not belong to Bienvenido Santos's tribe of "lovely people"—a patronizing epithet—whose consolation is that they (like artists) presumably have ready and immediate access to the eternal verities. No such luck. Not even for internal exiles such as Mikhail Bakhtin, Anna Akhmatova, Ding Ling, or for "beautiful" souls such as Jose Garcia Villa and their epigones in the miasmic salons of the empire.

\* \* \* \* \*

Why this obsessive quest for who came first? Is precedence a claim to authenticity and autochthonous originality? What if we came last, not "fresh off the boats," clinging to the anchors or even floating on driftwood? Does this entitle us less to "citizenship" or the right to inhabit our constructed place here? Who owns this land, this continent, anyway? Weren't the American Indians the stewards of communal land before the cartographer Amerigo Vespucci was recast as the name-giver to a whole continent?

In his semantic genealogy, Raymond Williams (in *Keywords*, 1983) traces the etymology of "native" to the Latin *nasci* (to be born); *nativus* means innate, natural; hence, "naive" as artless and simple. After the period of conquest and domination, "native" became equivalent to "bondman," or "villein," born in bondage. This negative age—the ascription of inferiority to locals, to non-Europeans—existed alongside the positive age when applied to one's own place or person. Williams observes further:

> Indigenous has served both as a euphemism and as a more neutral term. In English it is more difficult to use in the sense which converts all others to inferiors (to go indigenous is obviously less plausible than to go native). In French, however, indigenes went through the same development as English natives, and is now often replaced by autochtones [*sic*]. (1983, 215)

We may therefore be truly naifs if we ignore the advent of U.S. power in Manila Bay (not Morro Bay) in 1898. This is the inaugural event that started the process of deracination, the primordial event that unfolded in the emergence of the class of *pensionados* and the recruits of the Hawaiian Sugar Plantation up to the "brain drain" of the seventies, the political opportunists who sought asylum during the Marcos dictatorship, and the present influx of this branch of the Filipino diaspora. To shift to the romance of the Spanish galleons is to repress this birth of the Filipino in the womb of the imperial body, a birth that—to invoke the terms in which Petrarch conceived his exile as the physical separation from the mother's body—implies liberation. This is probably why Jose Marti, the revolutionary Cuban who lived in exile in the United States while Spain tyrannized over his Motherland, spoke of living in the "belly of the beast."

Here the metaphor becomes fertile for all kinds of movements, of embarkations and departures. For Petrarch, exile served as the fantasy of discontinuity that allowed the poet immense relief from the tremendous anxiety he felt because of his "belatedness," his advent after the decline of classic Roman civilization. Petrarch was "wounded" by his Greek precursors; he resolved to heal the wound by conceiving the act of writing as a process of digestion, of engulfing, regurgitating, and absorption. We find analogous strategies of sublimation in Virgil, Dante, Gramsci in his *Prison Notebooks*, and so on. This displacement of the original trauma, which assumed earlier Gnostic resonance as the imprisonment of the soul within the body, may perhaps explain the preponderance of oral and gustatory images, eating and digesting activities, in the fiction of Jessica Hagedorn, R. Zamora Linmark, and others.

Are Filipinos condemned to this fantasy of cannibalism as a means of compensation for the loss of the mother? Are we in perpetual mourning, unable to eject the lost beloved that is still embedded in the psyche and forever memorialized there? Are we, Filipinos scattered throughout the planet, bound to the curse of a repetitive compulsion, worshipping fetishes (like aging veterans of some forgotten or mythical battle) that forever remind us of the absent, forgotten, and unrecuperated Others?

That is perhaps the permanent stance of the exile, the act of desiring what is neither here nor there. This paradigm is exemplified in the last speech of Richard Rowan, the writer-hero of James Joyce's *Exiles*, addressing not only Bertha but also someone else, an absent person:

> I have wounded my soul for you—a deep wound of doubt which can never be healed. I can never know, never in this world. I do not wish to know or to believe. I do not care. It is not in the darkness of belief that I desire you. But in restless living wounding doubt. To hold you by no bonds, even of love, to be united with you in body and soul in utter nakedness—for this I longed. (1951, 112)

The quest for the mother as the cure for jealousy, for the illness accompanying the discovery that one cannot completely possess the body of the loved one (the mother-surrogate), is given an ironic twist by Joyce's meditation on women's liberation in his notes to *Exiles*:

> It is a fact that for nearly two thousand years the women of Christendom have prayed to and kissed the naked image of one who had neither wife nor mistress nor sister and would scarcely have been associated with his mother had it not been that the Italian church discovered, with its infallible practical instinct, the rich possibilities of the figure of the Madonna. (120–21)

I recall somewhere that photo or drawing of Rizal's mother, Teodora Alonzo, contemplating the urn containing the remains of her son. This *pieta* attitude symbolizes the longed-for fulfillment of the exile's wish to return to the homeland's bosom, the completion of his earthly journey.

\*    \*    \*    \*    \*

Come now, are we serious in all these melancholy reflections? Was Jose Rizal indulging in this when, in exile at Dapitan, he was preoccupied not just with Josephine Bracken but with a thousand projects of cultivation, teaching, polemical arguments with his Jesuit mentors, correspondence with scholars in Europe, ophthalmological practice, and so on? "What do I have to do with thee, woman?" Or Isabelo de los Reyes—our own socialist forebear—hurled not into the Heideggerian banality of our quotidian world but into the dark dungeon of Montjuich prison near Barcelona for his subversive connections: was he troubled by porous and shifting boundaries? And that perchance he was not really inside but outside, something like the in-between hybrid of postcolonial orthodoxy? Indeed, one may ask: for General Artemio Ricarte, self-exiled in Japan after the victory of the Yankee invaders, is imagining the lost nation a labor of mourning too?

Let us leave this topos of Freudian melancholia and ground our speculations on actual circumstances. Such postmodern quandaries concerning the modalities of displacement of time by space, of essences by contingencies, could not have cajoled the tempered will of Apolinario Mabini into acquiescence. A brilliant adviser to General Emilio Aguinaldo, president of the first Philippine Republic, the captured Mabini refused to swear allegiance to the sovereign power of the United States. This "sublime paralytic" conceived deportation as a crucible of his insurrectionary soul. Intransigent, he preferred the challenge of physical removal to Guam where he was incarcerated for two years.

Imagine the paralyzed Mabini being carried in a hammock along the shores of Guam at the threshold of the storm-wracked twentieth century. Scouring the horizon for a glimpse of his beloved *las islas Filipinas* across the Pacific Ocean, Mabini must have felt that we needed to bide our time because surrender/defeat was not a compromise but a strategy of waiting for the next opportunity. He envisioned a long march, a protracted journey, toward emancipation. One can only surmise that Mabini's shrewd and proud spirit was able to endure the pain of banishment because he was, by forging in his mind "the conscience of his race," writing his memoirs of the revolution, his wit and cunning deployed to bridge the distance between that melancholy island and the other godforsaken islands he was not really able to leave. Who cares now for Mabini? Or for Macario Sakay and the countless "brigands" whom the United States hanged for sedition?

At this point in our journey, we can't stop to savor the pleasure of nostalgia. We are on the way home—"Tomorrow, Manila!"

---

By the rivers of Babylon, there we sat down, yea, we wept when we remembered Zion. . . .
How shall we sing the Lord's song in a strange land?

—Psalm 137

Exile then is a ruse, a subterfuge of the temporarily weak subaltern against the master. It is a problem of deploying time against space—the classic guerilla stratagem against superior firepower. It is the cunning of conviction, of hope.

We thus have a replay of Hegel's choreography of master and slave in a new context. Long before Foucault and Michel de Certeau came around to theorize the performance of everyday resistance, Bertolt Brecht had already explored in his *Lehrstucke* the theme of Schweikian evasions and underminings. The moment of suspended regularity, the interruption of the normal and habitual, becomes the occasion to vindicate the sacrifices of all those who have been forgotten, invisible, silenced. In Peter Weiss's play *Trotsky in Exile*, in the scene before his execution, Trotsky expresses this hope amid setbacks, defeats, and losses of all kinds:

> I can't stop believing in reason, in human solidarity. . . . Failures and disappointments can't stop me from seeing beyond the present defeat to a rising of the oppressed everywhere. This is no Utopian prophecy. It is the sober prediction of a dialectical materialist. I have never lost my faith in the revolutionary power of the masses. But we must be prepared for a long fight. For years, maybe decades, of revolts, civil wars, new revolts, new wars. (1973, 156)

In times of emergency, Trotsky's strategic stance of waiting in exile proves to be the time of pregnancy, of gestation, and the emergence of new things.

Apart from being a symptom of defeat, exile then can also serve as a weapon of resistance. After the Jewish diaspora in the sixth century B.C., the captivity in Babylon, and the centuries of imperial devastation, now we have the situation of the Palestinians, deprived of their native habitat, finally on the way, in transit, to—we don't know yet. A nation-state: is that the harbor, the terminal, of the passage from darkness to light? Unless the transnational bourgeoisie conspire together in this post–Cold War era of intercapitalist rivalry, I hazard that after so much sacrifice the new social formation will not be a simple mimicry of the bourgeois nation-state. Let us hope so.

For so many years after World War II, the Palestinians were the "wandering Jews," also known as "terrorists" by their enemies. One of the most eloquent poets of this diaspora, Fawaz Turki, described how Palestinians in exile attest to "the transcendence . . . in the banal," how they agonized "over who is really in exile:/they or their homeland,/who left who/who will come back to the/other first/where will they meet." Exiles are like lovers then who yearn not for homecoming but for a meeting, another tryst, the long-awaited encounter and reunion. At first, the land was the loved one; later on, the land would metamorphose into events, places, encounters, defeats, and victories. And it is still being transfigured, undergoing transmutations.

For Edward Said, however, exile is the space of the "extraterritorial" where the Baudelairean streetwalker of modernity finally arrives. Said celebrates exile with a vengeance. In *After the Last Sky*, he recognizes the pain, bitter sorrow, and despair but also the unsettling and decentering force of the exile's plight, its revolutionary potential. Even though Said believes that "the pathos of exile is in the loss of contact with the solidity and the satisfaction of Earth: homecoming is out of the question" (2000, 166), he seems to counterpoint to it a Gnostic, even neo-Platonic, response by invoking Hugh of St. Victor, a twelfth-century monk from Saxony:

> It is, therefore, a source of great virtue for the practiced mind to learn, bit by bit, first to change about in visible and transitory things, so that afterwards it may be able to leave them behind altogether. The person who finds his homeland sweet is still a tender beginner; he to whom every soil is as his native one is already strong; but he is perfect to whom the entire world is as a foreign place. The tender soul has fixed his love on one spot in the world; the strong person has extended his love to all places; the perfect man has extinguished his. (2000, 166)

On second thought, this asceticism may be culture-bound, or it may be peculiar to a continental mentality overshadowed by surrounding mountains. Like our brothers in the Caribbean, we Filipinos are archipelagic creatures trained to navigate treacherous waters and irregular shoals. Our epistemic loyalty is to islands with their distinctive auras, vibrations, trajectories, fault lines. John Fowles is one of the few shrewd minds who can discern the difference between the continental and the archipelagic sensorium:

> Island communities are the original alternative societies. That is why so many islanders envy them. Of their nature they break down the multiple alienations of industrial and suburban man. Some vision of Utopian belonging, of social blessedness, of an independence based on cooperation, haunts them all. (1978, 36)

Islands signify our solidarity, even in this time of fragmentation and ceaseless transversality

With this Utopian motif, we may recall Shevek, in Ursula Le Guin's *The Dispossessed* (1974), for whom exile is the symbol for inhabiting an unfinished, incomplete world. It is a site where fulfillment (happiness, reunion, homecoming) is forever postponed. This sustained deferral is what exile means: "There was process: process was all. You could go in a promising direction or you could go wrong, but you did not set out with the expectation of ever stopping anywhere."

Meanwhile, consider the fate of partisans of the South African struggle now allowed reentry into their homeland. Exile for them always entailed a return to a national space to exercise the rights of reclamation and restitution. Yet when the "rendezvous of victory" arrived in 1992, we find "translated persons" and partisans of *metissage* (creolized) at the entry points. Commenting on Bessie Head's achievement, Rob Nixon (1995) considers the exiles as an invaluable asset for the construction of a new South Africa: "Re-entering exiles should thus be recognized as cross-border creations, incurable cultural misfits who can be claimed as a resource, rather than spurned as alien, suspect, or irrelevant."

Toward the predicament of uprooting, one can assume polarized stances. One is the sentimental kind expressed poignantly by Bienvenido Santos:

> All exiles want to go home. Although many of them never return, in their imagination they make their journey a thousand times, taking the slowest boats because in their dream world time is not as urgent as actual time passing, quicker than arrows, kneading on their flesh, crying on their bones. (1982, 11)

The antithesis to that is the understated, self-estranged gesture of Bertolt Brecht. Driven from Europe by Hitler's storm troopers, the path-breaking dramatist found himself a refugee, neither an expatriate nomad nor border-crossing immigrant. Crossing the Japanese Sea, he watched "the grayish bodies of dolphins" in the gaiety of dawn. In "Landscape of Exile," Brecht cast himself in the role of the fugitive who "beheld with joy . . . the little horsecarts with gilt decorations/and the pink sleeves of the matrons/in the alleys of doomed Manila" (1976, 117). His visit to the Philippines was short-lived, like those of Hemingway and Faulkner in the years of the Cold War. Situated on the edge of disaster, Brecht discovered that the oil derricks, the thirsty gardens of Los Angeles, the ravines and fruit market of California "did not leave the messenger of misfortune unmoved." By analogy, were the Pinoys/Pinays at the turn of the century messengers of a messianic faith, underwriting visions of apocalypse long before Brecht sighted the coast of the North American continent?

\* \* \* \* \*

From these excursions into delinquent and wayward paths, we return to the idea of transit, passage, a movement of reconnaissance in search of a home everywhere. And this "everywhere" points, and directs us, to wherever materials are available for building a shelter for work and community. This may be the ultimate philosophical mission in our time whose most provocative prophet is John Berger. Berger's meditations on home, migration, and exile in *And our faces, my heart, brief as photos* (1984) deserve careful pondering. By way of provisional conclusion to these notes, I want to interpolate here a few of his insights into the complex phenomenology of exile.

You can never go home again, Thomas Wolfe counseled us. But what do you mean by home? we respond. Berger speculates on what happens after the loss of home when the migrant leaves, when the continuity with the ancestral dead is broken. The first substitute for the lost, mourned object (kin, home) is passionate erotic love that transcends history. Romantic love unites two displaced persons, linking beginnings and origins, because it predates experience and allows memory and imagination free play. Such passion inspired the project of completing what was incomplete, of healing the division of the sexes—a substitute for homecoming. However, romantic love, like religion and the sacramental instinct, has suffered transmogrification in the modern world of secular rationality. It has been displaced by commodity-fetishism, the cash-nexus, and the cult of simulacra and spectacles. Berger then expounds on the other alternative historical hope of completion:

> Every migrant knows in his heart of hearts that it is impossible to return. Even if he is physically able to return, he does not truly return, because he himself has been so deeply changed by his emigration. It is equally impossible to return to that historical state in which every village was the center of the world. One hope of recreating a center is now to make it the entire earth. Only world-wide solidarity can transcend modern homelessness. Fraternity is too easy a term; forgetting Cain and Abel, it somehow promises that all problems can be soluble. In reality many are insoluble—hence the never-ending need for solidarity.
>
> Today, as soon as very early childhood is over, the house can never again be home, as it was in other epochs. This century, for all its wealth and with all its communication systems, is the century of banishment. Eventually perhaps the promise, of which Marx was the great prophet, will be fulfilled, and then the substitute for the shelter of a home will not just be our personal names, but our collective conscious presence in history, and we will live again at the heart of the real. Despite everything, I can imagine it.
>
> Meanwhile, we live not just our own lives but the longings of our century. (1984, 67)

Revolution, then, is the way out through the stagnant repetition of suffering and deprivation in the commodified business of everyday life. It is Walter Benjamin's *Jetzt-Zeit*, Now-Time, that will blast the continuum of reified history. It is an ever-present apocalypse whose presiding spirit in the past, Joachim da Fiore, finds many incarnations in the present: for one, the Filipino overseas contract worker and his unpredictable, unlicensed peregrinations.

Meanwhile look, stranger, on this planet Earth belonging to no single individual, our mother whom no one possesses. We find solidarity with indigenous peoples an inexhaustible source of comfort, inspiration, and creative renewal. The aboriginal Indians, dispossessed of their homelands and victimized by those merchants—agents of Faust and Mephistopheles— obsessed by private ownership and solitary hedonism, express for us also what I think can be the only ultimate resolution for human exile and diaspora for Filipinos as well as for other peoples: "We and the earth, our mother, are of one mind."

---

## DALIT NG BALIKBAYANG SINTA

Adios, dulce extranjera, mi amiga, mi alegria. . . .

—Jose Rizal, "Mi Ultimo Adios"

### I

*Lumipad ka na patungong Roma at London*
Balisang nakalingon sa ulap lulan ng naglaboy na panaginip
Lubog sa alaala ng kinabukasang unti-unting nalulunod

*Lumipad ka na patungong Riyadh at Qatar*
Sa pagkamulat kukurap-kurap sa pagtulog puso'y nagsisikip
Binabagabag ng sumpang naligaw sa salawahang paglalakbay

*Lumipad ka na patungong Toronto at New York*
Tinutugis ang biyayang mailap nabulusok sa patibong ng banyaga
Sa ulilang pugad anong maamong pag-asa ang nabulabog

*Lumipad ka na patungong Chicago at San Francisco*
Kumakaway ka pa tiwalang may katuparang babati ng
    "Mabuhay!"
Alinlangang luha'y naglambitin sa bahag-hari ng bawat yapos

*Lumipad ka na patungong Hong Kong at Tokyo*
"Di kita malilimot"—pumaimbulog ang tukso ng nabitiwang
    paalam
Nabakling pakpak usok sa bagwis inalagwang talulot ng bituing
    nasunog

*Lumipad ka na patungong Sydney at Taipei*
Ay naku, anong panganib ng gayumang sa pangarap nagkupkop
Ibon kang nagpumiglas alay mo'y talim ng paglayang nilalangit

Lumipad ka, O sintang mahal, ngunit saang kandungan ka lalapag?
Bumabalik sa dalampasigang hulog ng iyong hinasang pagtitiis
Aking kaluluwang hiniwa't ikinalat sa bawat sulok ng daigdig.

## II

Huli na raw ang lahat. Huli na, umalis na ang tren lulan ang
    gunita't pangarap.
Huli na, lumipas na ang kamusmusan ng balikbayang naglagalag.

Huli na, naiwan na tayo ng eruplanong patungong Tokyo at Los
    Angeles.
Huli na, nakaraan na ang oras ng kagampan at pagsisiyam.

Tumulak na, malayo na ang bapor patungong Hong Kong at
    Singapore.
Nagbabakasakaling aabot pa ang kable—Sayang, di biro,
    nakapanghihinayang.

Huli ka na sa pangakong pinutakti ng agam-agam at pag-uulik-ulik.
Huli na, nahulog na ang araw. Itikom ang labi, itiim ang bagang.

Kahuluga'y naanod—lumubog sa dagat Sargasso ng
    pagpapakumbaba't pagtitiis—
Pahabol ay di na magbubuhol—Tapos na ang pagsisisi't
    pagpapatawad.

Walang taga-ligtas ang lalapag sa tarmak mula sa lobo ng iyong
    pangarap.
Huli na nga, nakaraos na ang kasukdulan, di na maisasauli ang
    naibigay.

Sinong manlalakbay ang magkakaila upang mahuli ang
    katotohanan?
Mailap pa sa mabangis na hayop na nasukol, bumabalandra sa
    rehas—

Mailap pa sa hibong nagpupumiglas—Saan ka nanggaling? Saan
    pupunta?
Paos, hapo, dayukdok, gasgas ang siko't tuhod, gumagapang mula
    sa guwang—

Maghulihan tayo ng loob, Estranghera, hinihintay ang ligayang
    walang kahulilip.

## BALIKBAYAN BELOVED

—You will leave everything you love; this is the arrow first released by
the bow of your exile.

—Dante Alighieri, *The Divine Comedy*


### I

*You've flown to Rome and London*
Anxiously looking back to clouds loaded with dreams wandering
Sunk in memories of tomorrow     slowly drowning

*You've flown to Riyadh and Qatar*
On waking up  blinking   in sleep the heart's constricting
vexed by a vow lost in the flotsam and jetsam of the journey

*You've flown to Toronto and New York*
Pursuing wild blessings     plunged into the foreigner's trap
in a nest bereaved    what tame hope has been driven wild

*You've flown to Chicago and San Francisco*
Waving afar  trusting in a fulfillment that will greet you  "Long Live!"
Tears unmoored  swing from the rainbow of every embrace

*You've flown to Hong Kong and Tokyo*
"I'll never forget you"—the temptation of a farewell unclenched  soars
Wings broken  feathers smoking   floating petals of stars gutted

*You've flown to Sydney and Taipeh*
Ay, alas, what danger of seduction from dreams   encompassing
Bird struggling to escape     offering the edge of liberty       adored

You've flown, O beloved sweetheart, but on whose bosom will you
     land?
You return to the seashore   yielded by your sharpened forbearance
My soul cut up  and scattered   to all the corners of the planet.


### II

Late, they said everything is late. It's gone, that train loaded with
     memories and dreams
Late, they said it's gone—the nomadic Filipina migrant's innocence
     is gone.

Late, we've been left behind by the airplane headed for Tokyo and
  Los Angeles
Late, it's over—the hours of an infant's deliverance and funeral
  dirges

Already departed. So distant now is the ship sailing toward Hong
  Kong and Singapore
Taking a chance that the telegram will reach—what a pity, no
  kidding, a terrible waste

You're late—your promises rotting with anxiety and doubts. . . .
  Finished!
Too late, the sun has crashed! Close your mouth, squeeze your
  jaws' teeth—

The sense of it all floats and sinks in the Sargasso Sea of
  humiliation and suffering—it's over
Postscripts will not tie the knot—repentance and forgiveness are
  over

No savior will land on the airport tarmac from the balloon of your
  hopes
It's over, the orgasm's over, what's given cannot be returned

What traveler will disavow so as to catch the truth? It's finished—
More slippery than the wild beast trapped, banging on steel bars—

Wilder than desire struggling to escape—where did you come from?
  Where are you going?
Hoarse, exhausted, starved, elbows and knees bruised, crawling on
  all fours from the abyss. . . .
Beloved foreigner, let's catch what's left inside, waiting for joy in
  abeyance, nothing ahead or behind, endless. . . .

(Translated from the original Filipino by the author)

# 6

# Trajectories of
# Diaspora Survivors

Contemporary cultural studies posit the demise of the nation as an unquestioned assumption, almost a doctrinal point of departure for speculations on the nature of the globalization process. Are concepts such as the nation-state, national sovereignty, or nationalities, and their referents obsolete and useless? Whatever the rumors about the demise of the nation-state, or the obsolescence of nationalism in the wake of September 11, 2001, agencies that assume its healthy existence are busy: not only the members of the United Nations, but also the metropolitan powers, with the United States as its military spearhead, have all reaffirmed their civilizing nationalism with a vengeance.

In this epoch of counterterrorism, the local and the global find a meeting ground in the transactions among nation-states and diverse nationalities while global hegemony is negotiated among the metropolitan powers. Their instrumentalities—the World Trade Organization, NATO, the World Bank and the International Monetary Fund, and other consortia—are all exerting pressure and influence everywhere. Citizenship cards, passports, customs gatekeepers, and border patrols are still mundane regularities. Saskia Sassen has described the advent of the global city as a sign of the "incipient unbundling of the exclusive territoriality of the nation-state." At the same time, however, she adds that what we see looming in the horizon is the "transnational geography of centrality . . . consisting of multiple linkages and strategic concentrations of material infrastructure," a "grid of sites and linkages" (1998, 214) between North and South still comprised of nation-states.

With the World Trade Organization and finance capital in the saddle, the buying and selling of labor-power moves center stage once more. What has not escaped the most pachydermous epigones of free-market apologists who have not been distracted by the Gulf War, the carnage in Bosnia and Kosovo, and now in Afghanistan are the frequency and volume of labor migration, flows of bodies of color (including mail-order brides, children, and the syndicated traffic in prostitutes and other commodified bodies), in consonance with the flight of labor-intensive industries to far-flung industrial zones in Mexico, Thailand, the Philippines, Haiti, China, and other dependent formations. These regularities defy postmodernist concepts of contingency, ambivalence, and indeterminacy. Such bodies are, of course, not the performative parodists of Judith Butler in quest of pleasure or the aesthetically fashioned selves idealized by Foucault and the pragmatic patriot, Richard Rorty.

# In the Arena of Culture Wars

Culture wars are being conducted by other means through the transport and exchange of bodies of color in the international bazaars. And the scaling of bodies proceeds according to corporeal differences (sex, race, age, physical capacity, etc.). Other diasporas—in addition to the historic ones of the Jews, Africans, Chinese, Irish, and Palestinians—are in the making. The editors of the *South Atlantic Quarterly* special issue on "diaspora and immigration" celebrated the political and cultural experiences of these nomadic cohorts who can "teach us how to think about our destiny and how to articulate the unity of science with the diversity of knowledge as we confront the politics of difference" (Mudimbe and Engel 1999, 6). Unity, diversity, politics of difference—the contours and direction of diasporas are conceived as the arena of conflict among disparate philosophical/ideological standpoints. Contesting the European discourse on modernity and pleading for the "inescapability and legitimate value of mutation, hybridity, and intermixture," Paul Gilroy has drawn up the trope of the "Black Atlantic" on the basis of the "temporal and ontological rupture of the middle passage" (1993, 223). Neither the Jewish nor the African diasporas can, of course, be held up as inviolable archetypes if we want to pursue an "infinite process of identity construction." My interest here is historically focused: to inquire into how the specific geopolitical contingencies of the Filipino diaspora-in-the-making can problematize this infinitude of identity formation in the context of "third world" principles of national liberation, given the persistent neocolonial, not postcolonial, predicament of the Philippines today (San Juan 1996a).

Postmodern cultural studies from the counterterrorizing North is now replicating McKinley's gunboat policy of "Benevolent Assimilation" at the turn of the last century (Pomeroy 1992). Its missionary task is to discover how, without their knowing it, Filipina domestics are becoming cosmopolitans while working as maids (more exactly, domestic slaves), empowering themselves by devious tactics of evasion, accommodation, and making do. Obviously this task of naturalizing servitude benefits the privileged few, the modern slave masters. This is not due to a primordial irony in the nature of constructing their identity, which, according to Ernesto Laclau, "presupposes the constitutive split" between the content and the function of identification as such since they—like most modern subjects—are "the empty places of an absent fullness" (1994, 36). Signifiers of lack, these women from poverty-stricken regions in the Philippines are presumably longing for a plenitude symbolized by a stable, prosperous homeland/family that, according to postcolonial dogma, is forever deferred if not evacuated. Yet these maids (euphemized as "domestics") possess faculties of resourcefulness, stoic boldness, and ingenuity. Despite this, it is alleged that Western experts are needed for them to acquire self-reflexive agency, to know that their very presence in such areas as Kuwait, Milan, Los Angeles, Taipei, Singapore, and London and the cultural politics they spontaneously create are "complexly mediated and transformed by memory, fantasy and desire" (Hall 1992, 254). The time of labor has annihilated indeed the spaces of the body, home, community, and nation. The expenditure of a whole nation-people's labor-power now confounds the narrative of individual progress on which the logic of capital and its metaphysics of rationality are hitherto founded.

Space-time particulars are needed if we want to ascertain the "power-geometry" (Massey 1993) that scales diasporic duration, the temporality of displacement. I might state at the outset an open secret: the annual remittance of billions of dollars by Filipino workers abroad, now more than nine million, suffices to keep the Philippine economy afloat and support the luxury and privileges of less than 1 percent of the people, the Filipino oligarchy. Since the seventies, Filipino bodies have been the number one Filipino export, and their corpses (about three to five return in coffins daily) are becoming a serious item in the import ledger. In 1998 alone, according to the Commission on Filipinos Overseas, 755,000 Filipinos found work abroad, sending home a total of P7.5 billion; in the last three years, their annual remittance averaged $5 billion (Tujan 2001) and $14 billion today. Throughout the nineties, the average total of migrant workers is about one million a year; they remit over 5 percent of the national GNP, not to mention the millions of pesos collected by the Philippine government in myriad taxes and fees. Hence, these overseas cohorts are glorified as "modern heroes," "mga bagong bayani" (the "new heroes"), the most famous of whom are Flor Contemplacion who was falsely accused and hanged in Singapore, and Sarah Balabagan, flogged in Saudi Arabia for defending herself against her rapist-employer.

This global marketing of Filipino labor is an unprecedented phenomenon, rivaled only by the trade of African slaves in the previous centuries. More than one thousand concerned Filipino American students made this the central topic of the 1997 FIND Conference at the State University of New York–Binghamton, where I was the invited keynote speaker. These concerned youths were bothered by the reputation of the Filipina/o as the "domestic help," or glorified servant of the world. How did Filipinas/os come to find themselves scattered to the four corners of the earth and subjugated to the position of selling their selfhoods? What are we doing about it? In general, what is the meaning and import of this unprecedented traffic, millions of Filipinas/os in motion and in transit around the planet?

## Lifting the Embargo

Of the nine million Filipinos, there are more than one million Filipina domestics (also known as OCWs, or overseas contract workers) in Hong Kong, Singapore, and Taiwan today, employed under terrible conditions. News reports of brutal and inhumane treatment, slavery, rape, suicide, and murder suffered by these workers abound. The reason why thousands of college-educated women continue to travel to Hong Kong and other destinations—even as the procession of coffins of their sisters greet them at the ports of embarkation—is not a mystery. I can only sketch here the outline of the political economy of migrant labor as a subtext to the hermeneutics of diasporic representation.

Suffice it here to spell out the context of this transmigrancy: the accelerated impoverishment of millions of Filipino citizens, the oppressive unjust system (the Philippines as a neocolonial dependency of the United States and the transnational corporate power elite) managed by local compradors, landlords, and bureaucrat-capitalists who foster emigration to relieve unemployment and defuse mass unrest, combined with the economic enticements in Hong Kong and other newly industrializing countries, and so on—all these comprise the parameters for this ongoing process of the marketing of bodies. The convergence of complex global factors, including the internal conditions in the Philippines, has been carefully delineated by, among others, Bridget Anderson (2000), Delia Aguilar (2004), Grace Chang (2000), and Rhacel Parreñas (2001). We may cite, in particular, the devalorization of women's labor in global cities, the shrinking status of sovereignty for peripheral nation-states, and the new saliency of human rights in a feminist analytic of the "New World Order." In addition to the rampant pillage of the national treasury by corrupt Filipino compradors, bureaucrat-capitalists, and feudalistic landlords, the plunder of the economy by transnational capital has been worsened by the "structural conditionalities" imposed by the World Bank and the International Monetary Fund. Disaggregation of the economy has registered in the disintegration of ordinary Filipino lives (most from rural areas) due to forced migration because of lack of employment, recruiting appeals of governments and business agencies, and the dissolution of the homeland as psychic and physical anchorage in the vortex of the rapid depredation of finance capital.

In general, imperialism and the anarchy of the "free market" engender incongruities, nonsynchronies, and shifting subject-positions of the Other inscribed in the liminal space of subjugated territory. Capital accumulation is the matrix of unequal power (Harvey 1996; Hymer 1975) between metropolis and colonies. The historical reality of uneven sociopolitical development in a U.S. colonial and, later, neocolonial society like the Philippines is evident in the systematic Americanization of schooling, mass media, sports, music, and diverse channels of mass communication (advertisements, television and films, cyberspace). Backwardness now helps hi-tech corporate business. Since the seventies, globalization has concentrated on the exploitation of local tastes and idioms for niche marketing while the impact of the Filipino diaspora in the huge flow of remittances from OCWs has accentuated the discrepancy between metropolitan wealth and neocolonial poverty, with the consumerist habitus made egregiously flagrant in the conspicuous consumption of domestics returning from the Middle East, Europe, Hong Kong, Japan, and other places with *balikbayan* (returnee) boxes. Unbeknownst to observers of this postmodern "cargo cult," coffins of these workers (one of them martyred in Singapore, Flor Contemplacion, achieved the status of national saint) arrive in Manila at the rate of three to five a day without too much fanfare.

# New Heroines?

Notwithstanding this massive research into the structural and historical background of these "new heroes" (as President Corazon Aquino called them in acknowledgment of their contribution to the country's dollar reserves), their plight remains shrouded in bureaucratic fatuities. An ethnographic account of the lives of Filipina domestics celebrates their newfound subjectivity within various disciplinary regimes. Deploying Foucault's notion of "localized power," the British anthropologist Nicole Constable seeks "to situate Filipina domestic workers within the field of power, not as equal players but as participants" (1999, 11).

Ambivalence supposedly characterizes the narratives of these women: they resist oppression at the same time as they "participate in their own subordination." And how is their agency manifested? How else but in their consuming power? Consider this spectacle: During their Sundays off, Filipina maids gather in certain places such as the restaurants of the Central District in Hong Kong and demand prompt service or complain to the managers if they are not attended to properly. They also have the option of exercising agency at McDonald's if they ask for extra condiments or napkins. Apart from these anecdotal examples, the fact that these maids were able to negotiate their way through a bewildering array of institutions to secure their jobs is testimony to what Constable calls "the subtler and more complex forms of power, discipline and resistance in their everyday lives" (1999, 202). According to one reviewer, this scholarly attempt to ferret out signs of tension or conflict in the routine lives of domestics obfuscates the larger context that defines the subordination of these women and the instrumentalities that reproduce their subjugation. In short, functionalism has given way to neopositivism. To put it another way, Constable shares Foucault's dilemma of ascribing resistance to subjects while devaluing history as "meaningless kaleidoscopic changes of shape in discourse totalities" (see Habermas 1987, 277). Nor is Constable alone in this quite trendy vocation. Donna Haraway (1992), among others, had earlier urged the practitioners of cultural studies to abandon the politics of representation that allegedly objectifies and disempowers whatever it represents. She wants us to choose, instead, local struggles for strategic articulations that are always impermanent, vulnerable, and contingent. This precept forbids the critique of ideology—how can one distinguish truth from falsehood since there are only "truth effects" contrived by power? This populist and often demagogic stance promotes "a radical skepticism" (Brantlinger 1990, 102) that cannot discriminate truth-claims, nor establish a basis for sustained and organized political action.

The most flagrant erasure in Constable's postmodernist inventory of episodes seems more serious. This is her discounting of the unequal relation between the Philippines and a capitalist city such as Hong Kong, a relation enabled by the continuing neocolonial domination of Filipinos by Western corporate interests led by the United States (Sison and De Lima 1998). However, this microphysics of learning how to survive performed by Filipino maids cannot exonerate the ethnographist from complicity with this strategy of displacing causality (a technique of inversion also found in mainstream historians of the Philippines such as Glenn May, David Steinberg, Stanley Karnow) and apologizing for the victims by oblique patronage. Anne Lacsamana pronounces a felicitous verdict on this specimen of cultural studies: "To dismiss the broader history of Filipino OCWs in favor of more trivial pursuits (such as watching them eat at a fast food restaurant) reenacts a Western superiority that has already created (and is responsible for) many of the social, economic, and political woes that continue to plague the country" (1998, 42).

# Deracination Trauma

Now the largest constituency in the Asian American group in the United States, Filipinos have become the newest diasporic community in the whole world. United Nations statistics indicate that Filipinos make up the newest migrant assemblage in the world: nine million Filipino migrant workers (out of eighty million citizens), mostly female domestic help and semiskilled labor. They endure poorly paid employment under substandard conditions, with few or no rights, in the Middle East, Asia, Europe, North America, and elsewhere. It might be noted here that historically, diasporic groups are defined not only by a homeland but also by a desire for eventual return and a collective identity centered on myths and memories of the homeland. The Filipino diaspora, however, is different. Since the homeland has long been colonized by Western powers (Spain, United States) and remains neocolonized despite formal or nominal independence, the Filipino identification is not with a fully defined nation but with regions, localities, and communities of languages and traditions. Perceived as Others, they are lumped with familiar aliens: Chinese, Mexicans, Japanese, Indonesians, and so on. Newspaper reports have cited the Philippines as the next target of the U.S. government's global "crusade" against terrorism. Where is the nation alluded to in passports and other identification papers? How do we conceive of this "Filipino" nation or nationality, given the preemptive impact of U.S. domination and now, on top of the persistent neocolonizing pressure, the usurping force of abstractive, quantifying capital?

According to orthodox immigration theory, "push" and "pull" factors combine to explain the phenomenon of overseas contract workers. Do we resign ourselves to this easy schematic formulation? Poverty and injustice, to be sure, have driven most Filipinos to seek work abroad, sublimating the desire to return by regular remittances to their families; occasional visits and other means of communication defer the eventual homecoming. Alienation and isolation, brutal and racist treatment, and other dehumanized conditions prevent their permanent settlement in the "receiving" countries, except where they have been given legal access to obtaining citizenship status. If the return is postponed, are modes of adaptation and temporary domicile in nonnative grounds the feasible alternatives for these expatriates (as they are fondly called by their compatriots in Manila)?

The reality of "foreignness" cannot be eluded. Alienation, insulting treatment, and racist violence prevent their permanent resettlement in the "receiving societies," except where Filipino communities (as in the United States and Canada, for example) have been given legal access to citizenship rights. Individuals, however, have to go through abrasive screening and tests—more stringent now in this repressive neofascist ethos. During political crises in the Philippines, Filipino overseas workers mobilize themselves for support of local and nationwide resistance against imperial domination and local tyranny. Because the putative "Filipino" nation is in the process of formation in the neocolony and abroad, Overseas Filipino Workers have been considered transnationals or transmigrants—a paradoxical turn since the existence of the nation is problematic, and the "trans" label a chimera. This diaspora then faces the ineluctable hurdles of racism, ethnic exclusion, inferiorization via racial profiling, and physical attacks. Can Filipino migrant labor mount a collective resistance against globalized exploitation? Can the Filipino diaspora expose also the limits of genetic and/or procedural notions of citizenship? In what way can the Filipino diaspora serve as a paradigm for analyzing and critically unsettling the corporate globalization of labor and the reification of identities in the new millennium?

# Look Homeward, Angels

As a point of departure for future inquiry, we might situate the Filipino diaspora within its Asian American configuration—since the author is based here in this racial polity (San Juan 2002). My intervention proceeds from a concrete historic staging ground. First, a definition of "diaspora." According to Milton Esman, the term refers to "a minority ethnic group of migrant origin which maintains sentimental or material links with its land of origin" (1996, 316). Either because of social exclusion, internal cohesion, and other geopolitical factors, these communities are never assimilated into the host society; but they develop in time a diasporic consciousness that carries out a collective sharing of space with others, purged of any exclusivist ethos or proprietary design. These communities will embody a peculiar sensibility enacting a caring and compassionate agenda for the whole species that thrives on cultural difference. Unlike peoples who have been conquered, annexed, enslaved, or coerced in some other way, diasporas are voluntary movements of people from place to place, although such migrations may also betray symptoms of compulsion if analyzed within a global political economy of labor and interstate political rivalries. Immanuel Wallerstein (1995) feels that these labor migrants can challenge transnational corporations by overloading the system with "free movement," at the same time that they try to retain for themselves more of the surplus value they produce. But are such movements really free? And if they are cheap labor totally contingent on the unpredictable fortunes of business, isn't the expectation of their rebelliousness exorbitant? Like ethnicity, diaspora that is fashioned by determinate historical causes has tended to take on "the 'natural' appearance of an autonomous force, a 'principle' capable of determining the course of social action" (Comaroff and Comaroff 1992). Like racism and nationalism, diaspora presents multiform physiognomies open to various interpretations and articulations. Historical precedents may provide clues of what's to come.

Let us consider one late-modern interpretation of diaspora. For David Palumbo-Liu, the concept of "diaspora" performs a strategic function. It probably endows the slash in the rubric "Asian/American" with an uncanny performative resonance. Palumbo-Liu contends that diaspora affords a space for the reinvention of identity free from naturalized categories but (if I may underscore here) not from borders, state apparatuses, and other worldly imperatives. Although remarking that the concept of diaspora as an "enabling fiction" affords us "the ideological purchase different articulations of the term allow," Palumbo-Liu doesn't completely succumb to the rebarbative postcolonialist babble about contingency ruling overall. I want to quote a passage from his insightful book, *Asian/American*, which might afford parameters for the random reflections here apropos of the theme and discourse of Filipino diaspora:

> "[D]iaspora" does not consist in the fact of leaving Home, but in having that factuality available to representation as such—we come to "know" diaspora only as it is psychically identified in a narrative form that discloses the various ideological investments. . . . It is that narrative form that locates the representation of diaspora in its particular chronotope. This spatiotemporal construct approximates a psychic experience particularly linked to material history. It is only after the diasporic comes into contact with the material history of its new location that a particular discourse is enabled that seeks to mark a distance, a relation, both within and outside that constellation of contingency. (1996, 316)

Like the words "hybridity," border crossing, ambivalence, subaltern, and transculturation, the term "diaspora" has now become chic in polite conversations and genteel colloquia. A recent conference at the University of Minnesota, entitled "Race, Ethnicity, and Migration," lists as first of the topics one can engage with "Diaspora and Diasporic Identities," followed by "Genocide, Ethnic Cleansing, and Forced Migration." One indeed dreads to encounter in this context such buzzwords as "post-nation," "alterity," or ludic "differance" now overshadowed by "globalization" and everything prefixed with "trans" and assorted postalities. In fact I used the word "diaspora" as part of the title of my book, *From Exile to Diaspora: Versions of the Filipino Experience in the United States* (1998b). Diaspora becomes oxymoronic: a particularizing universal, a local narrative that subsumes all experiences within its fold. Diaspora enacts a mimicry of itself, dispersing its members around in a kaleidoscope of simulations and simulacras borne by the flow of goods, money, labor, and so on, in the international commodity chain.

Let me interject a personal note: I have lived in the United States for more than forty years (the greater part of my life), with frequent visits to the Philippines without too many *balikbayan* cargo, unfortunately. And in my various voyages in/out, I have encountered Filipinos in many parts of the world in the course of my research. In the early eighties I was surprised to meet compatriots at the footsteps of the post office in Tripoli, Libya, and later on in the streets and squares of London, Edinburgh, Spain, Italy, Greece, Tokyo, Taiwan, Hong Kong, and other places. Have I then stumbled onto some unheard-of enigmatic scandal as a "Filipino diaspora"? Or have I surreptitiously constructed this, dare I say, "reality" and ongoing experience of about eight million Filipinos around the planet? Not to speak of millions of displaced indigenous peoples in the Philippines itself, an archipelago of 7,100 islands, "one of the world's most strategically important land masses," according to geographer George Demko (1992).

For those not familiar with my other writings critical of poststructuralist approaches (1996a; 1998a), I want to state outright that I consider such views about the Filipino diaspora half-truths closer to rumor, if not sheer mystifications. Spurious distinctions about cognition and perception concerning ethnic identity will remain vacuous if they do not take into account the reality of imperial world-systemic changes and their concrete multilayered ramifications. Lacking any dialectical materialist analysis of the dynamics of colonialism and imperialism that connect the Philippines and its peoples with the United States and the rest of the world, conventional studies on Filipino immigration and resettlement are all scholastic games, at best disingenuous exercises in chauvinist or white-supremacist apologetics. This is because they rely on concepts and methodologies that conceal unequal power relations—that is, relations of subordination and domination, racial exclusion, marginalization, sexism, gender inferiorization, as well as national subalternity, and other forms of discrimination. I want to stress in particular unequal power relations among nation-states. Lest people be misled by academic gossip, I am not proposing here an economistic and deterministic approach, or a historicist one with a monolithic Enlightenment metanarrative, teleology, and essentialist or ethnocentric agenda. Far from it. What is intriguing are the dynamics of symbolic violence (Bourdieu 1977) and the naturalization of social constructs and beliefs that are dramatized in the plot and figures of diasporic happenings.

# Excavations in the Boondocks

The testimony of diasporic narrative may be a useful pedagogical device to ground my observations here on the experiences of Filipina migrant workers as synthesized in literary form. Prior to the disruption of the postcolonial impasse and to situate postcolonial difference in the Philippine context, I would like at this juncture to concretize the crisis of bourgeois metaphysics and its political implications in contemporary Filipino expression.

In two of my previous works, *The Philippine Temptation* (1996a) and *History and Form* (1996c), I have described the domination of U.S. symbolic capital on literary and critical discourse since the annulment of the Spanish language and the indigenous vernaculars as viable media of expression in the public sphere at the start of U.S. colonization in 1898. The ascendancy of the hegemonic discourse of liberal utilitarianism expressed in English prevailed throughout the period of formal independence and the Cold War until the martial law period (1972–1986) when an authoritarian order reinforced semifeudal and tributary norms. Meanwhile, Pilipino (now Filipino) had become a genuine lingua franca with the popularity of local films and television serials, aided by the prohibitive costs of imported Western cultural fare. As noted earlier, these cultural developments parallel the intense neocolonization, or even refeudalization, of the whole political-economic system.

Symptomatic of a disaggregated and uneven socioeconomic formation are the literary and journalistic narratives spun around the trauma of dislocation undergone by more than nine million OFWs, mostly women. I analyze one specimen of this genre in the next section. It should be recalled that this unprecedented hemorrhage of labor-power, the massive export of educated women whose skills have been downgraded to quasi-slavish domestic help, issues from a diseased body politic. The marks of the disease are the impoverishment of 75 percent of the population, widespread corruption by the minuscule oligarchy, criminality, military/police atrocities, and the intensifying insurgency of peasants, women, youth, workers, and indigenous communities. The network of the patriarchal family and semifeudal civil society unravels when women from all sectors (except the rich minority) alienate their "free labor" in the world market. While the prime commodity remains labor-power (singularly measured here in both time and space especially for lived-in help), OCWs find themselves frozen in a tributary status between serfhood and colonizing petite-bourgeois households. Except for the carceral condition of "hospitality" women in Japan and elsewhere overseen by gangsters, most Filipinas function as indentured servants akin to those in colonial settler societies in seventeenth-century Virginia, Australia, Jamaica, and elsewhere. Unlike those societies, however, the Middle East, Canada, Hong Kong, Singapore, and other receiving countries operate as part of the transnationalized political economy of global capitalism. These indentured cohorts are witnesses to the dismemberment of the emergent Filipino nation and the scattering of its traumatized elements to state-governed territories around the planet.

# Undomesticated Domestics

At this point I want to illustrate the phenomenon of neocolonial disintegration and ideological reconstitution of the "third world" subject as a symptom of uneven capitalist hegemony in a fictional account by a Filipina author
who writes in Filipino, the national language. Fanny Garcia (1994) wrote the
story entitled "Arriverderci" in 1982 at the height of the Marcos-induced
export of Filipina bodies to relieve widespread immiseration in all sectors of
society and curb mounting resistance in city and countryside.

Garcia's ascetic representation of this highly gendered diaspora yields
a diagnostic illustration of postcolonial schizophrenia. In the opening
scene, Garcia describes Filipina domestics in Rome, Italy, enjoying a week-
end break in an excursion outside the city. One of these domestics, Nelly,
meets a nondescript compatriot, Vicky (Vicenta), who slowly confides to
Nelly her incredible experience of physical hardship, loneliness, and frus-
trated ambition, including her desperate background in her hometown,
San Isidro. Vicky also reveals her fear that her employer might rape her,
motivating her to inquire about the possibility of moving in with Nelly
whose own crowded apartment cannot accommodate Vicky. Spatial confinement resembles incarceration for those who refuse the oppression of
live-in contracts, the latter dramatized in Vicky's earlier experience.

Dialogue begets intimacy and the shock of discovery. After trust has
been established between them, Nelly learns that Vicky has concealed the
truth of her dire situation from her relatives back home. Like others, Vicky
has invented a fantasy life to make her folks happy. After a short lapse
of time, Nelly and her companions read a newspaper account of Vicky's
suicide—according to her employer, she leaped from the fifth floor of the
apartment due to a broken heart caused by her sweetheart, a Filipino sea-
man, who was marrying another woman. Nelly, of course, knows the real
reason: Vicky was forced to kill herself to save her honor, to refuse bodily invasion by the Italian master. Nelly and her friends manage to gather funds
to send Vicky's body back home to the Philippines. When asked how she
would explain Vicky's death to the next of kin, everyone agrees that they
could not tell the truth. Nelly resolves their predicament with a fictive ruse:

> "Ganito na lang," sabi ni Nelly, "nabangga ang kotseng sinasakyan
> n'ya." Sumang-ayon ang lahat. Pumunta sa kusina si Nelly. Hawak
> ang bolpen at nakatitig sa blangkong putting papel na nakapatong
> sa mesa, naisip ni Nelly, dapat din niyang tandaan: sa San Isidro, si
> Vicenta at Vicky ay si Bising. (334–35)

> ["Let's do it this way," Nelly said, "she died when the car she
> was in crashed." Everyone agreed. Nelly entered the kitchen.

Holding a ballpoint pen and staring at the blank piece of paper on the table, Nelly thought that she should also remember: in San Isidro, Vicenta and Vicky were also Bising.]

In the triple personas of Vicky nurtured in the mind of Nelly, we witness the literal and figurative diaspora of the Filipino nation in which the manifold layers of experience occurring at different localities and temporalities are reconciled. They are sutured together not in the corpse but in the act of gendered solidarity and national empathy. Without the practices of communication and cooperation among Filipina workers, the life of the individual OFW is suspended in thrall, a helpless fragment in the nexus of commodity circulation. Terror in capitalist society reinscribes boundaries and renews memory.

# History and Agency

What I want to highlight, however, is the historicizing power of this narrative. Marx once said that capitalism conquers space with time (see Harvey 2000). The urgent question is: can its victims fight back via a counterhegemonic strategy of spatial politics? Here the time of the nationalizing imagination overcomes displacement by global capital. Fantasy becomes complicit with truth when Nelly and her friends agree to shelter Vicky's family from the terror of patriarchal violence located in European terrain. We see that the routine life of the Filipino community is defined by bureaucratized space that seems to replicate the schedule back home; but the chronological itinerary is deceptive because while this passage lures us into a calm compromise with what exists, the plot of attempted rape and Vicky's suicide transpires behind the semblance of the normal and the ordinary:

Ang buhay nila sa Italia ay isang relo—hindi nagbabago ng anyo, ng direksiyon, ng mga numero.

Kung Linggo ng umaga, nagtitipon-tipon sa loob ng Vaticano, doon sa pagitan ng malalaking haliging bato ng colonnade. . . .

Ang Papa'y lilitaw mula sa isang mataas na bintana ng isang gusali, at sa harap ng mikropono'y magsasalita't magdadasal, at matapos ang kanyang basbas, sila'y magkakanya-kanyang grupo sa paglisan. Karaniwa'y sa mga parke ang tuloy. Sa damuhan, sa ilalim ng mga puno, ilalabas ang mga baon. May paikot-ikot sa mga grupo, nagtitinda ng pansit na lemon ang pampaasim, litsong kawali na may ketsup, at iba pa. Umpisa na ng piknik. Magkakasama ang mga Ilokano, ang mga Batanggenyo, at iba pang hatiang batay sa wika o lugar. O kaya'y ang mga propesyonal at

di-propesyonal. Matapos ang kainan, palilipasin ang oras sa pa-
mamagitan ng kuwentuhan o kaya'y pagpapaunlak sa isang nag-
papasugal. Malakas ang tayaan. Mga bandang alas-tres o
alas-kuwatro ng hapon, kanya-kanyang alis na ang mga pangkat.
Pupunta sa mga simbahang pinagmimisahan ng mga paring Pinoy
na iskolar ng kani-kanilang order. Sa Ingles at Pilipino ang misa,
mga awit at sermon. Punong-puno ang simbahan, pulos Pilipino,
maliban sa isa o dalawa o tatlong puti na maaring kaibigan, nobio,
asawa o kabit ng ilang kababayan.

   Matapos ang misa, muling maghihiwalay ang mga
pangkat-pangkat. May pupunta muli sa mga parke, may mag-
didisco, may magsisine. Halos hatinggabi na kung maghiwa-hi-
walay patungo sa kanya-kanyang tinutuluyan. (329–30).

[Their lives in Italy resembled a clock—never changing in shape,
direction or numbers.

   On Sunday mornings they would gather inside the Vatican,
there between the huge rocky pillars of the colonnade. . . . The
Pope would appear at a window of the tall building, and would
pray and speak in front of a microphone, and after his bene-
diction, they would all join their groups upon leaving. Usually
they head for the parks. On the grass, under the trees, they will
spread their packs. Some will circle around selling noodles with
lemon slices, roast pork with catsup, and other viands. The pic-
nic begins. Ilocanos congregate among themselves, so do those
from Batangas, and others gather together according to language or region. Or they socialize according to profession or
lack of it. After eating, they will pass the time telling stories or
gambling. Betting proceeds vigorously. Toward three or four in
the afternoon, the cohorts begin their departure. They head toward the churches where Filipino priests, scholars of their or-
ders, hold mass in English and Filipino, together with songs and
sermon. The churches overflow, all Filipinos, except for one,
two or three whites, who may be friends, sweethearts, wives, or
paramours.

   After the mass, the groups will again separate. Some will return to the parks, others will go to discos or movie houses, until
around midnight they will go their separate individual ways to
wherever they are staying.]

Resignation is premature. This surface regularity conceals fissures and
discontinuities that will only disclose themselves when the death of Vicky
shatters the peace and complicates the pathos of indentured domesticity.

# Ludic Misrepresentations

The most telling symptom of uneven development caused by the new international division of labor is the schizoid nature of the Filipina response to serflike confinement. This response has been celebrated by postcolonial critics as the exemplary act of "sly civility," a tactic of outwitting the enemy by mimicry and ambivalent acts. We read a tabulation of this tactic in Garcia's description of Nelly's plans to tour Europe by touching base with friends and acquaintances throughout the continent, an escape from the pressure of responsibility or accountability to anyone. Here is the cartography of Nelly's "imagined community" that generates a new position: the deterritorialized citizen of global capital. The space of recreation may relieve the pressure of alienated time, but it cannot ultimately resolve the dilemma of spatiotemporal dislocation and dispersal. Asked by her friends what's going on between her and Vicky, Nelly simply smiles and shrugs her shoulders:

> Mas mahalaga sa kanya ang mga tanong ng sarili. Pulos Roma na lamang ba? Aling sulok at kanto pa ng Roma ang hindi niya natatapakan? Pulos pagkakatulong na lamang ba? Hindi siya nagpunta sa Europa upang paganapin lamang ang sarili sa mga istorya ng pagliliwaliw kung Linggo, na kabisadong-kabisado na niya ang simula't dulo. Hindi siya nangibang bansa upang makinig lamang sa mga usapang nakaangkla sa mga "nanay," "tatay," "anak," mga gawaing-bahay, hinaing at problema. Hindi upang sundan ang buhay at kasaysayan ng isang Vicenta. Ipinasya niyang umpisahan na ang paglilibot sa Europa. May sapat na siyang naiipon para sa ibang bansa. Bibili siya ng Eurail pass, mas mura sa tren. Unahin kaya muna niya ang France, West Germany at Netherlands? May mga kaibigan siya doon. Nasa Paris si Orly, may kuwartong inuupahan. Nagpunta ito sa Paris bilang iskolar, artist-observer sa loob ng tatlong buwan, ngunit tulad niya, hindi na ito bumalik sa Pilipinas. Ngayo'y nabubuhay ito sa pamamagitan ng pagpipinta at pagiging potograpo. Sa Frankfurt, makikituloy siya kay Nora at sa Alemang napangasawa nito, dating pen pal. Nasa Amsterdam si Angie, kahera sa department store, at ka-live-in ang isang Dutch. Sapat na marahil ang isang buwang paglalakbay. Saka naman iplano ang mga ibang bansa. Sinulatan niya ang tatlong kaibigan. (333)

[More valuable for her are the questions addressed to herself. Am I to be confined to Rome alone? What corner and crossroad of Rome has she not covered already? Am I to be tied to domestic work? She didn't travel to Europe in order to let herself play a role in the stories of killing time on Sundays, whose beginning and end she knew thoroughly. She didn't go abroad only to listen to talk anchored to "mother," "father," "child," domestic chores, grumblings and problems. Nor to pursue the life and history of a certain Vicenta. She decided to start her travels around Europe. She already has enough savings for the trip to other countries. She'll buy a Eurail pass, it's cheaper by train. Should she begin with France, West Germany, and the Netherlands? She has friends there. Orly is in Paris, with a rented room. He went to Paris as a scholar, artist-observer, for three months, but like her he never returned to the Philippines. Now he's supporting himself by painting and photography. In Frankfurt she'll stay with Nora and her German husband, her former pen pal. Angie is in Amsterdam, a cashier at a department store, with a live-in Dutch partner. Perhaps a month's journey will be enough. She'll plan visiting other lands later. She wrote her three friends.]

In this passage, we discern the contradictions immanent in Filipina agency as she negotiates her position in the locus between wage-labor under serflike conditions and the mobility promised by the "free market" of late capitalist Europe. This situation may provide us the source of scaling the postcolonial dilemma suffered by Filipinas, conceiving scale as, in Neil Smith's definition, "the geographical resolution of contradictory processes of competition and co-operation" (1984, 99). But the chance for an escape to resolve the contradictions is foiled for the moment when Nelly and her friends learn of Vicky's death.

# Tragic Comedy

Contrary to postcolonial alibis concerning decentered subject-positions, Garcia's narrative posits an interrogation of presumed agency: Is the charm of adventure enough to heal the trauma of dislocation and obviate the terror of rape? Are the opportunities of consuming images and experiences offered by the wages of indentured labor enough to compensate for the nullity of citizenship and the loss of intimacy and the support of family and community? Is this postcolonial interstitiality the new name of servitude under the aegis of consumerist transnationalism where physical motion transcending fixed locality becomes a surrogate for the achievement of dignity and freedom?

What is clear is the dialectical unity of opposites embedded in the geopolitical predicament of OCWs captured in Garcia's narrative. The homeland (or its internalized cartography) is cannibalized and grafted onto sites of potential reconstitution. The Filipino diaspora here is defined by the Filipinas' social interaction and its specific differentiated geography, an interaction characterized by family/kinship linkages as well as solidarity based on recursive acts of mutual aid and struggle for survival. The political struggle over the production of scale in global capitalism is translated here in Nelly's mapping of her coordinates as she plans her tour of Europe, a translation of abstract space into places indexed by Filipino friends and acquaintances. This is not postcolonial ambivalence or hybridity because it is centered on the organic bonds of experience with oppressed compatriots and their continuous resuscitation. Nelly's affiliation with Vicky is tied to a web of shared stories of intimacy, dehumanization, and vulnerability. The Eurocentric fabrication of Otherness is qualified if not neutralized by Nelly's collectively assigned task of communication with Vicky's family, a task that prefigures and recuperates even if only in symbolic terms the interrupted struggle for national autonomy and sovereignty on the face of disintegration by transnational corporate aggression. Postcolonial disjunctures are reproduced by acts of revolt and sustained resistance. Such acts constitute a bad example for metropolitan citizen subjects of industrialized democracies. Racism still prevents them from uniting with their victims. While it would be exorbitant to claim that global capitalism has been dealt a blow by Filipina agencies of coping and life maintenance, I would suggest here that this mode of representation—which I would categorize as a type of allegorical realism grounded in the confluence of vernacular poetics and selective borrowings from the Western avant-garde (Brecht, Mayakovsky, Neruda)—enables us to grasp the totalizing virtue of Filipino nationalism as it interpellates diasporic subjects. Perhaps this virtue manifests itself only as a potential reservoir of energies that can be mobilized in crisis situations; still, the cultural and ideological resistance of neocolonized Filipinos overseas testifies to its immanent presence in what Lenin called "the weak links" of the imperialist chain around the planet, not only in the peripheral dependencies but also in the margins now transposed to the centers of empire.

# Extrapolations and Reconfigurations

In summary, I venture the following theses for further discussion. My first thesis on the phenomenon of the Filipino dismemberment is this: Given that the Philippine habitat has never cohered as a genuinely independent nation—national autonomy continues to escape the nation-people in a neocolonial setup—Filipinos are dispersed from family or kinship webs in villages, towns, or provincial regions first, and loosely from an inchoate, even "refeudalized," nation-state. This dispersal is primarily due to economic coercion and disenfranchisement under the retrogressive regime of comprador-bureaucratic (not welfare-state) capitalism; migration is seen as freedom to seek one's fortune, experience the pleasure of adventure, libidinal games of resistance, and other illusions of transcendence. So the origin to which one returns is not properly a nation-state but a village, a quasi-primordial community, kinship network, or even a ritual family/clan. In this context, the state is viewed in fact as a corrupt exploiter, not a representative of the masses, a comprador agent of transnational corporations and Western (specifically U.S.) powers.

Second thesis: What are the myths enabling a cathexis of the homeland? They derive from assorted childhood memories and folklore together with customary practices surrounding municipal and religious celebrations; at best, there may be signs of a residual affective tie to national heroes like Rizal, Bonifacio, and latter-day celebrities such as singers, movie stars, athletes, and so on. Indigenous food, dances, and music can be acquired as commodities whose presence temporarily heals the trauma of removal; family reunification can resolve the psychic damage of loss of status or alienation. In short, rootedness in autochthonous habitat does not exert a commanding sway, experienced only as a nostalgic mood. Meanwhile, language, religion, kinship, the aura of family rituals, and common experiences in school or workplace function invariably as the organic bonds of community. Such bonds demarcate the boundaries of the imagination but also release energies and affects that mutate into actions—as performed by Garcia's characters—serving ultimately national-popular emancipatory projects.

Third thesis: Alienation in the host country is what unites Filipinos, a shared history of colonial and racial subordination, marginalization, and struggles for cultural survival through hybrid forms of resistance and political rebellion. This is what may replace the nonexistent nation/homeland, absent the liberation of the Filipino nation-state.

In the thirties, Carlos Bulosan once observed that "it is a crime to be a Filipino in America." Years of union struggle and political organizing in interethnic coalitions have blurred if not erased that stigma. Accomplishments in the Civil Rights struggles of the sixties have provided nourishment for ethnic pride. And, on the other side, impulses of "assimilationism" via the "model minority" umbrella have aroused a passion for multiculturalism divorced from any urge to disinvest in the "possessive investment in whiteness" (Lipsitz 1998). However, compared to the Japanese or Asian Indians, Filipino Americans as a whole have not made it; the exceptions prove the rule. Andrew Cunanan (the serial killer who slew the famous Versace) is the specter that continues to haunt "melting pot" Filipino Americanists who continue to blabber about the "forgotten Filipino" in the hope of being awarded a share of the obsolescent welfare-state pie. Dispossession of sovereignty leads to shipwreck, natives drifting rudderless, or marooned on islands all over the planet. Via strategies of community preservation and other schemes of defining the locality of the community in historical contexts of displacement, the Filipino diaspora defers its return—unless and until there is a Filipino nation that they can identify with. This will continue in places where there is no hope of permanent resettlement as citizens or bona fide residents (as in Japan, Hong Kong, Taiwan, Singapore, and elsewhere). This is the disavowed terror of globalization.

Fourth thesis: Some Filipinos in their old age may desire eventual return only when they are economically secure. In general, Filipinos will not return to the site of misery and oppression—to poverty, exploitation, humiliated status, despair, hunger, and lack of dignity. Of course, some are forcibly returned: damaged, deported, or dead. But OFWs would rather move their kin and parents to their place of employment, preferably in countries where family reunification is allowed, as, for example, in the United States, Italy, and Canada. Or even in places of suffering and humiliation, provided there is some hope or illusion of future improvement. Utopian longings can mislead but also reconfigure and redirect wayward adventures.

Fifth thesis: Ongoing support for nationalist struggles at home is sporadic and intermittent during times of retrenchment and revitalized apartheid. Do we see any mass protests and collective indignation here in the United States at the Visiting Forces Agreement, for example, and the invasion (ca. 1998–2008) of the country by several thousand U.S. Marines in joint U.S.–Philippines military exercises? Especially after September 11 and the Arroyo sycophancy to the Bush regime, the Philippines—considered by the U.S. government as the harbor of homegrown "terrorists" such as the Abu Sayyaf—will soon be transformed into the next "killing field" after Afghanistan. During the Marcos dictatorship, the politicized generation of Filipino American youth here was able to mobilize a large segment of the community to support the national-democratic mass struggles, including the armed combatants of the New People's Army (led by the Communist Party of the Philippines), against U.S.-supported authoritarian rule. Filipino nationalism blossomed in the late sixties and seventies, but suffered attenuation when it was rechanneled to support the populist elitism of Aquino and Ramos, the lumpen populism of Estrada, and now the mendacious Arroyo regime. This precarious balance of class forces at this conjuncture is subject to the shifts in political mobilization and calculation, hence the intervention of Filipino agencies with emancipatory goals and socialist principles is crucial and strategically necessary.

Sixth thesis: In this time of emergency, the Filipino collective identity is in crisis and in a stage of formation and elaboration. The Filipino diasporic consciousness is an odd species, a singular genre: it is not obsessed with a physical return to roots or to land where common sacrifices (to echo Ernest Renan) are remembered and celebrated. It is tied more to a symbolic

homeland indexed by kinship or particular traditions and communal practices that it tries to transplant abroad in diverse localities. So, in the moment of Babylonian captivity, dwelling in "Egypt" or its modern
surrogates, building public spheres of solidarity to sustain identities outside
the national time/space "in order to live inside, with a difference" may be
the most viable route (or root) of Filipinos in motion—the collectivity in
transit, although this is, given the ineluctability of differences becoming
contradictions, subject to the revolutionary transformations emerging in
the Philippine countryside and cities. It is susceptible also to other radical
changes in the geopolitical rivalry of metropolitan powers based on nation-states. There is indeed deferral, postponement, or waiting—but history
moves on in the battlefields of Luzon, Visayas, and Mindanao where a
people's war rooted in a durable revolutionary tradition rages on. This
drama of a national-democratic revolution will not allow the Filipino diaspora and its progeny to slumber in the consumerist paradises of Los Angeles, New York, Chicago, San Francisco, or Seattle. It will certainly
disturb the peace of those benefiting from the labor and sacrifices of OFWs
who experience the repetition-compulsion of globalized trade and endure
the recursive traumas of displacement and dispossession.

# From Prologue to Epilogue

Caught in the crosscurrents of global upheavals, I can only conclude with
a very provisional and indeed temporizing epilogue—if I may beg leave
from those Filipina bodies in coffins heading home: Filipinos in the United
States (and elsewhere, given the still hegemonic Western dispensation amid
allegations of its disappearance) are neither "Oriental" nor "Hispanic," despite their looks and names. They might be syncretic or hybrid subjects with
suspect loyalties. They cannot be called fashionable "transnationals" or
flexible transmigrants because of racialized, ascribed markers (physical appearance, accent, peculiar nonwhite folkways, and other group idiosyncra-
cies) that are needed to sustain and reproduce white supremacy in this racial
polity. Bridget Anderson (2000) has cogently demonstrated how the international labor market consistently racializes the selling of Filipina selfhood;
thus, not only gender and class but, more decisively, "racial identities" conditioned by immigrant status, inferiorized nationality, and so on, are reproduced through the combined exploitation and oppression taking place
in the employer's household. Slavery has become redomesticated in the age
of reconfigured mercantilism—the vampires of the past continue to haunt
the cyberprecinct of finance capital and its futurist hallucinations. The trajectory of the Filipino diaspora remains unpredictable. Ultimately, the rebirth of Filipino agency in the era of global capitalism depends not only on

the vicissitudes of social transformation in the United States but, in a dialectical sense, on the fate of the struggle for autonomy and popular-democratic sovereignty in the Philippines where *balikbayans* (returnees) still practice, though with increasing trepidation interrupted by fits of amnesia, the speech-acts and durable performances of *pakikibaka* (common struggle), *pakikiramay* (collective sharing), and *pakikipagkapwa-tao* (reciprocal esteem). Left untranslated, those phrases from the "Filipino" vernacular address a gradually vanishing audience. Indeed, this chapter itself may just be a wayward apostrophe to a vanished dreamworld—a liberated homeland, a phantasmagoric refuge—evoking the utopias and archaic golden ages of myths and legends. Wherever it is, however, this locus of memories, hopes, and dreams will surely be inhabited by a new collectivity as befits a new objective reality to which Susan Buck-Morss, in her elegiac paean to the catastrophe that overtook mass utopia, alludes to "the geographical mixing of people and things, global webs that disseminate meanings, electronic prostheses of the human body, new arrangements of the human sensorium. Such imaginings, freed from the constraints of bounded spaces and from the dictates of unilinear time, might dream of becoming, in Lenin's words, 'as radical as reality itself'" (quoted in Buck-Morrs 2000, 278). That was already approximated by Marx in his view that "the coincidence of the changing of circumstances and of human activity or self-changing can be conceived and rationally understood only as revolutionary practice" (quoted in Fischer 1996, 170). Or, to translate in the proverbial idiom warranted by the experience of all diasporic bodies and ventriloquized by the Angel of history (invoked by Walter Benjamin [1969]) surveying the ruins before and after: *De te fabula.*

# Tracking the Exile's Flight: Mapping a Rendezvous

... my adored land, region of the sun caressed,
Pearl of the Orient Sea, our Eden lost ...

—Jose Rizal, "Mi Ultimo Adios"

Early in 2006 I had occasion to address a gathering of alumni of the Philippine Studies Program, Filipino Americans recently graduated from college, who had all been inspired by their summer sojourn at the University of the Philippines studying Philippine culture and history and immersing themselves in the thick of turbulent political and social events in the home of their parents or grandparents. It was the time of the ominous declaration of a "national emergency" by President Arroyo, thus making the occasion charged with portentous significance and challenge. My remarks thus provoked the alumni to reassess their experience to enable them to elucidate "the signs of the times."

I dwelled on the theme that we are living at a time when so many events in the United States and in the Philippines—disasters, crises, emergencies— are forcing us to think what we should do to advance social justice and equality, to make another world possible, a better world if possible. Because this talk, in retrospect, sums up also the themes and moral/ethical concerns discussed in the previous chapters, I would like to reproduce a substantial part of the text here and open the space for "conscientization" and action.

---

Given the intensifying crisis in the Philippines, our diverse responses will decide the direction of our lives and perhaps the future of our community.

139

It confirms my belief that experience and social practice, not mere ideas, can precipitate change. But of course, without thought and critical reflection, we will surely leave ourselves open to the encroachment of the corporate media—FOX, Disney World, MTV, the infinite glamour of images, shopping malls, commodity fetishism all around—until we have become robotized consumers of the globalized transnational market. In the spirit of collaborative exchange, I offer the following comments to provoke thought and critical reflection. What's the end in view? To make a better world if possible.

# I

In October 1997, I was invited to speak at the FIND (Filipino InterCollegiate Networking Dialogue) at State University of New York–Binghamton; the theme of the two-day conference was: "Re-examining the Filipino Diaspora." Many students I met in passing were seriously disturbed by the image of Filipinos around the world shown as "domestics" and "servants," if not mail-order brides, prostitutes, and so on. But, on the whole, the more than one thousand delegates were more seriously engaged in exploring how to achieve "success," or "agency," in the trendy postmodernist lexicon. They were saturated with readings about the excess or "spectral presences" of overseas Filipinos and the "shamelessness" of the *balikbayans*. No wonder, the FIND Conference could not "find" a feasible direction for common action, with the Fil Ams generally conditioned still by the decades-long neoconservative indoctrination of the Reagan and Bush regimes.

This generation of Fil Ams, all born after the end of the Vietnam War, differs from the generation I was acquainted with. They were politicized in the mid-sixties and seventies, learning mass politics in the activities of the antimartial law organizations, the Union of Democratic Filipinos, and other interethnic coalitions. They supported the Manongs (such as Philip Vera Cruz) at the forefront of the Farm Workers' Union struggles in Cali-fornia and the ILWU struggles in Seattle, Hawaii, and elsewhere. While teaching in California and Connecticut, I was politicized by the Civil Rights struggles in the late sixties and early seventies, as well as the national-democratic struggle in the Philippines, together with these young Fil Ams who discovered Bulosan and Bonifacio, who visited the Philippines on their own or in small groups to affiliate with the Kabataang Makabayan and other progressive sectors during the First Quarter Storm, before the declaration of martial law and after.

During the long night of the U.S.–Marcos dictatorship, a generation of Filipino Americans matured, found or lost themselves after the 1986

February Revolution. The resurgence of neoconservatism beginning with the Reagan administration in 1980, the decline of national-liberation struggles in Latin and Central America, up to the collapse of the Soviet Union in 1989, however, produced a demoralizing effect that exacerbated the internal divisions in the organizations of Filipino Americans and resulted in their dismantling.

We no longer have the "Manongs" as examples for young Fil Ams to learn from. In fact, few young Fil Ams now read Bulosan's writings, much less the biography of Ka Philip Vera Cruz. We have "model minority" Filipinos like General Taguba, the White House cook, Lea Salonga, celebrities in television and other media casinos, and so on. What else is new? You belong to a new generation in which the ideal of becoming the model "multicultural American," while a ruse for suppressing critical impulses, seems to have become obligatory. It has effectively sublimated any claim for collective recognition of qualities other than the acquisitive or possessive. "Identity politics" in the sense of ethnic pride, and so forth has been easily co-opted by Establishment charity. But given the economic difficulties faced by the post–1965 immigrants, and the refurbished ethos of "white supremacy," Filipinos cannot so easily follow the path of the Japanese, Korean, Indian, or Taiwanese technocrats, for one simple reason: the Philippines, our country of origin, remains a subordinated, dependent, neocolonized society, technologically backward (in comparison with Japan, Taiwan, China, Singapore, Malaysia, or Thailand), even culturally incoherent and certainly politically disintegrated.

It is worse now because the Marcos period severely retarded the country's development, set us back many decades from the time when we were the leading industrializing country in Asia next to Japan. Today the Philippines has one of the lowest per capita income in the region, over 75 percent of Filipinos are desperately impoverished. Now the largest Asian exporter of cheap labor, the Philippines relies on the remittance of more than nine million overseas contract workers, precariously dependent on the international labor market so vulnerable to crises, wars, currency fluctuations, and other unpredictable contingencies. The entire Filipino people and its territorial home have become collectively hostaged to an inherently unstable global capitalist economy driven to profit accumulation, heedless of their dignity, health, or survival.

What distinguishes your generation and the one before you is, I think, the fact of the disappearance of a radical socialist alternative now being addressed by the antiglobalization movement. The welfare state is no more. The end-of-the-century milieu was characterized by the reign of cynical neoconservatism (with strong Anglo fundamentalist contempt of other cultures), which has recently been challenged by the antiglobalization movement and jolted by the post–9/11 attack from Islamic fundamentalist extremists.

One might ask: How do you situate yourself as young Filipino Americans (or, if you prefer, Filipinos based in the United States) in this current conjuncture? For those fired up by your visit and eager to contribute to transforming the social order in the Philippines by trying to change traditional practices and institutions, the urgent question is: Where are you coming from? What is your competence and capability? Understandably you feel compelled to intervene, tell folks what to do, how to do it, thereby enacting the role of the superior civilized taskmaster, a latter-day "Thomasite," who once accompanied U.S. troops in the pacification campaigns. But there's already an entire corps of U.S.-educated cadres of teachers and technocrats already doing that back home, reproducing their ilk every day.

To be sure, the condition of chronic poverty, corruption, daily practices of social injustice and inequality should properly be grasped as systemic effects. They are symptoms of the decay of political and economic structures accumulated in the long history of colonialism and neocolonialism, something that cannot be done away with overnight. And since these are also processes—the process of the comprador elite doing everything to maintain the iniquitous order (with U.S. support), and the masses struggling against everyday situations of exploitation and oppression—groups, not individuals, are the actors and protagonists involved, fighting for what are long-range stakes in the fierce class war. We need to take our bearings by trying to achieve a total, in-depth picture of these complex processes, the contradictions we need to take into account, the realities and possibilities for change, in the light of local and international political alignments.

But in this task, we will not find any constructive help from the academic experts. Let me give you an example why. In Professor Yen Le Espiritu's recent book, *Home Bound* [2003], we find this Vietnamese scholar inspired by three Fil Am women who recently joined the Integrate-Exposure Program of the League of Filipino Students in Los Angeles. Upon their return, one felt "proud to be a Pinay." They all rediscovered their "motherland" and their ethnic identity. They felt privileged in having participated in transnationalist border-crossing, which Espiritu claims to be "transgressive" in itself. It is as though frequent travels, remittances, and visits to the Philippines, accompanied with conspicuous *balikbayan* boxes now conceived as "symbolic" capital—the French sociologist Pierre Bourdieu is called in to lend theoretical finesse to simple acts of coping and routine survival tactics—already served as "acts of resistance" that successfully trounced the disciplinary normative regime of U.S. capital. In effect, *balikbayan* packages undermined the localizing regime of the U.S. Homeland Security State. Amazing! Fantastic!

Now, please don't mistake me as indulging in personality bashing. I am interested primarily in ideological mystification and knowledge-production, or error-production. I am not the only one to suspect how this academic metaphysics of imagining resistance to racial and gendered subjugation, influenced by fashionable cult figures such as Foucault, Derrida, Negri, and a whole slew of scholastic libertarians and anarchists in Europe and North America, has produced all kinds of wrong-headed wish-fulfillment. It has led to the temporary marginalization of the more radical critique provided by historical materialism, by critical Marxism.

Lesson One: Study history from the viewpoint of the masses, the working people and their struggle for freedom, equality and dignity. Apply this popular-democratic, historical materialist perspective to the study of U.S. history, its evolution as a class society, as a political system based on the division of its inhabitants into social classes.

Up to now, Cold War propaganda continues to caricature Marxist critical analysis as economic determinist, sexist, Eurocentric, not sensitive to personal needs, and so forth. Consequently, in the last three decades, the question of identity has been separated from its socioeconomic and historical contexts, becoming more a question of individual psychology, sexual-affective relations, a New Age concern with the body or matter as such. This has led to the point where any account of Philippine–American relations becomes an instance of negotiation, a power game in which colonizer and colonized are positioned on a level playing field, veritably equal combatants. Hence Stanley Karnow (author of the best-selling *In Our Image* [1989]) and other American experts on Filipino tutelage can diagnose Filipino backwardness as caused by the natives' own folly, recalcitrance, ineptitude, and so on.

For her part, Espiritu believes that by postulating an alleged "multiple subject position" of the immigrant, she has thereby disrupted the U.S. state's strategy of differential inclusion. By presuming that Filipino subjectivity acquires self-making power or agency through travel, border crossing, consumption habits, reinventing traditional customs, and so on, it has already overcome white nativistic racism, class subordination, and homogenizing imperialism.

One may ask: Isn't this belief precisely what the whole system of neoliberal pluralism has programmed everyone into believing—namely, that we are free to do whatever we want as long as it does not subvert consumerist individualism, or white supremacist standards? You cannot talk about agency, or meaningful subjectivity, of a racialized group (such as Filipinos, who—I might emphasize—are not just an ethnic group like Italian Americans, Swedish Americans, etc.) in a system pervaded by class inequality, alienation in the workplace and neighborhoods, and historic exclusions.

It is silly to denounce white supremacy and at the same time ascribe to Filipinos such wonderful virtues as disruptive border-crossers, especially now when we have witnessed hundreds of Filipinos summarily deported after 9/11 in humiliating conditions. We have seen thousands of Filipino airport workers laid off, Filipino World War II veterans still neglected and Filipinos racially profiled owing to the stigmatization of the Philippines as home to terrorist groups such as the Abu Sayyaf, the New People's Army, and so on. Ironically, this is how Filipinos are "recognized" today, despite the publicity in *Filipinas* magazine and other self-serving media. "Living their lives across borders"—to quote Espiritu—does not automatically render the Filipino a transgressor, a transnationalist rebel against the white supremacist order, despite inventing her own ethnic traditions of difference. We will, as usual, only be celebrated as charming icons or spectacles, exotic curiosities for global circulation and consumption.

But what's crucially misguided is a fundamental premise informing Espiritu's and other studies, and this is what I want to underscore here. They assume that the Filipino nation or nation-state is truly sovereign, that Filipinos have sufficiently acquired a sense of critical wisdom and autonomy enough to understand and outgrow the crippling legacies of colonialism and white supremacy, so that we are fully responsible for our actions. The whole society is still profoundly neocolonized, the large majority still trammeled by subaltern attitudes and dispositions. (Recent opinion polls show that of all nationalities that one can choose from, Filipinos prefer to be American—what else?)

To return to Espiritu's disabling mistake. The wrong premise of Filipino national sovereignty distorts all talk of a boundary-breaking transnationalism, together with the postmodernist babble that accuses the essentializing nationalism of Rizal, Aguinaldo, and so on, as the force that has repressed the hybrid, fragmented, vernacularizing "Filipino" identity. Wait a moment: was Aguinaldo victorious over the Americans? Did the people enjoy a sovereign truly independent nation-state after the devastation of the Filipino-American War? Who won the war, in the first place?

Who indeed can capture the essence of "Filipino-ness," if there is one? Speaking a native language or vernacular by itself won't do it; maybe, eating *balut*, *bagoong*, and other native delicacies might help. Depending on what social class is articulating it, the term "Filipino" can be "the name of a sovereign nation" that is fictitious, or it can designate the group of overseas contract workers with Philippine passports dependent on the employing state. The reason why elite Filipinos feel embarrassed when mistaken for OCWs in Singapore or Italy is the fact that they claim to represent the nation or nation-state, whereas the thousands of Filipina domestics we met in the railroad stations of Rome and Taipeh, who may be modern heroes, do not really represent what is distinctive about the "Filipino," notwithstanding that stupid remark that we have been blessed by "intelligent design" to be super nannies. Remember those Internet-circulated lists of mannerisms and habits that supposedly identify the Filipino?

Before we can take action, we need to grasp concrete historical reality and its contingencies. And the first thing to comprehend is the profoundly neocolonized situation of Filipino society and polity, the continuing dominance of the neoliberal ideology (with feudal encrustations) over the system, the effective hegemony of U.S. world outlook over civil society and state. Contrary to Stuart Hall [1997b] and others, it is not just culture that constitutes the terrain for producing diasporic, subaltern identity; it is the political and economic order—the class system—that determines the cultural or ideological domain of representation, subjectivity, values, attitudes, and so on, which in turn reciprocally reinforces the sociopolitical hierarchy and reproduces its mechanisms and actors.

Throughout Espiritu's book, as well as in dozens of recent studies of the "damaged" Filipino society and culture, you will encounter criticisms of racism, gender, intersections of this and that, even the evils of global capitalism. But you will not find a serious critical analysis of social class, the extraction of surplus value from labor-power (I need to stress here that Filipina domestics as "modern slaves" not only sell labor-power but also their personhood), which is the key to grasping the complex phenomena of racial colonial subordination of the Philippines to the United States and the neoliberal global market.

Given our neocolonial status, it goes without saying that the subordinate position of the Philippines in the international division of labor, our share in the distribution of accumulated capital (surplus value), determines our image, our identity, and our notion of our future, to a larger degree than any ethnic particularism we can boast of.

The pedagogical message here might be put thus: We need to undergo real "brainwashing," that is, getting rid of these poisonous beliefs and assumptions that will make us naive if well-meaning lackeys of capitalist modernization, equipped with the program of "Benevolent Assimilation" (McKinley) and imperial philanthropic arrogance. We need to acquire a Marxist orientation. This means that if you want to help liberate the Philippines from the U.S. neocolonial stranglehold, or express your solidarity with the mass struggles going on, you will want to fight the class enemy right here, in Washington and in the corporate headquarters. You will want to help destroy a parasitic class system that requires for its nourishment militarist imperialist interventions in the Philippines, Iraq, Afghanistan, Colombia, and throughout the world.

Our struggle here is neither primary nor secondary to the struggle for national democracy and independence in the Philippines; it is an integral part of the internationalist struggle against global capitalism. But because of our limitations as individual agents, or as members of collectivities, we need to concentrate our energies on what we can do best in our specific time and place. You decide where, which collective project, you think you can contribute your energies and skills to good effect. This resolves those perennial squabbles among Filipino American activists about which task is primary—supporting the struggle back home, or building a revolutionary vanguard party here, debates that drained their energies while their party-building dreams collapsed with that of the Soviet Union and the restoration of bourgeois rule in China.

Lesson Two: Study Philippine history from a progressive point of view, in particular the period of U.S. colonization and neocolonization of the country up to today. And together with that, the rise of the U.S. empire and its current hegemony in a globalized market/commodity–dominated planet.

The first thing I would emphasize in any historical overview of ourselves is the contemporary political conjuncture: the ascendancy of an extremely militarist and racist ruling section in the United States. This rightist power bloc has continued to exploit the 9/11 attack in a global war on terrorism, utilizing all its weapons of violence and coercion to produce "regime change" and impose a retooled hegemony, a "new American Century," on the backs of millions of people of color in the South, in the underdeveloped societies that were former colonies or dependent formations. This is happening at a time when the "socialist alternative" has disappeared with the collapse of the Soviet Union, even while the growth of anti-imperialist forces in Latin America in general is intensifying. In short, global contradictions are sharpening to the point of regional wars, wholesale extermination of peoples, relentless destruction of the environment, and so on. There is one hopeful sign counterpointing that doomsday scenario: the birth of the antiglobalization movement that is now beginning to mobilize more forces while national liberation movements in Venezuela, Mexico, Nepal, the Philippines and elsewhere continue to gain ground in the face of U.S. state terrorism.

We who live in "the belly of the beast" need to take account of the USA PATRIOT Act and its elaborate regulations, a repressive legal machinery sanctioning surveillance of citizens and extrajudical torture for dissenters judged as "enemy combatants." We are today living in a regime worse than the Cold War and the McCarthy persecutions of the fifties experienced by Carlos Bulosan, Chris Mensalvas, and other Filipino union activists. The Abu Ghraibs, Guantanamos, and others are completely new decadent symptoms of the crisis of U.S. global hegemony. We need to use whatever civil liberties still exist to mobilize the broadest united front to defend and advance participatory democracy beyond formal citizenship rights. We need to defeat fundamentalist religious reactionaries fomenting a "clash of civilizations" to entrench the supremacy of global capital.

As Filipinos in the Homeland Security State, how do we enact or put into play our solidarity with our compatriots in the Philippines and in the worldwide diaspora?

# II

Unfailingly, as in the past, the Philippines grabs the headlines when disasters, natural and/or man-made, inflict untold devastation, misery, and death on our brothers, sisters, parents, and friends back home. Just on the tail of the seventy-one persons killed and five hundred injured at the Wowowee ABS-CBN event on February 4, [2006], we soon confront the tragedy of eighteen hundred people killed in Guinsaugon, Leyte, with over 376 homes destroyed by a mud slide. These repeated flooding incidents may be traced back to decades of wanton deforestation allowed, even abetted, by the local politicians and the central government. Of course, news analysis will never help us understand the historical context, much less the political and social causality, of these catastrophes. The beleaguered president Arroyo appeared on television mainly to urge everyone to send prayers to the survivors in Leyte, while U.S. warships and thousands of marines converged on the island as though in a repeat of General Douglas MacArthur's 1944 landing on that island to signal the fulfillment of his vow, "I Shall Return."

Indeed, the return of U.S. troops was marked by the approval of the Visiting Forces Agreement during Fidel Ramos's presidency, after the 1992 scrapping of the Clark Field and the Subic Naval Bases by a coalition of nationalist-democratic forces. But from February 20 to March 5, 2006, the largest gathering of U.S. troops (fifty-five hundred soldiers) landed for the 22nd RP–US Balikatan Exercise, purportedly to train twenty-eight hundred Filipino soldiers to hunt "terrorists," mainly the Abu Sayyaf, but also of course the guerillas of the New People's Army (which has been classified by the U.S. State Department as a "terrorist" organization). The presence of U.S. troops flagrantly mocks the putative sovereignty of the Philippines—indeed, even after formal independence in 1946, as everyone knows, the Philippines was saddled with so many treaties, obligations, and contracts that made it a genuine neocolony up to today. So forget all this pretentious postcolonial babble—the Philippines is still an appendage of Washington, despite all symptoms to the contrary.

With Secretary Colin Powell's decision to stigmatize as "terrorist" the major insurgent groups that have been fighting for forty years for popular democracy and independence—the Communist Party of the Philippines and the New People's Army, the introduction of thousands of U.S. troops, weapons, logistics, and supporting personnel has become legitimate. More is involved than simply converting the archipelago to instant military bases and facilities for the U.S. military—a bargain exchange for the strategic outposts Clark Air Base and Subic Naval Base that were scrapped by a resurgent Filipino nationalism a decade ago. With the military officials practically managing the executive branch of government, the Philippine nation-state will prove to be more an appendage of the Pentagon than a humdrum neocolony administered by oligarchic compradors, which it has been since nominal independence in 1946. On the whole, Powell's stigmatizing act is part of the New American Century Project to reaffirm a new pax Americana after the Cold War.

The telling evidence surfaced recently when a twenty-two-year-old Filipina was gang-raped by six U.S. soldiers on leave from the aircraft carrier USS *Essex* last November 1, 2005. The U.S. Embassy refused to surrender to the local court four of the accused on the grounds of the Visiting Forces Agreement. This would be a national scandal in Korea or Japan; but in the Philippines, it seems routine for the United States to lord it over their "subalterns." After all, this follows the hallowed pattern of Filipinos beaten, raped, and killed—some were suspected as "wild boars"—in or around the U.S. military bases. There is, of course, a long history of Filipino victimage, dating back to the "water cure" and other forms of torture during the Filipino-American War of 1899 lasting up to the second decade of the last century.

Allow me to encapsulate the theme of the struggle for national democracy and independence in the Philippines.

When U.S. occupation troops in Iraq continued to suffer casualties every day after the war officially ended, academics and journalists began to supply capsule histories comparing their situation with those of troops in the Philippines during the Filipino-American War (1899–1902). A *New York Times* essay summed up the lesson in its title, "In 1901 Philippines, Peace Cost More Lives Than Were Lost in War" [July 2, 2003, B1], while an article in the *Los Angeles Times* contrasted the simplicity of McKinley's "easy" goal of annexation (though at the cost of 4,234 U.S. soldiers killed and 3,000 wounded) with George W. Bush's ambition to "create a new working democracy as soon as possible" [July 20, 2003, M2].

What is the real connection between the Philippines and the current U.S. war against terrorism? What is behind the return of the former colonizer to what was once called its "insular territory" administered then by the Bureau of Indian Affairs?

# III

Is the postcolonial agenda of abrogation and appropriation of colonial discourse still valid for understanding the Philippine situation after 9/11? This may be answered by considering the controversy on the U.S. genocide in the Philippines sparked by Gore Vidal in his commentary in the *New York Review of Books* (ca. 2005–2008). Vidal addressed the "Filipino genocide" thus:

> Between the years 1899 and 1913 the United States of America wrote the darkest pages of its history. The invasion of the Philippines, for no other reason than acquiring imperial possessions, prompted a fierce reaction of the Filipino people. 126,000 American soldiers were brought in to quell the resistance. As a result, 400,000 Filipino "insurrectos" died under the American fire and one million Filipino civilians died because of the hardship, mass killings and scorched earth tactics carried out by the Americans. In total the American war against a peaceful people who fairly ignored the existence of the Americans until their arrival wiped out 1/6 of the population of the country. One hundred years have passed. Isn't it high time that the USA army, Congress and Government apologised [*sic*] for the horrendous crimes and monstrous sufferings that inflicted upon the peoples of Filipinas? It was American policy at the turn of the century to kill as many Filipinos as possible. . . .
>
> The comparison of this highly successful operation with our less successful adventure in Vietnam was made by, among others, Bernard Fall, who referred to our conquest of the Philippines as "the bloodiest colonial war (in proportion to population) ever fought by a white power in Asia; it cost the lives of 3,000,000 Filipinos." (cf. E. Ahmed's "The Theory and Fallacies of Counter-Insurgency," *The Nation*, August 2, 1971). General Bell himself, the old sweetheart, estimated that we killed one-sixth of the population of the main island of Luzon—some 600,000 people. (2005)

Scholars and lay readers objected to Vidal's charge. They accused him of exaggerating, even distorting, the facts, historical truths that Mark Twain, William Howard Taft, Theodore Roosevelt, and the U.S. Congress had publicly commented on. A scholar of the subject, Professor Stephen Shalom (1981), inferred from census statistics that 10 percent of the 1901 population of 3,666,822 Filipinos died from the "benevolent pacification" of which General J. Franklin Bell was a zealous executor. Vidal responded to his critics: "Our policy in the Philippines was genocide. We were not there to liberate or even defend a 'liberty-loving' people, we were there to acquire those rich islands and if we had to kill the entire population we would have done so. Just as we had killed the Indians in the century before (some of our best troops in the Philippines were former Indian fighters) and as we would kill Southeast Asians later in this century" (1981). Part of this "pacification" strategy was the "water cure" practiced on Filipino rebels, now known as "water boarding" tactics approved by the Bush administration in the "global war on terror" (Katz 2007). Postcolonial scholars refuse or shirk from engaging with this brutish picture since it lacks ambiguity; the bloody subjugation of Filipinos seems too straightforward, bereft of enigmatic nuances, perhaps too vulgar or just repetitious of previous imperial adventures.

The emergence of a U.S. "Homeland" consensus or climate of thought (codified, for example, in the USA PATRIOT Act and Military Commissions Act) seems to have rendered suspect the deconstructive axiom of postcolonial theory. Part of this trend is to insist as a reflexive mantra the news about the death of the "nation-state," the self-identical subject, and all totalizing forms of rationality (including varieties of Marxist critiques of the "free market" and neoliberal ideology). Born of the Cold War reaction to the utopian critique of capital, postcolonial thought has so far invested its chief energies in the analysis of difference as manifest in the "fractured and ambivalent discourse of colonial power." Premised on nominalist-relativist axioms, deconstruction and its variants congratulate themselves on being more radical than classical Marxism. Negri and Hardt's *Empire* (2000), in fact, seeks to pass itself off as the authentic "communist" manifesto! With imperialism banished with a stroke of the pen, we are free to fantasize on the shape of our private utopias founded on paper money, credit, and financial speculation.

Postcolonialists may be the prescient heralds of neoliberal finance-capital globalization now in irreversible crisis. Postcolonialist punditry (e.g., Bhabha, Spivak, Ashcroft, and other epigones) reject the universalist claims of national-liberation struggles as forms of Eurocentric mimicry. It celebrates the ideals of hybridity, in-between or borderland experience, and other fantasmatic performances of agency parasitic on the neoliberal market and the circulation of heterogeneous commodities. Consequently, it found itself endorsing the war against Islamic fundamentalism (the "internal enemies" of the pluralist order). It unwittingly became complicit with the decentering program of the World Bank, the International Monetary Fund, and the World Trade Organization.

What needs attention today is the exposure of this complicity, together with a practical critique of U.S. hegemonic imperial discourse legitimized by the current "war on terrorism" (a euphemism of predatory globalization). In my *Beyond Postcolonial Theory, Working Through the Contradictions,* and *In the Wake of Terror,* I elaborated on how postcolonial criticism can renew its oppositional and emancipatory vision by addressing aspects of the "terrorism" *problematique*, among others: (1) the ethos and pragmatic schemes of the new American Century ideologues; (2) the globalizing strategy of finance capital as mediated through the World Trade Organization, the International Monetary Fund, and the World Bank; and (3) the intellectual apologetic and rationalization of the "clash of civilization" scholasticism that functions as the postmodern reincarnation of "Manifest Destiny" and the "civilizing mission" of the old-style colonialists before humanitarian imperialism was ever dreamed of. Themes of the Other/alterity, subaltern identity, the question of difference, materialist locality, performative bodies, and other conjunctural phenomena have been thoroughly interrogated from a historical-materialist point of view in the works of Peter McLaren, Arif Dirlik, Fredric Jameson, Teresa Ebert, Masu'd Zavarzadeh, and many others.

Perhaps one last recalcitrant problem sidetracked by the postality syndrome is nationalism, the "national question."

Are we seeing American troops in the boondocks (*bundok*, in the original Tagalog, means "mountain") again? Are we experiencing a traumatic attack of déjà vu? A moment of reflection returns us to what Bernard Fall called "the first Vietnam." As everyone now knows, U.S. pacification slaughtered 1.4 million Filipinos, not counting the thousands of Moros who died in the infamous genocidal pacification campaign. The campaign to conquer the Philippines was designed in accordance with President McKinley's policy of "Benevolent Assimilation" of the uncivilized and unchristian natives, a "civilizing mission" that Mark Twain considered worthy of the Puritan settlers and the pioneers in the proverbial "virgin land."

Pressured by the sugar-beet lobby and persistent rural insurrections, the Philippine Commonwealth of 1935 was established, constituted with a compromise mix of laws and regulations then being tried in Puerto Rico, Cuba, and Hawaii. Eventually the islands became a model of a pacified neocolony complete with brown-skinned legislators, judges, policemen, tax collectors, teachers, and so on. Except for the preliminary studies of Renato Constantino, Virgilio Enriquez, and others, nothing much about the revealing effects of that process of subjugation of Filipinos have registered in the Philippine Studies or American Studies archive. This is usually explained by the theory that the U.S. did not follow the old path of European colonialism, and its war against Spain was pursued to liberate the natives from Spanish tyranny. If so, that war now rescued from the dustbin of history signaled the advent of a globalizing U.S. interventionism whose latest manifestation, in a different historical register, is Bush's "National Security Strategy" of "exercising self-defense [of the Homeland] by acting preemptively," assuming that might is right when spreading "democracy" by military occupation and bombs.

Despite these changes, the old frames of intelligibility have not been modified or reconfigured to understand how nationalist revolutions in the colonized territories cannot be confused with the nationalist patriotism of the dominant or hegemonic metropoles, or how the mode of U.S. imperial rule in the twentieth century differs in form and content from those of the British or French in the nineteenth century. The received consensus of a technological modernizing influence from the advanced industrial powers remains deeply entrenched. Consider, for example, the observation by Paul Wong and Tania Azores that one reason why Filipino nurses emigrate to the United States is found in "the belief in the right of personal choice that is deeply embedded in the political ideology inherited from the United States" [1994, 174]. How does this explain the poor working conditions and the lack of jobs with decent pay for nurses in the Philippines?

The demise of the independent nation-state purportedly caused by globalization has caused some demoralization among middle elements. Even postcolonial and postmodernist thinkers commit the mistake of censuring the decolonizing projects of the subjugated peoples because these projects (in the superior gaze of these thinkers) have been damaged, or are bound to become perverted into despotic postcolonial regimes, like those in Ghana, Algeria, Vietnam, the Philippines, and elsewhere. The only alternative, it seems, is to give assent to the process of globalization under the aegis of the World Bank/IMF/WTO, and hope for a kind of "benevolent assimilation." Without a truly independent nation-state representing the masses, not an oligarchic elite, what is the defense against predatory transnational corporations?

The case of the national-democratic struggle in the Philippines may be taken as an example of one historic singularity. Because of the historical specificity of the Philippines' emergence as a dependent nation-state controlled by the United States in the twentieth century, nationalism as a mass movement has always been defined by events of anti-imperialist rebellion. U.S. conquest entailed long and sustained violent suppression of the Filipino revolutionary forces for decades. The central founding "event" (as the philosopher Alain Badiou would define the term) is the 1896 revolution against Spain and its sequel, the Filipino-American War of 1899–1902, and the Moro resistance (up to 1914) against U.S. colonization. Another political sequence of events is the Sakdal uprising in the thirties during the Commonwealth period followed by the Huk uprising in the forties and fifties—a sequence that is renewed in the First Quarter Storm of 1970 against the neocolonial state. While the feudal oligarchy and the comprador class under U.S. patronage utilized elements of the nationalist tradition formed in 1896–1898 as their ideological weapon for establishing moral-intellectual leadership, their attempts have never been successful. Propped by the Pentagon-supported military, the Arroyo administration today, for example, uses the U.S. slogan of democracy against terrorism and the fantasies of the neoliberal free market to legitimize its continued exploitation of workers, peasants, women, and ethnic minorities.

Following a long and tested tradition of grassroots mobilization, Filipino nationalism has always remained centered on the peasantry's demand for land closely tied to the popular-democratic demand for equality and genuine sovereignty. For over a century now, U.S.-backed modernization and neoliberal programs have utterly failed in the Philippines. The resistance against globalized capital and its neoliberal extortions is spearheaded today by a national-democratic mass movement of various ideological persuasions. We have a durable Marxist-led insurgency that seeks to articulate the "unfinished revolution" of 1896 in its demand for national self-determination against U.S. control and social justice for the majority of citizens (ninety million) 10 percent of whom are now migrant workers abroad.

In the wake of past defeats of peasant revolts, the Filipino culture of nationalism constantly renews its anti-imperialist vocation by mobilizing new forces (women and church people in the sixties, and the indigenous communities in the seventies and eighties). It is organically embedded in emancipatory social and political movements whose origin evokes in part the Enlightenment narrative of sovereignty as mediated by third world nationalist movements, but whose sites of actualization are the local events of mass insurgency against continued U.S. hegemony. The Philippines as an "imagined" and actually experienced ensemble of communities, or multiplicities in motion, remains in the process of being constructed primarily through modes of political and social resistance against corporate globalization and its technologically mediated ideologies, fashioning thereby the appropriate cultural forms of dissent, resistance, and subversion worthy of its people's history and its collective vision.

# IV

Uneven, unequal development may also illuminate the new reconfiguring of the Philippines as an Asian/Pacific formation occupying the borderline between the Orientalist imaginary and the Western racializing gaze. But its geopolitical inscription in the South makes Filipinos more akin to the inhabitants of the "fourth world," the aboriginal and indigenous peoples of the Americas, the Hawaiians, the Maoris, and so on. The reconfiguring of the Philippines as a terrain of contestation finds its historic validity in the transitional plight of Filipinos migrating to the United States in the years before the establishment of the Philippine Commonwealth in 1935: they were neither aliens nor citizens but "nationals," denizens of the twilight zone, the borderland between the core and the periphery.

We live in a racial polity, a political order with a deep and long history of racist practice, of which the "model minority" myth is just one revealing symptom. Whether you were born here or recently arrived, you are perceived by the dominant society as someone "alien," not quite "American, somehow a strange "other." This is the inherent racial politics of the territory we happen to inhabit.

Contrary to what postmodernists label "transmigrants," Filipinos in the United States are now beginning to grasp the fact that it is the invasion of the Philippines by the United States in 1898, the destruction of the revolutionary Philippine Republic, the annexation of the islands and the colonial subjugation of its people that explains why we Filipinos are somehow tangibly present in this continent. Whether we like it or not—and here I address the emergent community of "Filipinos" in the United States—Filipinos surfaced in the American public's consciousness not as museum curiosities (indeed, the "indigenous types" exhibited at the St. Louis exposition of 1904 contributed to the fixation of a Filipino primitive stereotype, specifically "dogeaters," in popular lore) but as a nation of resisters to U.S. colonial aggression.

We cannot go back without masochistic self-denial to the fugitives of the Spanish galleons who settled in Louisiana to reawaken us from the American dream of success. (Those interested in the antiquarian topics of the Louisiana "Manillamen" or the Indios who supposedly stumbled into California, will surely not belabor the sordid genocide of their countrymen in the Filipino-American War of 1899–1902—a nice escape for these would-be historians.) Surely if our project is the vindication of a people's dignity and democratic empowerment, not just ethnic competition with Native Americans for precedence, we need to recover the history of resistance, of insurrection, that can resolve the problem of identity— identity is not a matter of antique relics or quaint folkways, it is a matter of the political project you are engaged with, the collective project of community vindication that you have committed to pursue.

It goes without saying, though often forgotten, that the chief distinction of Filipinos from other Asians residing in the United States is that their country of origin was the object of violent colonization and unrelenting subjugation by U.S. monopoly capital. It is this foundational process, not the settling of Filipino fugitives in Louisiana or anywhere else, that establishes the limit and potential of the Filipino lifeworld here. Without understanding the complex process of colonial subjugation and the internalization of dependency, Filipinos will not be able to define their own specific historical trajectory here as a dual or bifurcated formation— one based on the continuing struggle of Filipinos for national liberation and popular democracy in the Philippines, and the other based on the exploitation and resistance of immigrants here (from the "Manongs" in

Hawaii and on the West Coast to the post–1965 "brain drain" and the present diaspora worldwide). These two distinct histories, while geographically separate, flow into each other and converge into a single multilayered and mutually determining narrative that needs to be articulated around the principles of national sovereignty, social justice, and equality.

So far this has not been done because, among other reasons, the mainstream textbook approaches distort both histories across the realms of lived experience characterized by class, gender, race, nationality, and so on. In the wake of the poststructuralist trend among intellectuals, a theory of Filipinos as transnational migrants or transmigrants has been introduced to befog the atmosphere already mired by the insistence on contingency, aporia, ambivalence, indeterminacy, disjunction, liminality, and so on. To avoid the "nihilism of despair or Utopia of progress," we are told to be transnational or transcultural, or else. But the notion of Filipinos as transnational subjects assumes that all nation-states are equal in power, status, and so on. Like assimilationism, this theory of transmigrants and transnationals obfuscates imperial domination and the imperative of rebellion. It reinforces the marginalization and dependency of "third world" peoples. It erases what David Harvey calls historical "permanences" and aggravates the Othering of people of color into racialized minorities—cheap labor (like OFWs) for global corporations and autocratic households. It rejects their history of resistance and their agency for emancipating themselves from the laws of the market and its operational ideology of white supremacy.

Let me conclude by repeating what I submit is the central argument, the controlling vision, of my discourses on Philippines–American relations.

Filipinos in the United States possess their own historical trajectory, one with its own singular profile but always linked in a thousand ways to what is going on in the Philippines. To capture the contours of this trajectory, we need to avoid two pitfalls: first, the nostalgic essentializing nativism that surfaces in the fetishism of folk festivals and other commodified cultural products that accompany tourist spectacles, college Filipino Nights, and official rituals. To avoid this error, we need to connect folklore and such cultural practices to the conflicted lives of the Igorots, Moros, and masses of peasants and workers.

Second, more dangerous perhaps, we should guard against minstrelsy, self-denial by mimicry, the anxiety of not becoming truly "Americanized," that is, defined by white supremacist norms. My view is that we don't want to be schizoid or ambidextrous performers forever, in the fashion of Bienvenido Santos's "you lovely people" [1982]. This drive to assume a hybrid "postcolonial" identity, with all its self-ingratiating exoticism and aura of originality, only reinforces the pluralist/liberal consensus of "rational choice theory" (the utilitarian model of means and ends that promotes alienation and atomistic individualism) and fosters institutional racism. On the other hand, the submerging of one's history into a pan-ethnic Asian American movement or any other ethnic absolutism violates the integrity of the Filipino people's tradition of revolutionary struggle for autonomy, our outstanding contribution to humankind's narrative of the struggle for freedom from all modes of oppression and exploitation.

Becoming Filipino then is a process of dialectical struggle, not a matter of wish-fulfillment or mental conjuring. As I said earlier, it is ultimately a collective political project. For Filipinos to grasp who they are, more importantly what they can become—for humans, as Antonio Gramsci once said [1971], can only be defined in terms of what they can become, in terms of possibilities that can be actualized—we need to examine again the historical circumstances that joined the trajectory of the Philippines and the United States, of Americans and Filipinos, constituting in the process the dialectical configuration we know as Filipino American in its collective or group dimension. The Filipino in the United States is thus a concrete historical phenomenon understandable neither as Filipino alone nor American alone but as an articulation of the political, social, economic, and cultural forces of the two societies with their distinct but intersecting histories.

We need to grasp the dialectics of imperial conquest and anticolonial revolution, the dynamics and totality of that interaction, as the key to how, and for what ends, the Philippines and its diasporic citizenry—nearly ten million strong, sending $12 billion last year, which made Gloria Arroyo ecstatic at the success of her neoliberalizing scheme—is being reconfigured for the next millennium.

# Afterword

Our project is essentially transformative: how to confront reality to change it. But this confrontation requires an attempt to make sense of facts. The facts when repeated sound now to be more a matter of bad taste or inept mannerism than a banality: over nine million Filipinos (out of a total population of ninety million) now work abroad, 75 percent of them women, chiefly as domestics and semiskilled contract workers, in two hundred different countries. Over four million more leave, without proper/legal travel and work permits, for unknown destinations. Three thousand leave every day, about three to five coffins of these OFWs return to the Manila International Airport every day. Obviously, the reason is not for adventure or tourism, or even for an exciting, less constrained life (Pagaduan 2006). Frankly, it is for livelihood (any income-generating work, including "sex work") and a materially improved future.

After a visit to the United Nations, President Gloria Macapagal-Arroyo met some OFWs at the Waldorf Astoria Towers in Manhattan, New York, to thank them for their remittance. Almost every Filipino now knows that OFWs contribute more than enough to relieve the government of the onerous foreign debt payments to the World Bank/International Monetary Fund and financial consortiums: in 2006, they remitted $12.8 billion, this year the projection is $14 billion. In 2004, OFWs sent $8.5 billion, a sum equal to half of the country's national budget. Arroyo tried to honor these expatriates: "We take pride in our overseas Filipinos . . . for your sacrifice and dedication to your work, your family and your nation" (GMA News.TV, October 7, 2006). Such an "honor" is, as they say, more recognized in the breach than in its fulfillment.

Victimization of Filipinos (beating, starvation, rape, nonpayment of wages, etc.) by employers from Europe to the Middle East to Singapore, Hong Kong, and Japan have been documented in detail since the seventies when the export of "warm bodies" began. The situation continues, with more horrendous impact. The fates of Flor Contemplacion, Sarah Balabagan, Maricris Sioson, and others have become public scandals and occasions for mass indignation. As of this writing (2008), there are several hundred OFWs in jail, thirty-four Filipinos in Saudi Arabia awaiting

157

execution, and thirty-four more worldwide (to cite two: Marilou Ranario in Kuwait and Rodelo Lanuza in Saudi Arabia). In March 2005, four OFWs—Sergio Aldana, Antonio Alvesa, Wilfredo Bautista, and Miguel Fernandez—were executed in Saudi Arabia for unclear reasons. On June 13, 2007, Reynaldo Cortes was beheaded in Saudi Arabia for allegedly killing a Pakistani taxi driver. In the majority of cases, the Arroyo government never lifted a finger, much less even consoled the relatives, provoking cries of outrage from the organization MIGRANTE and concerned citizens (Makilan 2007a). Should we charge Arroyo with hypocrisy and deceit or credit her for diplomatic savvy?

The Philippines is not exceptional for providing a large reserve army of cheap labor to global capitalism. Other countries such as India, Mexico, Pakistan, Egypt, Sri Lanka, Indonesia, Thailand, and other strapped "third world" hinterlands also serve as reservoirs of labor power.

About two hundred million migrant workers from the underdeveloped zones of the periphery, what globalization experts call "the South," sent $150 billion to their home countries—nearly twice what those poor nations received in terms of aid from the rich governments of the "North." In 2004, Mexico enjoyed $17 billion in remittances, a total equal to the value of its oil trade, while India received $14 billion, an amount larger than the revenue earned by its flourishing software industry. But these funds are mainly spent on consumables; they are not used for large-scale investment or long-term job creation. Those countries remain poor, without jobs for millions. Moreover, they are vulnerable to the contingencies of a crises-prone system of global capitalism, as proved by the cases of Somalia, the Philippines, and others hit by post–9/11 strictures on money-transferring and hiring. And so, despite this influx of wealth, according to World Policy scholars Benjamin Pauker and Michele Wucker, in exchange for those transfers, Mexico, the Philippines, and other nations "pay an inestimable human cost, one that will become only more onerous with time. . . . [Unless those nations concentrate their efforts in developing their own economies] remittances will continue to be part of the very reason workers leave in the first place: a vicious economic trap that condemns people to emigrate in order to survive, even as their exodus deprives home economies of the workforce that might make it possible for others to remain" (2005, 68–69). A local survey of the government's labor export policy by Ernesto Pernia (2007) stresses its apparent benefits in increasing household consumption and solving fiscal and trade deficits while underplaying the social costs—breakup of families, drugs, long-term dependence on perilous labor-market funding, and other social costs that erode sovereignty and the unquantifiable loss of "national integrity."

Given the tide of barbarization attendant on the putative benefits of global capitalism—celebrated by such pundits as Thomas Friedman and epigones, we have witnessed a paradigm shift among social scientists studying the phenomenon of the Filipino diaspora. Critical intelligence has been hijacked to serve vulgar apologetics. For example, the employment of Filipina women as domestics or nannies to care for children, old people, the chronically infirm or disabled, and so on, has been lauded as altruistic care. Generally, this exploitation of enslaved human labor-power escapes criticism because of its philanthropic facade. With most female domestics coming from impoverished, formerly colonized societies, we perceive that the hierarchical structure of global inequality among nation-states has something to do with this trend. It is a legacy of the unjust and unequal division of international labor. This "global care chain," as trendy sociologists would put it, is household work managed as a thoroughgoing capitalist industry. In an anthology entitled *Global Woman*, the editors Barbara Ehrenreich and Arlie Hochschild tried to contextualize the exploitation of third world women in the new epoch of flexible, neoliberal globalized capitalism. But their picture misses one stark difference, a telling omission.

The stark disparity is sharply delineated by Bridget Anderson in her penetrating critique, *Doing the Dirty Work?* Opposing scholars who streamline if not euphemistically glamorize the job of caring, Anderson exposes how domestics from the Philippines, Sri Lanka, and other subaltern nations function as "legal slaves." She invokes the United Nations definition of slavery as "any institution or practice which, by restricting the freedom of the individual, is susceptible of causing severe hardship and serious deprivation of liberty." Anderson shows how this came about through the economic conquest of third world societies by the wealthy industrialized North. This has given the middle class of the First World "materialistic forms of power over them" (2000, 149). Earlier, institutionally imposed norms of race and gender have naturalized the migrant worker's subjugation. But in the new field of globalized capital, the fact of a lack of citizenship rights and the status of subordinated or inferiorized nationality both contribute to worsening the degradation of third world women.

But there is something more pernicious that eludes the orthodox scholastic. What Anderson argues is that domestic work commodifies not only labor power—in classic political economy, labor power serves as the commodity that produces surplus-value (profit)—but, more significantly, the personhood of the domestic. Indentured or commodified personhood is the key to understanding what globalization is really all about. Consequently, what is needed is not only an analysis of the labor-capital relation, but also the savage asymmetry of nation-states, of polities that hire these poor women and the polities that collude in this postmodern slave trade. Brutalized migrant labor throughout the world thrives on the intensified inequality of nation-states, particularly the intense impoverishment of "third world" societies in Africa, Latin America, and Asia.

The political economy of globalized migrant labor involves the dialectics of production and reproduction. We need to examine how the dynamics of capital accumulation hinges on, and subtends, the sustained reproduction of iniquitous social relations. Unlike the conventional immigration researcher, Anderson foregrounds social reproduction at the center of her inquiry, allowing her to assert how gender, race, and nation are tightly interwoven into the mistress/domestic class relationship. In short, the Filipina domestic is what enables European bourgeois society and, by extension, the relatively prosperous societies of the Middle East and Asia, to reproduce themselves.

The reproduction of the race (in Europe, North America, Japan, etc.) integral to the perpetuation of the unjust social order is connected with the historical development of nation-states, whether as imagined or as geopolitically defined locus. Historically, membership in the community was determined by race in its various modalities, a circumscription that is constantly being negotiated. It is in this racialized setting that European women's positioning as citizen acquires crucial significance. This is the site where third world domestics play a major role, as Anderson acutely emphasizes: "The fact that they are migrants is important: in order to participate *like men* women must have workers who will provide the same flexibility as wives, in particular working long hours and combining caring and domestic chores" (2000, 190). This is where we discern that care as labor is the domestic's assignment, whereas the experience of care as emotion is the employer's privilege (Ehrenreich and Hochschild 2003). The distinction is fundamental and necessary in elucidating the axis of social reproduction rooted in socially productive praxis. Such a vital distinction speaks volumes about migrant domestic labor/care as the key sociopolitical factor that sustains the existing oppressive international division of labor, a fact that undermines all claims that globalized capitalism has brought, and is bringing, freedom, prosperity, and egalitarian democracy to everyone.

The plight of Filipina domestics and other OFWs has become the topic of numerous academic studies as well as innumerable journalistic pieces (see, for example, Rowe 2003). Rolando B. Tolentino has ably explored how Filipina bodies "have been integrated into the circuits of transnationalism" in both national and international spaces," in particular the geopolitical inscription of mail-order brides." Although he is critical of the nostalgic drive of imperialist nations to imagine their past as coherent families, Tolentino still manages to believe that those narratives of emplacement of Filipina bodies, their diasporic movement in transnational space, "attests to the flexibility, versatility, resilience and endurance of their owners' stories" (1999, 65–66). What needs rigorous interrogation, however, in this post–9/11 millennial impasse is the interface of globalization and immigrant rights, of global capitalism and the struggle of peoples for social justice, dignity, and a measure of national self-determination. Here we behold the new racializing strategy of globalized capital, of transnationalist neoliberalism in its barbaric phase.

We are supposedly in this new wonderful age of transnationalism overseeing the dissolution of nations or nation-states and the triumphalist ascendancy of transnational corporations spreading beatific blessings on everyone. Even the communists Antonio Negri and Michael Hardt celebrated this new face of finance capitalism in their highly touted book, *Empire* (2000). Capital has presumably broken down national borders or boundaries; frontiers have been dissolved by the uncontrolled flow of capital, money, goods, and, of course, human bodies. Neocolonized Filipino academics have bought into this whole package of rejecting all totalizing metanarratives, all "essentializing claims and regulatory compulsions" that come from nationalism, national-liberation struggles, sovereignty demands, and so on. In their obsession with looking for postnational agency, subjectivity, abolition of inside/outside, and so forth, they absolutize their quite idealized forms of the local, the vernacular, the indigene, as though one can so easily reinvent the "native" from a blank slate, the mythical tabula rasa. Consequently, what or who is Filipino cannot be answered except relatively or playfully, through a series of vernacular/local acts to constitute modern plural, performative subjects with "partial and changeable subjectivities" (Campomanes 2003). But why bother with nationality or ethnic identity at all?

An accessible version of this fashionable eclectic position may be found in Barbara Posadas's empiricist description of Filipino Americans as characterized by cohesion, fragmentation, and multiple identities. Her account replicates a whole library of sociological investigations of the Filipino community subscribing to the hoary doctrine of American Exceptionalism. She rehearses familiar ground in recapitulating the identity politics of the last three decades with a pseudo-objective stance: "Being Philippine- or American-born, being an FOB (fresh off the boat) or an ARF (American-reared Filipino); being a pre-war, a post-war, a post-1965, or a very recent immigrant; being a child born in the United States to an old-timer, to a post-1965 professional, or to a TNT—all these factors of place, time, and circumstance can work, along with class, education, occupation, gender, sexual orientation, cultural awareness, political preference, and so many other factors, in simple and complex combinations, to forge bonds among some, while dividing them from others" (1999, 149). This claim to a layered, multitudinous identity echoed by another observer is immediately belied by the assertion that Filipinos "constitute yet another immigrant success story [next to Mexicans in the United States], with a median annual family income of more than $72,000 and able to remit nearly $5 billion a year to the Philippines" (Francia 2007). Notwithstanding the questionable statistics, we note how the old utilitarian calculus of balancing pain/pleasure has been drastically reduced here to a matter of reified dollar amounts so diametrically opposed to the same author's own pious demand for a more complex, historically nuanced portrayal of the community.

We need to return to the rough process of lived experience, beyond the reification of dollar remittances and the mirage of possessive/acquisitive freedom. The case of Flor Contemplacion who was wrongfully hanged in March 1995 by the Singapore government has been replicated in numerous cases of OFWs jailed, tortured, and executed in the Middle East, and in their murdered bodies found accidentally in other countries. The latest is that of twenty-seven-year-old Filipina live-in caregiver Jocelyn Dulnuan whose body was found on the premises of a Doulton Place mansion in Toronto, Ontario, Canada. Dulnuan was a native of Namulditan, Ifugao; she received a degree in criminology from the University of Baguio, Philippines. Seeking to support her family (a husband and three-year-old daughter), she worked first as domestic help in Hong Kong before moving to Canada in November 2006 under the auspices of the Canadian government's Live-in Caregiver Program. According to the National Alliance of Philippine Women in Canada, that program is racist and antiwomen, perpetuating "a cycle of poverty, debt, isolation, and vulnerability to physical, sexual, and verbal abuse" (Makilan 2007b). This Canadian "nonevent" stirred no big outcry in the Philippines or a call for investigation from the public officials who continue to extoll these domestics as "modern-day heroes" (Calugay 2007).

Despite these horror stories, thirty-four hundred Filipinos continue to leave every day for work abroad. Most rely on the good faith of their recruiters and prospective employers; others on fortune or luck. One recent testimony of how "heroic" OFWs have faced the rigors of life abroad is the revelation before the U.S. Congress of the abusive treatment of fifty-one Filipinos and other third world nationals by the First Kuwaiti Company at the U.S. Embassy construction site. They tried to escape but failed. Based on the detailed testimonies of two former American employees, the workers were treated like slaves, deceived by unscrupulous recruiters, government officials, airport and immigration personnel, security forces, and private contractors—the familiar syndicate of human traffickers. One commentator bewailed the failure of the Philippine government to protect the rights of its citizens after more than thirty years of exporting their warm bodies, a "benign neglect" due to the "insatiable greed" for their remittances. As noted earlier, the $12–14 billion remittance of OFWs keeps the Philippine economy afloat by paying for the huge $55 billion foreign debt accrued by the corrupt, illegitimate Arroyo regime and the parasitic oligarchy. But this commentator lacks that requisite historical perspective and political perspicacity to situate this tragedy in the larger picture I have suggested throughout, characterized by the unconscionable legacy of colonial underdevelopment and the profound subordination of the whole society to U.S. imperial dictates and the insatiable greed of global finance-capital represented by the World Bank, the International Monetary Fund, and other multilateral agencies.

So many incidental, symptomatic problems distract us from grounding ourselves in the reality of international conflicts that it is time to sound the alarm. One recent distraction is the furor caused by the racist slur in the ABC-Disney TV comedy-drama *Desperate Housewives* in which the quality of Philippine medical schools was questioned. So what else is new? Thousands of Filipinos in the United States and other stakeholders elsewhere felt offended, but the gatekeepers, including Arroyo's bureaucrats, had no choice but to accept ABC's mild apology for fear of alienating investors, policy makers, and so on. The National Alliance for Filipino Concerns, however, refused to settle with the verbal excuse. It argued that the remark "maligned not only the integrity and competence of Filipino medical practitioners and health care providers in the United States, the Philippines, and all over the world but also constitutes immigrant bashing that warrants condemnation not only by the victims but by all defenders of freedom as well." Unless a "sincere, appropriate, and satisfactory apology" is given by ABC, the National Alliance will call for an international boycott of all ABC-Disney products and continuous mass picketing (CENPEG 2007). This campaign would be truly educational and promote a genuine militant consciousness of global politics if it went beyond simply reforming corporate culture. Unfortunately, it is bound to channel the energies of the community into some safe liberal compromise that would go the way of all such Band-Aid remedies. Judging from all the comments offered by various Filipino organizations and their leaders, it is easy to see how the Filipino Americans' knowledge of the historical foundations of U.S. racism is rudimentary, to say the least; and one is sorely at a loss to find any trace of a genuine comprehension of the function of racist ideological practices and institutions in maintaining the exploited subaltern position of the Filipino nationality in the United States.

On the other hand, one is encouraged by the signs of a renewal of critical intelligence and political sagacity that once prevailed in the community during the seventies and eighties, at the height of the anti-Marcos dictatorship movement. During that time, antimartial law coalitions (one thinks of the Union of Democratic Filipinos [KDP] and UGNAYAN, among others) were able to mobilize substantial numbers of youth and professionals to organize and protest the U.S. support of the Marcos regime and its brutal authoritarian excesses. After the February 1986

"People Power" revolt, radical mobilization subsided. What replaced it is a narrow, individualist-centered consumerism and mimicry that revived a residual colonial mentality complete with clannish, sectarian, parochial habits and a heavy dose of patriarchal authoritarianism. This is still the lethargic inertia of marginality plaguing the Filipino immigrant associations and its spokespersons.

With the phenomenal victimization of Filipinos in the wake of the protofascist policies of the Bush administration, especially after September 11, 2001, the Filipino community seems to be waking up. Amid the crescendo of racist attacks against Muslim communities, and the stigmatization of Arabs and "undocumented" Latinos, Filipinos were subjected to further racialized stigmatization when the Philippines became the "second battleground" in the U.S.-led "war against terrorism," thanks to the mendacious servility of the Arroyo regime. What has made the Filipino community exceptional, once again, as a target of racist institutional violence is the identification of the Philippines as a haven of Abu Sayyaf and other Muslim terrorist groups. This is partly instigated by the Arroyo administration's desire to obtain U.S. political and financial support, in particular weapons and logistics for the military and police forces that ultimately prop up the decadent rule of a beleaguered oligarchy of landlords, compradors, and bureaucrat-capitalists—clients of the former colonial ruler responsible for the worsening impoverishment of the country. Eighty percent of ninety million Filipinos survive on less than $2 a day—forty-six million go hungry every day. As of 2006, according to the study made by BAYAN (2007), the net worth of the ten richest Filipinos—US$12.4 billion (in 2006)—has grown to become equivalent to the combined annual income of forty-nine million Filipinos, while unemployment totals 11.3 percent and underemployment 18.7 percent; a clear sign of deepening inequality and immiseration of the majority of citizens.

Contradictions pervade the Filipino community, reflecting the larger contradictions of U.S. society as a whole. The older generation of professionals seeks to impose its assimilationist worldview on their children as well as on over half of the community of about three to four million, most of whom are newly disembarked and unable to find opportunities for mobility as easily as doctors and nurses. The entry of this group of professionals has now been limited—except for selected hires in the health care sector—as the U.S. economy becomes further de-skilled and deindustrialized. The preponderant batch of Filipinos in this new millennium will no longer enjoy the space of relative economic ease found during the onset of Reagan neoconservatism in the eighties and nineties. In this adversarial climate, Filipinos are now targeted as sacrificial offerings. This is a new sociopolitical alignment that eludes the prudential "sly civility" of the gatekeepers and guardians of ethnic morality.

Fortunately, we have younger Filipinos today who have not succumbed to postmodernist nihilism and ludic games of neoliberal rhetoric and sophistry. A group of Filipino/a academics known as the Critical Filipina and Filipino Studies Collective (CFFSC) has initiated what I think is the sharpest, provocative analysis of the crucial problem facing the Filipino community in the United States today. Their report entitled *Resisting Homeland Security: Organizing Unjust Removals of U.S. Filipinos* is the first in-depth study I have seen that analyzes the new predicament Filipinos face under the aegis of "homeland security." It is worth more than a dozen traditional sociological or political dissertations on immigration and multiculturalism flooding the mainstream academy.

With their peculiar colonial background and the long, durable history of racialized indoctrination, Filipinos now are subject to "removal," a fate worse than the criminalization suffered by the "Manongs" in the plantations of Hawaii, the canneries of Alaska, or the harbors of the West Coast. Based on the harassments, arrests, and deportations of Filipinos after 9/11, the report contextualizes the current plight of Filipinos in this new climate of State terrorism, with a whole apparatus of State surveillance and disciplinary classification brought to bear on their existence. What is distinctive here is not simply a critique of racist practices (such as the symptomatic racial slur in *Desperate Housewives*) but a total picture of the sedimented historical relations between colonizer-colonized, and the persisting symptoms of such a relationship in contemporary social and political transactions across the board. This dynamic, historically informed approach corrects the positivistic tautology of most journalistic and scholarly accounts. In short, the racialization and inferiorization of Filipinos as a national group, not just an ethnic fragment of multicultural America, cannot be diagnosed and appraised apart from the continuing domination of the Philippines by the United States.

With the founding of the Homeland Security State, a new set of laws and state apparatuses has been put in place that changes the old "rules of the game" operationalized by the 1965 immigration law that abolished the criterion of national origins. Today the rules are determined by the Homeland Security regime defending itself from global enemies, peoples and states around the world that are labeled "terrorists" or members of the "axis of evil." A Manichean world has been demarcated, with civilizations and cultures battling each other to the death. As Dr. Peter Chua and others in the CFFSC argue, a "historical shift in the U.S. practice of imperialism" has taken place witnessed by new legislation. "The 1996 Illegal Immigration Reform and Immigrant Responsibility Act (IIRAIRA), implemented by President William Clinton, dramatically shifted immigrant rights. IIRAIRA curtailed unauthorized immigration and regulated immigrants, regardless of status, making a home in the United States. The passing of the USA PATRIOT Act and the establishment of Homeland Security subsume the regulation of immigration into national security" (CFFSC 2004, 1). Developments in the Philippines are part of this new regulated scenario. The collaboration of the Philippine government under President Arroyo with Bush's antiterror campaign has proved fatal in allowing the Philippines to be categorized as a society/territory harboring Al-Qaeda–linked terrorists (the Abu Sayyaf bandits), thus indirectly stigmatizing Filipino migrants and even ordinary Filipino tourists or travelers. This has reinforced the historical legacy of Filipino "colonials" as "Oriental criminals," or undesirable aliens polluting the body politic, dangerous contaminants that should be expelled or removed.

A new paradigm is imperative. In this framework, the question of immigration and immigrant rights—as Jay Mendoza (2004) puts it—cannot be grasped simply as a matter of amnesty, legalization, access to public services, family unification, citizenship advocacy, and the like. Rather, it has to be articulated and analyzed in the larger context of war, "renditions," national security, clandestine operations, prisons and torture as state instrumentalities, and foreign policy. In short, the position of the Filipino community in the United States—its current status, role, viability, welfare, survival in the future—is part and parcel of the way the Philippines as a sovereign nation is defined in the hierarchical alignment of nation-states in the global field. As long as the Philippines lacks genuine sovereignty and economic self-sufficiency, and its government continues to serve the hegemonic interests of the U.S. ruling class, Filipinos in the United States will remain subjects, rather objects, for removal, for detention, or summary deportation. Realist political wisdom and commitment to humanist-socialist principles need to replace Realpolitik and mendacity.

If this is the case, then, we are confronted with a new theme for exploration beyond the limits of this discourse. Now the problem of exile, displacement, and deterritorialization so astutely described by Darko Suvin (2004), Edward Said (1993), and Julia Kristeva (1991), among others, no longer has any resonance. We are faced with a new arena of battle, one between humanity and barbarism, between oppressed third world peoples fighting for survival and the rule of a dehumanized global capital. For this new stage of the fight, we need new weapons, new ideas or concepts, for which I hope this book has supplied materials for the initial experimental groundwork.

# References

Abraham, Itty. 2006. "Filipinos in the U.S." *Economic and Policitcal Weekly* (Feb. 25).

Acuna, Rodolfo. 1988. *Occupied America: A History of Chicanos*. New York: Harper and Row.

Agoncillo, Teodoro, and Oscar Alfonso. 1967. *History of the Filipino People*. Quezon City, Philippines: Malaya Books.

Aguilar, Delia D. 2000. *Globalization, Labor and Women*. No. 9 of Working Papers Series on Historical Systems, Peoples and Cultures. Bowling Green, OH: Department of Ethnic Studies, Bowling Green State University.

Aguilar-San Juan, Karin, ed. 1992. *The State of Asian America*. Boston, MA: South End Press.

Aijaz, Ahmad. 1982. "Who is the Moro?" and "Class and Colony in Mindanao." *Southeast Asia Chronicle* (Feb.): 2-10.

Aizenman, Nurith. 2004. "A Taste of Distant Home for D.C. Area Nannies." *Washington Post*, October 4. <http://www.washingtonpost.com/ac2/wp=dyn/contentID=A20273>.

Alcuitas, Hetty C. 2002. "Seven Years after Flor . . . Conditions of Overseas Filipino Workers Worsen." <http://www.newfilipina.org/htm>.

Anderson, Benedict. 1994. "Imagined Communities." In *Nationalism*, ed. John Hutchinson and Anthony D. Smith. New York: Oxford University Press.

———. 2005. *Under Three Flags*. London: Verso.

Anderson, Bridget. 2000. *Doing the Dirty Work? The Global Politics of Domestic Labor*. London: Zed Press.

Aquino, Belinda. 2005. "Filipinos in Hawaii Celebrate Centennial." *Philippine Journal Inquirer* (Dec. 28). http://www.inquirer.com/htm.

Arcilla, Jose S., S.J. 1971. *An Introduction to Philippine History*. Quezon City, Philippines: Ateneo de Manila University Press.

Asad, Talal. 2002. "Some Thoughts on the WTC Disaster." *ISIM Newsletter 9* (January).

Ashcroft, Bill et al. 1998. *Key Concepts in Post-Colonial Studies*. London: Routledge.

Bakhtin, Mikhail. 1981. *The Dialogic Imagination*, ed. Michael Holquist. Austin: University of Texas Press.

Bakhtin, Mikhail, and N. Voloshinov. 1986. *Marxism and the Philosophy of Language*. Cambridge, MA: Harvard University Press.

167

Balagtas, Francisco. 1978. *Florante at Laura*, trans. E. San Juan Jr. Manila, Philippines: Art Multiples. (Orig. pub. 1838.)

Balibar, Etienne, and Immanuel Wallerstein. 1991. *Race, Nation, Class: Ambiguous Identities*. London: Verso.

Bardache, Frank. 1993. "Cesar's Ghost: Decline and Fall of the U.F.W." *Nation* (July 26/Aug. 2): 130–35.

Bauman, Zygmunt. 1996. "From Pilgrim to Tourist—Or a Short Story of Identity." In *Questions of Cultural Identity*, ed. Stuart Hill and Paul Du Gay. London: Sage.

Bautista, Maria Cynthia Rose Banzon. 2002. "Migrant Workers and Their Environments: Insights from the Filipino Diaspora." <http://www.unu.edu/HQ/japanese/gs-j/gs2002j/shonan18/Bautista4abstE.pdf/2002>.

Bauzon, Kenneth. 1991. *Liberalism and the Quest for Islamic Identity in the Philippines*. Durham, NC: Acorn Press.

BAYAN. 2007. "National Situation." Unpublished paper of the BAYAN National Council Meeting, September 28–October 2. <http://www.bayan.org>.

Beltran, Crispin. 2004. *Resolution Introduced to the 13th Congress*. First Regular Session, Republic of the Philippines. House Resolution No. 103 (filed Aug. 5).

Beltran, Ruby, and Gloria Rodriguez. 1996. *Filipino Women Migrant Workers: At the Crossroads and Beyond Beijing*. Quezon City, Philippines: Giraffe Books.

Benjamin, Walter. 1969. *Illuminations*. New York: Schocken.

Bensaid, Daniel. 2002. *Marx for Our Time*. London: Verso.

Berger, John. 1984. *And our face, my heart, brief as photos*. New York: Pantheon Books.

Bloch, Ernst. 1970. *A Philosophy of the Future*. New York: Herder and Herder.

Bloch, Maurice. 1983. *Marxism and Anthropology*. New York: Oxford University Press.

Bogardus, Emory. 1976. "Anti-Filipino Race Riots." In *Letters in Exile*, ed. Jesse Quinsaat. Los Angeles: UCLA Asian American Studies Center.

Bonner, Raymond. 1987. *Waltzing with Dictators*. Quezon City, Philippines: KEN.

Boot, Max. 2002. *The Savage Wars of Peace: Small Wars and the Rise of American Power*. New York: Basic Books.

Bourdieu, Pierre. 1977. *Outline of a Theory of Practice*. London: Cambridge University Press.

———. 1991. *Language and Symbolic Power*. Cambridge, MA: Harvard University Press.

Bourdieu, Pierre, and Loic J. D. Wacquant. 1992. *An Invitation to Reflexive Sociology*. Chicago: University of Chicago Press.

———. 2000. *Pascalian Meditations*. Stanford, CA: Stanford University Press.

Brantlinger, Patrick. 1990. *Crusoe's Footprints*. New York: Routledge.

Brecht, Bertolt. 1976. *Poems 1913-1936*, ed. John Willett and Ralph Mannheim. New York: Methuen.

Brent, Joseph. 1998. *Charles Sanders Peirce: A Life*. Bloomington: Indiana University Press.

Buci-Glucksman, Christine. 1994. *Baroque Reason*. London: Sage.

Buck-Morss, Susan. 2000. *Dreamworld and Catastrophe*. Cambridge, MA: MIT Press.

Bulosan, Carlos. 1944. *The Laughter of My Father*. New York: Harcourt, Brace.

———. 1944. "Manuel L. Quezon—The Good Fight!" *Bataan Magazine* (Aug.): 13–15.

———. 1952. "Terrorism Rides the Philippines." *1952 Yearbook: International Longshoremen and Warehousemen's Union Local 3*. Seattle, WA: ILWU.

———. 1960. *The Sound of Falling Light*, ed. Dolores Feria. Quezon City: University of the Philippines Press.

———. 1973. *America Is in the Heart*. Seattle: University of Washington Press. (Orig. pub. 1946.)

———. 1978. *The Philippines Is in the* Heart, ed. E. San Juan Jr. Quezon City, Philippines: New Day Press.

———. 1982. *Selected Works and Letters*, ed. E. San Juan and Ninotchka Rosca. Honolulu, HI: Friends of the Filipino People.

———. 1988. "The Writer as Worker." *Midweek* (July 27): 30-31.

———. 1995a. *The Cry and the Dedication*. Philadelphia, PA: Temple University Press.

———. 1995b. "My Education." In *On Becoming Filipino: Selected Writings of Carlos Bulosan*, ed. E. San Juan Jr. Philadelphia, PA: Temple University Press.

———. 1996. "The Romance of Magno Rubio." In *Asian American Literature*, ed. Shawn Wong. New York: Longman.

———. 1998. *All The Conspirators*. Pasig City, Philippines: Anvil. (The attribution of this novel to Bulosan is still problematic.—ESJ)

Calugay, Joey. 2007. "Prospects for Filipinos in Canada under the North American Security and Prosperity Partnership (SPP)." Unpublished speech at the Immigrant Workers Center, Montreal, Quebec, Canada, August 13.

Campomanes, Oscar. 1998. "Carlos Bulosan." In *Encyclopedia of the American Left*, ed. Mari Jo Buhle, Paul Buhle, and Dan Georgakas. 2nd ed. New York: Oxford University Press.

———. 2003. "The Vernacular/Local, the National, and the Global in Filipino Studies." *Kritika Kultura* 3 (July). <http://www.kritikakultura.org/>.

Campomanes, Oscar, and Todd Gernes. 1988. "Two Letters from America: Carlos Bulosan and the Act of Writing." *MELUS* 15.3 (Fall): 15–46.

Capulong, Romeo T. 2004. "A Century of Crimes against the Filipino People." Unpublished lecture presented at the World Tribunal for Iraq Trial in New York City, August 25.

Casanova, Pascale. 2005. "Literature as a World." *New Left Review* 31 (Jan.–Feb.): 71–90.

Cashmore, E. Ellis. 1984. *Dictionary of Race and Ethnic Relations*. London: Routledge.

CENPEG (Center for People Empowerment in Governance). 2007. "Double Jeopardy in America." Issue Analysis No. 19 (Series of 2007) (Oct. 13). <http://www.cenpeg.org>.

Chan, Sucheng. 1991. *Asian Americans: An Interpretive History*. Boston, MA: Twayne.

Chang, Grace. 2000. *Disposable Domestics*. Boston, MA: South End Press.

Chekhov, Anton. 1979. *Anton Chekhov's Short Stories*. New York: Norton.

Chomsky, Noam. 2001. "The United States Is a Leading Terrorist State." Interview by David Barsamian. *Monthly Review* 53.6 (Nov.): 10–19.

Chung, S. F. 1996. "Review of *The Cry and the Dedication* and *On Becoming Filipino*." *Journal of Asian Studies*: 1148–49.

Cimatu, Frank. 2002. "Remembering Carlos Bulosan." *Philippine Daily Inquirer* (Sept. 25): A17.

Clifford, James. 1997. "Diaspora." In *The Ethnicity Reader*, ed. Montserrat Guibernau and John Rex. Cambridge: Polity Press.

———. 2006. "Diasporas." In *The Post-Colonial Studies Reader*, ed. Bill Ashcroft, Gareth Griffiths, and Helen Tiffin. London: Routledge.

Comaroff, John, and Jean Comaroff. 1992. *Ethnography and the Historical Imagination*. Boulder, CO: Westview Press.

Constable, Nicole. 1997. *Maid to Order in Hong Kong: Stories of Filipina Workers*. Ithaca, NY: Cornell University Press.

———. 1999. "At Home but Not at Home: Filipina Narratives of Ambivalent Returns." *Cultural Anthropology* 14: 203–228.

Constantino, Renato. 1966. *The Filipinos in the Philippines and Other Essays*. Quezon City, Philippines: Malaya Books.

———. 1974. *Identity and Consciousness: The Philippine Experience*. Quezon City, Philippines: Malaya Books.

———. 1975. *The Philippines: A Past Revisited*. Quezon City, Philippines: Tala Publishing Services.

———. 1978. *Neocolonial Identity and Counter-Consciousness: Essays on Cultural Decolonization*. White Plains, NY: Sharpe.

Critical Filipina and Filipino Studies Collective. 2004. *Resisting Homeland Security: Organizing against Unjust Removes of U.S. Filipinos*. San Jose, CA: CFFSC.

Cutshall, Alden. 1964. *The Philippines: Nation of Islands*. Princeton, NJ: Van Nostrand.

De Leon, Ferdinand M. 1999. "Revisiting the Life and Legacy of Pioneering Filipino Writer Carlos Bulosan." *Seattle Times*, August 8. <http://www.reflectionsofasia.com/carlosbulosan.hmt>.

Deleuze, Gilles, and Felix Guattari. 1986. *Kafka: Toward a Minor Literature*. Minneapolis: University of Minnesota Press.

Demko, George. 1992. *Why in the World: Adventures in Geography*. New York: Anchor Books.

Denning, Michael. 1997. *The Cultural Front*. New York: Verso.

De Vera, Arleen. 1994. "Without Parallel: The Local 7 Deportation Cases, 1949–1955." *AmerAsia Journal* 20.2: 1-25.

Diamond, David. 1999. "One Nation, Overseas." <http://wired.com/wired/archive/10.06>.

Dickhut, Willi. 1986. *Crises and Class Struggle*. Dusseldorf, Germany: Neuer Weg Verlag und Druck.

Dirlik, Arif. 1997. *The Postcolonial Aura*. Boulder, CO: Westview Press.

Docker, John. 2001. *1492: The Poetics of Diaspora*. London: Continuum.

Dostoevsky, Fyodor. 1971. *The Idiot*. Middlesex, UK: Penguin.

Doty, Roxanne Lynn. 1996. *Imperial Encounters*. Minneapolis: University of Minnesota Press.

Ducrot, Oswald, and Tzvetan Todorov. 1979. *Encyclopedia Dictionary of the Sciences of Language*. Baltimore, MD: Johns Hopkins University Press.

Dunne, John Gregory. 1971. *Delano*. New York: Farrar, Straus and Giroux.

Dussel, Enrique. 2007. "Alterity and Modernity (Las Casas, Vitoria, and Suarez: 1514–1617). In *Postcolonialism and Political Theory*, ed. Nalini Persram. Lanham, MD: Lexington Books.

Ehrenreich, Barbara, and Arlie Russell Hochschild, eds. 2003. *Global Woman*. New York: Metropolitan Books.

Emerman, Jimmy. 1991. "War of Words: Language, Colonialism and English Only." *Breakthrough* 15.1: 22–27.

Engel, Stefan. 2003. *Twilight of the Gods—Gotterdammerung over the "New World Order."* Essen, Germany: Verlag Neuer Weg.

Enriquez, Virgilio. 1981. "Decolonizing the Filipino Psyche: Philippine Psychology in the Seventies." *Philippine Social Sciences and Humanities Review* 45.1–4 (Jan.–Dec.): 191–216.

———. 1989a. *Filipino Psychology in the Third World*. Quezon City, Philippines: Philippine Psychology Research House. (Orig. pub. 1977.)

———. 1989b. "Sikolohiyang Pilipino: Perspektibo at Direksyon." In *Sikolohiyang Pilipino: Teorya, Metodo, at Gamit*, ed. Rogelia Pe-pua. Quezon City: University of the Philippines Press.

———. 1992. *From Colonial to Liberation Psychology*. Quezon City: University of the Philippines Press.

Enriquez, Virgilio, Sandra Herrera, and Emir Tubayan. 1991. *Ang Sikolohiyang Malaya Sa Panahon ng Krisis*. Quezon City: Akademya ng Sikolohiyang Pilipino.

Enriquez, Virgilio, and Elizabeth Protacio-Marcelino. 1989. *Neo-Colonial Politics and Language Struggle in the Philippines*. Quezon City: Akademya ng Sikolohiyang Pilipino. (Orig. pub. 1984.)

Erikson, Erik. 1975. *Life History and the Historical Moment*. New York: Norton.

Esman, Milton. 1996. "Diasporas and International Relations." In *Ethnicity*, ed. John Hutchins and Anthony Smith. New York: Oxford University Press.

Espiritu, Yen Le. 1995. *Filipino American Lives*. Philadelphia, PA: Temple University Press.

———. 2003. *Home Bound*. Berkeley and Los Angeles: University of California Press.

Estrada, George. 2005. "75 Years Later, Works of Filipino Author Still Shine." *News Tribune* (July). <http://www.thenewstribune.com/news/northwest/story/5045836p-4601431c.html>.

Estrada-Claudio, Sylvia. 1995. "Ang Sikolohiya ng Kababaihan." In *Mga Idea at Estilo*, ed. Lilia Quindoza Santiago. Quezon City: University of the Philippines Press.

Etulain, Richard, ed. 2002. *Cesar Chavez: A Brief Biography with Documents*. Boston, MA: Bedford/St. Martins.

Evangelista, Patricia. 2004. "Filipino Diaspora." <http://www.inq7.com/>.

Evangelista, Susan. 1985. *Carlos Bulosan and His Poetry*. Quezon City, Philippines: Ateneo de Manila University Press.

Fall, Bernard B. 1985. *Hell in a Very Small Place*. New York: Da Capo Press.

Feria, Dolores. 1957. "Carlos Bulosan: Gentle Genius." *Comment* 1: 57–64.

Fischer, Ernst. 1996. *How to Read Karl Marx*. New York: Monthly Review Press.

Fischer, William C. et al. 1997. *Identity, Community, and Pluralism in American Life*. New York: Oxford University Press.

Fishman, J. A. 1972. "The Sociology of Language." In *Language and Social Context*, ed. Pier Paolo Giglioli. Baltimore, MD: Penguin Books.

Fitt, Yann, Alexandre Faire, and Jean-Pierre Vigier. 1980. *The World Economic Crisis: U.S. Imperialism at Bay*. London: Zed Press.

Foner, Eric. 2004. "Rethinking American History in a Post–9/11 World." *History News Network* (Sept. 12). <http://hnn.us/articles/6961.html>.

Fowles, John. 1978. *Islands*. Boston, MA: Little Brown.

Frake, Charles. 1998. "Abu Sayyaf: Displays of Violence and the Proliferation of Contested Identities among Philippine Muslims." *American Anthropologist* 100.1: 41–54.

Francia, Luis H. 2007. "The Artist Abroad: Windows to the Fil-American's Layered Past." *Inquirer.net* (Jan. 2). <http://globalnation.inquirer.net/mindfeeds/mindfeeds/view_article.php? article_id=41247>.

Freire, Paulo. 1985. *The Politics of Education*. South Hadley, MA: Bergin and Garvey.

Garcia, Fanny. 1994. "Arrivederci." In *Ang Silid na Mahiwaga*, ed. Soledad Reyes. Pasig, Rizal, Philippines: Anvil Publishing.

Garcia, Hermie. 2007. "A Challenge to the Community." *Philippine Reporter* (Oct. 16). <http://www.philreporter.com/Issue-10-16-31-07/Notebook/20community.doc>.

Geron, Tomio. 1995. "Filipino Prophet." *AsianWeek*, August 4, 13.

Gilroy, Paul. 1993. *The Black Atlantic*. Cambridge, MA: Harvard University Press.

Godelier, Maurice. 1986. *The Mental and the Material*. London: Verso.

Gonzalez, Eduardo T. 1999. *Reconsidering the East Asian Model: What's Ahead for the Philippines?* Pasig City: Development Academy of the Philippines.

Gramsci, Antonio. 1971. *Selections from Prison Notebooks*. New York: International Publishers.

Griswold del Castillo, Richard, and Richard A. Garcia. 1995. *Cesar Chavez: A Triumph of Spirit*. Norman: University of Oklahoma Press.

Guattari, Felix. 1995. *Chaosmosis: An Ethico-Aesthetic Paradigm*. Bloomington: Indiana University Press.

Guerrero, Leon Maria. 1969. *The First Filipino: A biography of Jose Rizal*. Manila, Philippines: National Historical Commission.

Guillermo, Emil. 2002. "America Was in the Heart, but the FBI Was in His Life." *San Francisco Chronicle*, October 8: 8.

Guyotte, Roland L. 1997. "Generation Gap: Filipinos, Filipino Americans and Americans, Here and There, Then and Now." *Journal of American Ethnic History* (Fall): 64–70.

Habermas, Jürgen. 1987. *The Philosophical Discourse of Modernity*. Cambridge, MA: MIT Press.

Hall, Stuart. 1992. "New Ethnicities." In *Race, Culture and Difference*, ed. James Donald and Ali Rattansi. London: Sage.

———. 1997a. "The Local and the Global: Globalization and Ethnicity." In *Dangerous Liaisons*, ed. Anne McClintock et al. Minneapolis: University of Minnesota Press.

———. 1997b. "Making Diasporic Identities." In *The House that Race Built,* ed. Wahneema Lubiano. New York: Pantheon.

———. 2005. "Thinking the Diaspora: Home-Thoughts from Abroad." In *Postcolonialisms: An Anthology of Cultural Theory and Criticism,* ed. Gaurav Desai and Supriya Nair. New Brunswick, NJ: Rutgers University Press.

Haraway, Donna. 1992. "The Promises of Monsters: A Regenerative Politics for Inappropriate/d Others." In *Cultural Studies*, ed. Lawrence Grossberg et al. New York: Routledge.

Harper, Peter, and Laurie Fullerton. 1994. *Philippines Handbook*. Chico, CA: Moon Publications.

Harris, Marvin. 1979. *Cultural Materialism: The Struggle for a Science of Culture.* New York: Random House.

Hartman, Andrew. 2003. "Language as Oppression: The English-Only Movement in the United States." *Socialism and Democracy* 17.1: 187–208.

Harvey, David. 1989. *The Condition of Postmodernity*. Oxford, UK: Blackwell.

———. 1996. *Justice, Nature and the Geography of Difference*. Malden, MA: Blackwell.

———. 2000. *Spaces of Hope*. Berkeley and Los Angeles: University of California Press.

Hearn, Lafcadio. 1883. "Saint Malo: A Lacustrine Village in Louisiana." *Harper's Weekly*, March 31: 146-52.

Hernandez, Butch. 2004. "Commentary: Filipino Diaspora." <http://news.inq7.net/opinion/index.php?index=2&story-id=73505ch=75>.

Hollnsteiner, Mary Racelis. 1979. "The Filipino Family Confronts the Modern World." In *Society, Culture and the Filipino,* ed. Mary R. Hollnsteiner. Quezon City: Institute of Philippine Culture.

Hymer, S. 1975. "The Multinational Corporation and the Law of Uneven Development." In *International Firms and Modern Imperialism*, ed. Hugo Radice. Baltimore, MD: Penguin Books.

IBON. 2006. *OFW Remittances: Lifeline of the Economy*. Quezon City, Philippines: IBON Foundation.

Ignacio, Abe, Enrique de la Cruz, Jorge Emmanuel, and Helen Toribio. 2004. *The Forbidden Book: The Philippine-American War in Political Cartoons*. San Francisco, CA: T'Boli Publishing and Distribution.

Instituto del Tercer Mundo. 1999. *The World Guide 1999/2000*. Oxford, UK: New Internationalist Publications.

Ives, Peter. 2006. "Global English: Linguistic Imperialism or Lingua France?" *Studies in Language and Capitalism* I, 121–41. <http://www.languageandcaptialism.info>.

Jacobson, David, ed. 1998. *Immigration Reader*. Oxford, UK: Blackwell.

Jalandoni, Luis G. 2002. "Why the CPP and NPA Are Not Terrorist Organizations." *Press Release of the National Democratic Front of the Philippines* (Sept. 3). <http://home.wanadoo.nl/ndf>.

Jameson, Fredric. 2000. "Third World Literature in the Era of Multinational Capitalism." In *The Jameson Reader*, ed. Michael Hardt and Kathi Weeks. Oxford, UK: Blackwell.

Janiewski, Dolores. 1995. "Gendering, Racializing and Classifying: Settler Colonization in the United States." In *Unsettling Settler Societies*, ed. Daiva Stasiulis and Nira Yuval-Davis. London: Sage.

Joyce, James. 1951. *Exiles*. New York: Viking Press. (Orig. pub. 1918.)

Kaplan, Amy. 2004. "Violent Belongings and the Question of Empire Today: Presidential Address to the American Studies Association, October 17, 2003." *American Quarterly* 56.1 (Mar.): 1–18.

Kaplan, Fred. 2003. "From Baghdad to Manila: Another Lousy Analogy for the Occupation of Iraq." <http://slate.msn.com/id/2090114/>.

Karnow, Stanley. 1989. *In Our Image*. New York: Random House.

Katz, William Loren. 2004. "Splendid Little War; Long Bloody Occupation; Iraq, the U.S. and an Old Lesson." <http://www.williamkatz.com/>.

———. 2007. "Water Boarding in U.S. History." (Jan. 6). <http://www.hnn.us/articles/44411.html>.

Kintanar, Thelma, and Associates. 1996. *Cultural Dictionary for Filipinos*. Quezon City: University of the Philippines Press and Anvil Publishing.

Koshy, Susan. 2004. *Sexual Naturalization*. Stanford, CA: Stanford University Press.

Kristeva, Julia. 1991. *Strangers to Ourselves*. New York: Columbia University Press.

Kushner, Sam. 1975. *Long Road to Delano*. New York: International Publishers.

Laclau, Ernesto. 1994. "Minding the Gap." *The Making of Political Identities*. London: Verso.

Lacsamana, Anne. 1998. "Academic Imperialism and the Limits of Postmodernist Discourse: An Examination of Nicole Constable's Maid to Order in Hong Kong: Stories of Filipina Workers." *Amerasia Journal* 24.3 (Winter): 37–42.

Lagmay, Alfredo V. 1977. "Bahala na." In *Ulat ng Ikalawang Pambansang Kumperensya sa Sikolohiyang Pilipino* (Proceedings of the Second National Conference on Filipino Psychology), ed. L. F. Antonio et al. Quezon City: Pambansang Samahan ng Sikolohiyang Pilipino.

Lee, Rachel. 1999. *The Americas of Asian American Literature: Gendered Fictions of Nations and Transnation*. Princeton, NJ: Princeton University Press.

Le Guin, Ursula. 1974. *The Dispossessed*. New York: Avon Books.

Lenin, Vladimir. 1983. *Lenin on Language*. Moscow, Russia: Raduga.

Levy, Jacques. 1975. *Cesar Chavez: Autobiography of La Causa*. New York: Norton.

Libretti, Tim. 1998. "First and Third Worlds in U.S. Literature: Rethinking Carlos Bulosan." *MELUS Journal* 23.4: 135–55.

Lingis, Alphonso. 1994. *Foreign Bodies*. New York: Routledge.

Lipsitz, George. 1998. *The Possessive Investment in Whiteness*. Philadelphia, PA: Temple University Press.

London, Joan, and Henry Anderson. 1970. *So Shall Ye Reap*. New York: Crowell.

Lowy, Michael. 1998. *Fatherland or Mother Earth?* London: Pluto Press.

Luci, Charissa. 2004. "What Lies Ahead: The Plight of Filipino Seafarers." *Manila Bulletin* (Aug. 8).

Lukacs, Georg. 1972. *Marxism and Human Liberation*, ed. E. San Juan. New York: Dell.

Luxemburg, Rosa. 2008. "Martinique." *Kominform.at* (Nov. 14). First published in *Leipziger Volkszeitung*, May 15, 1902.

Lynch, Frank. 1969. "Social Acceptance." In *Four Readings on Philippine Values*, ed. F. Lynch. Quezon City, Philippines: Ateneo de Manila University Press.

———. 1979. "Big and Little People: Social Class in the Rural Philippines." In *Society, Culture and the Filipino*, ed. Mary R. Hollnsteiner. Quezon City: Institute of Philippine Culture.

Macedo, Donaldo. 2000. "English Only: The Tongue-Tying of America." In *Race and Ethnicity in the United States*, ed. Stephen Steinberg. Oxford, UK: Blackwell.

Mahajan, Rahul. 2002. *The New Crusade: America's War on Terrorism*. New York: Monthly Review Press.

Makilan, Aubrey S. C. 2006. "Modern Heroes as Milking Cows." *Bulatlat* 6.24 (July 23–29). <http://www.butlatlat.com>.

———. 2007a. "Beheaded OFW in Saudi Adds to Long List of Migrants Neglected by RP Government." *Bulatlat* 7.19 (Jan. 17–23).

———. 2007b. "Filipina Caregiver in Canada Killed, Another Dream Ending in Tragedy." *Bulatlat* 7.35 (October 7–13). <http://www.bulatlat.com>.

Mann, Eric. 2002. *Dispatches from Durban*. Los Angeles, CA: Frontlines Press.

Martin, Isabel Penfianco. 2002. "Pedagogy: Teaching Practices of American Colonial Educators in the Philippines." *KritikaKultura*. <http://www.kritikakultura.org/html.1-8>.

Marx, Karl. 1993. *Grundrisse*. New York: Anchor Books.

Marx, Karl, and Friedrich Engels. 1978. *The Marx–Engels Reader*, ed. Robert Tucker. New York: Norton.

Massey, Doreen. 1993. "Politics and Space/Time." In *Place and the Politics of Identity*, ed. Michael Keith and Steve Pile. London: Routledge.

Matthiessen, Peter. 1969. *Sal Si Puedes: Cesar Chavez and the New American Revolution*. New York: Random House.

Maurer, Armand. 1962. "Saint Augustine." *Medieval Philosophy*. New York: Random House.

Mazrui, Alamin. 2003. "The World Bank, the Language Question and the Future of African Education." In *The Language, Ethnicity and Race Reader*, ed. Roxy Harris and Ben Rampton. London: Routledge.

McKenna, Thomas M. 1998. *Muslim Rulers and Rebels*. Berkeley and Los Angeles: University of California Press.

McWilliams, Carey. 1997. "Most Filipino Immigrants Do Not Want Repatriation." In *Asian Americans: Opposing Viewpoints*, ed. William Dudley. San Diego, CA: Greenhaven Press.

Mendoza, Jay. 2003. "War, Immigrants, and the Economy: Filipinos in a Post–9/11 World." *Inform! Special Report* (Jan. 25): 1–28.

———. 2004. Afterword to *Resisting Homeland Security*. San Jose, CA: CFFSC.

Merleau-Ponty, Maurice. 1969. *The Essential Writings of Merleau-Ponty*, ed. Alden Fisher. New York: Harcourt, Brace and World.

Merrell, Floyd. 1997. *Peirce, Signs and Meaning*. Toronto: University of Toronto Press.

Meszaros, Istvan. 2001. *Socialism or Barbarism*. New York: Monthly Review Press.

Miller, Stuart Creighton. 1982. *"Benevolent Assimilation": The American Conquest of the Philippines, 1899–1903*. New Haven, CT: Yale University Press.

Mills, Charles W. 1999. "The Racial Polity." In *Racism and Philosophy*, ed. Susan Babbitt and Sue Campbell. Ithaca, NY: Cornell University Press.

Montinola, Aurelio R. III. 2006. "Mapping the Future: Economic Impact of Filipino Migration." *Philippine Daily Inquirer*, April 17, B2–2.

Mudimbe, V. Y., and Sabine Engel. 1999. Introduction to special issue, *South Atlantic Quarterly* (Winter-Spring): 1–8.

Mulhern, Francis. 2000. *Culture/Metaculture*. London: Routledge.

Myrdal, Gunnar. 1974. *An American Dilemma*. New York: McGraw Hill.

National Statistics Office, R.P. 2008. "Census of the Philippines." <http://www/census.gov.ph>.

Nearing, Scott, and Joseph Freeman. 1966. *Dollar Diplomacy*. New York: Monthly Review Press. (Orig. pub. 1925.)

Negri, Antonio, and Michael Hardt. 2000. *Empire*. Cambridge, MA: Harvard University Press.

Nguyen, Viet Thanh. 1996. "Home of the Brave." *A. Magazine*: 65-66.

Nixon, Rob. 1995. "Refugees and Homecoming: Bessie Head and the End of Exile." *Late Imperial Culture*, ed. Roman de la Campa, E. Ann Kaplan, and Michael Sprinker. New York: Verso.

Nunberg, Geoffrey. 2000. "Lingo Jingo: English-Only and the New Nativism." In *Race and Ethnicity in the United States*, ed. Stephen Steinberg. New York: Blackwell.

OFW Philippines Online. 2002. "Overseas Filipino Workers." <http://www.seasite.niu.edu/Tagalog/Modules/Modules/PhilippineEconomy/ofws.htm>.

Paddock, Richard C. 2006. "The Overseas Class." *LATimes.com*. <http://www.latimes.com/news/nationworld/world/la-fg-remit20,0,3918689.story>.

Pagaduan, Maureen. 2006. "Leaving Home: Filipino Women Surviving Migration." In *Poverty, Gender and Migration*, ed. Sadhana Arya and Anupama Roy. Volume 2 of *Women and Migration in Asia*. New Delhi, India: Sage.

Palumbo-Liu, David. 1999. *Asian/American*. Stanford, CA: Stanford University Press.

Parreñas, Rhacel S. 2001. *Servants of Globalization*. Stanford, CA: Stanford University Press.

Pauker, Benjamin, and Michele Wucker. 2005. "Diminishing Returns," *Harper's Magazine* (Dec.): 68–69.

Peirce, C. S. 1958. *Selected Writings,* ed. Philip Wiener. New York: Dover.

———. 1998. *The Essential Peirce*, ed. Edward C. Moore. Amherst, NY: Prometheus Books.

Peplow, Evelyn. 1991. *The Philippines: Tropical Paradise*. Lincolnwood, IL: Passport Books.

Pe-pua, Rogelia, ed. 1989. *Sikolohiyang Pilipino: Teorya, Metodo at Gamit*. Quezon City: University of the Philippines Press.

Pe-pua, Rogelia, and Elizabeth Protacio-Marcelino. 2000. "*Sikolohiyang Pilipino* (Filipino Psychology): A Legacy of Virgilio G. Enriquez." *Asian Journal of Social Psychology* 3: 49–71.

Pernia, Ernesto. 2007. "Is Labor Export Policy Good for RP's Development?" *Inquirer.net* (May 1). <http://globalnation.inquirer.net/mindfeeds/ mindfeeds/view_article.php?article_id=63476>.

Pido, Antonio. 1997. "Macro/Micro Dimensions of Pilipino Immigration to the United States." In *Filipino Americans*, ed. Maria P. P. Root. Thousand Oaks, CA: Sage.

Pomeroy, William. 1992. *The Philippines: Colonialism, Collaboration, and Resistance!* New York: International Publishers.

Posadas, Barbara. 1999. *The Filipino Americans*. Westport, CT: Greenwood Press.

Price Waterhouse. 1981. *Doing Business in the Philippines*. Manila, Philippines: Price Waterhouse Center for Transnational Taxation.

Ray, Ellen, and William H. Schaap. 2003. *Covert Action: The Roots of Terrorism*. Melbourne, Australia: Ocean Press.

Readings, Bill. 1996. *The University in Ruins*. Cambridge, MA: Harvard University Press.

Retamar, Roberto Fernandez. 1989. *Caliban and Other Essays*. Minneapolis: University of Minnesota Press.

Ricoeur, Paul. 1983. "Self as Ipse." In *Freedom and Interpretation*, ed. Barbara Johnson. New York: Basic Books.

Rifaterre, Michael. 1983. *Text Production*. New York: Columbia University Press.

Rizal, Jose. 1912. *The Reign of Greed. [el Filibusterismo]* Trans. Charles Derbyshire. Manila: Philippine Education Company. (Orig. pub. 1891.)

———. 1961. *Cartas entre Rizal y sus colegas de la propaganda*. Manila, Philippines: Jose Rizal Centennial Commission.

———. 1976. *Quotations from Rizal's Writings*. Manila, Philippines: National Historical Institute.

Robertson, Roland. 1994. *Globalization: Social Theory and Global Culture*. Thousand Oaks, CA: Sage.

———. 1995. "Glocalization: Time-Space and Homogeneity-Heterogeneity." In *Global Modernities*, ed. Mike Featherstone et al. London: Sage.

Roces, Alfredo, and Grace Roces. 1985. *Culture Shock! Philippines*. Singapore: Times Books International.

Rochberg-Halton, Eugene. 1986. *Meaning and Modernity*. Chicago: University of Chicago Press.

Rosca, Ninotchka. 2000. "Living in Two-Time Zones." *Legacy to Liberation*, ed. Fred Ho. San Francisco, CA: AK Press.

Root, Maria P. P., ed. 1997. *Filipino Americans*. Thousand Oaks, CA: Sage.

Rowe, Jonathan. 2003. "Maid to Order: The Third World Women Who Leave Their Children to Take Care of Ours." *Washington Monthly* (Nov.).

Roybal-Allard, Lucille. 1994. "In Honor of a Filipino American who Struggled for the Unionization of Farm Workers." *Library of Congress Records*. <http:Icereport.loc.gov/cgi-bin/query/z?r103:E21JY4-286>.

Rushdie, Salman. 1983. *Shame*. New York: Knopf.

Said, Edward. 1993. *Culture and Imperialism*. New York: Knopf.

———. 2000. *Reflections in Exile and Other Essays*. Cambridge, MA: Harvard University Press.

Salazar, Zeus, ed. 1989. "Ilang Batayan Para sa Isangt Sikolohiyang Pilipino." In *Sikolohiyang Pilipino: Teorya, Metodo at Gamit*, ed. Rogelia Pe-pua. Quezon City: University of the Philippines Press.

———. 2004. *Sikolohiyang Panlipunan-at-Kalinangan*. Quezon City, Philippines: Palimbagan ng Lahi.

Saleeby, Najeeb M. 1913. *The Moro Problem*. Manila, Philippines: Bureau of Printing.

San Juan, E. Jr. 1994a. *Allegories of Resistance*. Quezon City: University of the Philippines Press.

———. 1994b. "Carlos Bulosan." *The American Radical*, ed. Mari Jo Buhle, Paul Buhle, and Harvey Kaye. New York: Routledge.

———. 1995. "In Search of Filipino Writing: Reclaiming Whose 'America?'" In *The Ethnic Canon*, ed. David Palumbo-Liu. Minneapolis: University of Minnesota Press.

———. 1996a. *The Philippine Temptation*. Philadelphia, PA: Temple University Press.

———. 1996b. "Searching for the Heart of 'America.'" In *Teaching American Ethnic Literatures*, ed. John Maitino and David Peck. Albuquerque: University of New Mexico Press.

———. 1996c. *History and Form*. Quezon City, Philippines: Ateneo University Press.

———. 1998a. *Beyond Postcolonial Theory*. New York: St Martins Press.

———. 1998b. *From Exile to Diaspora: Versions of the Filipino Experience in the United States*. Boulder, CO: Westview Press.

———. 1999. "The Filipino Diaspora and the Centenary of the Philippine Revolution." In *Journey of 100 Years*, ed. Cecilia Manguera Brainard and Edmundo F. Litton. Santa Monica, CA: Philippine American Women Writers and Artists.

———. 2000. *After Postcolonialism*. Lanham, MD: Rowman and Littlefield.

———. 2002. *Racism and Cultural Studies*. Durham, NC: Duke University Press.

———. 2002–2003. "The Imperialist War on Terrorism and the Responsibility of Cultural Studies." *Arena Journal* 20: 45–56.

———. 2004a. "Inventing Vernacular Speech-Acts: Articulating Filipino Self-Determination in the U.S." *KritikaKultura* 5 (Dec.): 70–86. <http://www.ateneo.edu/kritikakultura>.

———. 2004b. *Working through the Contradictions*. Lewisburg, PA: Bucknell University Press.

———. 2007a. *In the Wake of Terror: Class, Race, Nation, Ethnicity in the Postmodern World*. Lanham, MD: Lexington Books.

———. 2007b. *U.S. Imperialism and Revolution in the Philippines*. New York: Palgrave Macmillan.

Santos, Bienvenido. 1982. "Words from a Writer in Exile." In *Asian Writers on Literature and Justice*, ed. Leopoldo Yabes. Manila: Philippine Center of International PEN.

Sartre, Jean-Paul. 1974. *Between Existentialism and Marxism*. New York: Morrow.

Sassen, Saskia. 1998. *Globalization and Its Discontents*. New York: New Press.

Schirmer, Daniel B., and Stephen Rosskamm Shalom, eds. 1987. *The Philippines Reader*. Boston, MA: South End Press.

Shalom, Steve. 1981. "Death in the Philippines." *New York Review of Books* (Dec. 17).

———. 2004. "Continuity and Change in Two Turn-of-the-Century Wars." Unpublished paper read at the Annual Conference of the Association of Asian American Studies, Boston, MA, March 27.

Siewert, Pauline Agbayani, and Linda Revilla. 1995. "Filipino Amerians." In *Asian Americans: Contemporary Trends and Issues*, ed. Pyong Gap Min. Thousand Oaks, CA: Sage.

Simmel, Georg. 1950. "The Stranger." In *The Sociology of Georg Simmel*, ed. Kurt H. Wolff. Glencoe, IL: Free Press.

Sison, Jose Maria, and Julita de Lima. 1998. *Philippine Economy and Politics*. Manila, Philippines: Aklat ng Bayan.

Smith, Neil. 1984. *Uneven Development*. New York: Blackwell.

Solarz, Stephen. 1997. "Against Official English: A U.S. Representative Explains Why There Should not Be an English Language Constitutional Amendment, 1988." In *Identity, Community, and Pluralism in American Life*, ed. William C. Fischer et al. New York: Oxford University Press.

Solberg, Sam. 1991. "An Introduction to Filipino American Literature." In *Aiiieeeee!*, ed. Frank Chin, Jeffery Paul Chan, Lawrence Fusao Inada, and Shawn Wong. New York: New American Library.

Sontag, Susan. 2002. "Real Battles and Empty Metaphors." Op-Ed Contribution. *New York Times*, September 10. <http://www/nytimes/com>.

Spears, Arthur K. 1999. *Race and Ideology*. Detroit, MI: Wayne State University Press.

Sta. Maria, Madelene. 1993. *Die Indigenisierung in den Sozialwissenshaften und der Versuch einer Resolution in Sikolohiyang Pilipino*. Inaugural dissertation, Faculty of Philosophy, University of Cologne, Germany.

Stauffer, Robert. 1981. "The Politics of Becoming: The Mindanao Conflict in a World-System Perspective." *Dependency Series* No. 31. Quezon City: University of the Philippines, Third World Studies Center.

Sturtevant, David. 1976. *Popular Uprisings in the Philippines, 1840–1940*. Ithaca, NY: Cornell University Press.

Surin, Kenneth. 1999. "Afterthoughts on Diaspora." *South Atlantic Quarterly* 98.1/2 (Winter–Spring): 275–326.

Suvin, Darko. 2004. "Exile as Mass Outrage and Intellectual Mission: Miseries and Splendours of Forced Displacement." Unpublished paper.

Takaki, Ronald. 1989. *Strangers from a Different Shore*. Boston, MA: Little, Brown.

Tan, Michael. 2004. "World without Filipinos." *Philippine Daily Inquirer* (June 16). <http://www.inq7.net/opi/2004/jun/16/opi_mltan-1.htm>.

Teodoro, Luis. 1985. "Notes on the Power of the People" [*The Cry and the Dedication*]. *Mithi* 1: 3–14.

Tolentino, Rolando B. 1999. "Bodies, Letters, Catalogs: Filipinas in Transnational Space." In *Transnational Asia Pacific: Gender, Culture and the Public Sphere*, ed. Shirley Geok-Lin Lim, Larry E. Smith, and Wimaldisanayake. Urbana: University of Illinois Press.

Tuazon, Bobby et al. 2002. *Unmasking the War on Terror: U.S. Imperialist Hegemony and Crisis*. Manila, Philippines: Center for Anti-Imperialist Studies.

Tujan, Antonio. 2001. "Globalization Boosts the Trafficking of Filipino OCWs." *Bulatlat* 39 (Nov. 11–17): 1–9. http://www.bulatlat.com.

Twain, Mark. 1992. "Thirty Thousand Killed a Million." *Atlantic Monthly* (Apr.): 52–56.

Valledor, Sid Amores. 2006. *The Original Writings of Philip Vera Cruz*. Indianapolis, IN: Dog Ear Publishing.

Vallejo, Cesar. 1976. *Selected Poems*. New York: Penguin.

Vera Cruz, Philip (with Craig Scharlin and Lilia Villanueva). 2000. *Philip Vera Cruz: A Personal History of Filipino Immigrants and the Farmworkers Movement*. Seattle: University of Washington Press. (An earlier 1992 edition was issued by the UCLA Labor Center and the Asian American Studies Center of UCLA.)

Vidal, Gore. 1973. "The Filipino Genocide." *New York Review of Books* (Nov. 8).

———. 1981. "Death in the Philippines." *New York Review of Books* (Dec. 17).

Volpp, Leti. 2000. "American Mestizo: Filipinos and Atimiscegenation Laws in California." *U.C. Davis Law Review* 33.4 (Summer): 795–835.

Wallerstein, Immanuel. 1995. "Revolution as Strategy and Tactics of Transformation." In *Marxism and the Postmodern Age*, ed. Antonio Callari et al. New York: Guilford.

Weightman, George. 1970. "The Philippine Intellectual Elite in the Post-Independence Period." *Solidarity* (Jan.): 20–25.

Weiss, Peter. 1973. *Trotsky in Exile*. New York: Pocket Books.

Wikipedia. 2006. "Overseas Filipino." <http://www.en.wikipedia.org/wik/Filipino.diaspora>.

Williams, Raymond. 1983. *Keywords*. New York: Oxford University Press.

Williams, William Appleman. 1962. *The Tragedy of American Diplomacy*. New York: Dell.

Wong, Paul, and Tania Azores. 1994. "The Migration and Incorporation of Filipino Nurses." In *The New Asian Immigratin in Los Angeles and Global Restructuring*, ed. Paul Ong, Edna Bonacich, and Lucie Cheng. Philadelphia, PA: Temple University Press.

Yap, Cecille. 2006. "2005 Overseas Workers Remittances $10.B, up 25%." <http://money.inq7.net/breakingnews/view_breakingnews.php?yyy=2006&mon>.

Zelinsky, Wilbur. 2001. *The Enigma of Ethnicity*. Iowa City: University of Iowa Press.

Zialcita, Fernando. 2005. *Authentic Though Not Exotic: Essays on Filipino Identity*. Quezon City, Philippines: Ateneo University Press.

Zinn, Howard. 1984. *The Twentieth Century: A People's History*. New York: Harper and Row.

Zwick, Jim. 1992. Introduction to *Mark Twain's Weapons of Satire*, ed. Jim Zwick. Syracuse, NY: Syracuse University Press.

# Index

181